T3-BOB-744

Between
Reformed Scholasticism
and Pan-Protestantism

Between Reformed Scholasticism and Pan-Protestantism

Jean-Alphonse Turretin (1671–1737)
and Enlightened Orthodoxy
at the Academy of Geneva

Martin I. Klauber

SUP

Selinsgrove: Susquehanna University Press
London and Toronto: Associated University Presses

© 1994 by Associated University Presses, Inc.

All rights reserved. Authorization to photocopy items for internal or personal use, or the internal or personal use of specific clients, is granted by the copyright owner, provided that a base fee of $10.00, plus eight cents per page, per copy is paid directly to the Copyright Clearance Center, 27 Congress Street, Salem, Massachusetts 01970. [0-945636-57-1/94 $10.00 + 8¢ pp, pc.]

BX
9439
.T85
K57
1994

Associated University Presses
440 Forsgate Drive
Cranbury, NJ 08512

Associated University Presses
25 Sicilian Avenue
London WC1A 2QH, England

Associated University Presses
P.O. Box 338, Port Credit
Mississauga, Ontario
Canada L5G 4L8

The paper used in this publication meets the requirements of the American National Standard for Permanence of Paper for Printed Library Materials Z39.48-1984.

Library of Congress Cataloging-in-Publication Data

Klauber, Martin I., 1956–
    Between reformed scholasticism and pan-Protestantism : Jean-Alphonse Turretin (1671–1737) and enlightened orthodoxy at the Academy of Geneva / Martin I. Klauber.
        p.   cm.
    Includes bibliographical references and index.
    ISBN 0-945636-57-1 (alk. paper)
    1. Turretin, Jean-Alphonse, 1671–1731.   2. Reformed Church—Doctrines—History.   3. Académie de Genève.   4. Formula consensus ecclesiarum Helveticarum.   I. Title.
BX9439.T85K57   1994
230'.42'092—dc20   92-51005
                                                                                CIP

PRINTED IN THE UNITED STATES OF AMERICA

Contents

Between
Reformed Scholasticism
and Pan-Protestantism

Introduction

The enlightened orthodoxy of Jean-Alphonse Turretin (1671–1737), professor of theology at the Academy of Geneva, represents an important development in the Reformed theology of Geneva.[1] His career reflected the views of an entire generation of Reformed scholars who attempted to reconcile orthodox Calvinism with the growth of rationalism.

Jean-Alphonse was the son of Francis Turretin and the grandson of Benedict Turretin, both prominent professors of theology at the Academy of Geneva. The Turretin family were from Lucca and were quite prosperous, since several family members served as chief standard-bearers there. The family left Italy during the Inquisition. Jean-Alphonse's great-grandfather, François, settled in Geneva in 1592 and joined the ranks of the bourgeoisie in 1627. This made it possible for family members to receive the best education Geneva had to offer.

Jean-Alphonse's father died in 1687, just before the young Turretin began his formal theological training at the Academy of Geneva. This meant that young Jean-Alphonse studied under theologians with far more liberal tendencies than his father, foremost of whom was Louis Tronchin (1629–1705).[2] He was the most prominent Genevan advocate of the Saumur Academy.[3] Jean-Alphonse Turretin also studied philosophy under a former professor at Saumur, Jean-Robert Chouet (1642–1731), the leading Cartesian among the faculty at the Academy of Geneva.[4]

Jean-Alphonse Turretin began his career as professor of church history at the Academy of Geneva in 1696, was appointed rector there in 1701 and then also professor of theology in 1705. He resigned from the post of rector due to ill health in 1711. From such influential positions, he opposed the traditional Reformed emphasis on tightly defined creeds and the intricacies of the doctrine of predestination. He developed a new "enlightened" form of theology that kept the basic elements of orthodoxy which agreed with the dictates of reason.

The primary sources for Turretin's theological system are found in the *Opera*[5] (1776) and in the *Dilucidationes philosophico-theo-*

9

logico-dogmatico-morales (1748).[6] Both works contain Turretin's *Theses de theologia naturali,* the primary source for his views on natural theology, and his *De Veritate religionis Judaicae et Christianae,*[7] in which he discusses his beliefs about special revelation. Both editions also include a series of Turretin's academic orations, his treatise on the essence of Christian belief, *De Articulis fundamentalibus,*[8] and his *De Pyrrhonismo pontifico,*[9] which is a critique of the French Bishop Jacques Bénigne Bossuet's polemics against Protestant theology. The Franeker edition contains Turretin's commentaries on Romans and Thessalonians. In addition, the *Bibliothèque publique et universitaire de Genève* houses several unpublished treatises of Turretin, including his commentary on the Sermon on the Mount, various collections of his sermon notes, and part of his personal correspondence.

In both his published and unpublished works, Turretin exhibited a disdain for the Reformed theology of the Synod of Dort and of his own father. He preferred to focus on what he called the fundamental articles of the faith that the German Lutherans and the Anglicans shared with the Reformed church. Turretin also became quite friendly with some of the faculty of the Remonstrant Seminary in Amsterdam, most notably the former Genevan Jean LeClerc (1657–1736)[10] In fact, Turretin used the same apologetic approach as the Remonstrants, who emphasized "external proofs"[11] to establish the authority of Scripture. Turretin, therefore, virtually ignored the traditional Calvinist argument that the Holy Spirit confirms the divine origin of Scripture in the heart of the Christian. He acknowledged the importance of biblical mystery, but, in his system of natural theology, he attempted to prove as much about the nature of God as possible through the use of reason. For him, natural revelation was common to all men of all cultures and formed a basis for Christian belief independent of biblical revelation. Although Turretin did not replace revelation with natural religion, he gave rational arguments an equal footing with biblical revelation, claiming that both are in complete harmony. Hence, the importance of biblical revelation was significantly diminished.

The use of rational thought was not new to Protestant theology. Both Calvin and Luther had advocated some degree of rationalism in their theological treatises. The Calvinist and Lutheran traditions believed that the use of reason must be limited, since it was almost completely marred by the Fall. They used reason to support biblical revelation, especially in biblical exegesis. However, they accepted doctrines such as the Trinity, the Incarnation, and the decrees of God as "mysteries" that seemed to defy reason, and felt they went beyond the comprehension of man. They believed the teachings of Scripture should be accepted in all instances, even when they seem to contradict rational thought.

Although Turretin adopted the Reformed concept of "biblical mystery" as it applied to the Trinity and the Incarnation, he virtually ignored the difficult aspects of predestination. He deemed it a secondary doctrine and unnecessary for salvation. His successors at the Academy of Geneva, such as Jacob Vernet (1698–1789), who followed Turretin as professor of theology, applied reason to all aspects of "biblical mystery" and rejected the necessity for belief in the Trinity or the Incarnation of Christ.[12]

Fundamental to the relationships of reason to revelation and of natural theology to special revelation is the issue of religious authority. It forms the very basis for knowledge about God. Protestant-Roman Catholic polemics, from the time of the Reformation, centered on debates concerning the subject of religious authority. The Roman Catholic church, as early as Eck's disputations with Luther, taught that the church itself validated the trustworthiness and the true interpretation of the Bible. Roman Catholic theologians emphasized the power and right of church traditions and papal pronouncements to formulate judgments about biblical doctrine and interpretation.[13] The Lutheran and Reformed camps of the Protestant Reformation upheld a shift of religious authority away from the traditions of the church to Holy Scripture itself. Both Martin Luther and John Calvin based their concept of religious authority on a divinely inspired Bible. The authority of Scripture was based on its divine origin as well as the confirming power of the Holy Spirit in the hearts and minds of believers.[14]

The Roman Catholic response to the Protestant defense of scriptural authority challenged such an emphasis on the role of the Holy Spirit. Richard Popkin outlines the development of a Roman Catholic apologetic argument that employed a modified form of "Pyrrhonism"[15] to undermine the Protestant belief in an infallible, authoritative Bible. The Catholic Pyrrhonist argument stated that the Bible could not serve as the final authority for the Christian faith because it could not be interpreted with any consistency. The Bible alone could not provide true knowledge about God because of its obscurity. Instead, one should rely on a firmer, more certain basis for religious knowledge: the church itself. True knowledge about God, the Catholic Pyrrhonists argued, could only come from the church, which provides the official interpretation of Scripture. The believer does not use reason, since it cannot be trusted, and

accepts the precepts of the church through the eyes of faith. Such
Roman Catholic scholars as François Veron used this argument
and attacked the Protestant emphasis on the confirming power of
the Holy Spirit. Protestant scholars responded by stressing the
power of redeemed reason, which enables the individual to learn
truth about God. Woodbridge describes such an argument:

> When Protestant apologists insisted that regenerated reason (and right
> reason *per se)* helped them to know that the Bible was authoritative,
> they often did so apologetically because Roman Catholic disputants
> had challenged the criterion of the witness of the Holy Spirit to confirm
> biblical authority. These same Protestants often understood that the
> witness of the Holy Spirit was the primary means whereby the faithful
> come to a conviction of the Bible's authority. When the Roman Catho-
> lic Oratorian Jean Morin highlighted difficult passages to exegete the
> Scripture, he did so with the intention of forcing Protestants to ac-
> knowledge that without Church traditions, they could never arrive at
> a proper interpretation of the text. Protestants argued in response that
> the Bible was a sure, infallible word and that Scripture interprets
> Scripture.[16]

In the late 1680s, when Turretin attended the Academy of Geneva, simple reliance upon the witness of the Holy Spirit would
not adequately support the view that the Bible was divinely inspired and without error. In addition to Roman Catholic skepticism, early textual critical studies of biblical manuscripts, as well
as the geographical and historical studies done by scholars such
as Isaac de la Peyrère (1594–1676),[17] raised questions about the
historical accuracy of the Bible. Turretin hoped to establish the
doctrine of *sola Scriptura* on a more certain footing by harmoniz-
ing scriptural truth with all the new discoveries in textual criticism,
geography, and history and thereby maintain a historically accurate and trustworthy Bible. He used the same methods of criticism
in evaluating the Bible as he would for any other work of literature
or history. He also allowed for the possibility of what he considered
minor errors of relatively unimportant historical or geographical
details in the text. He wanted a fideistic acceptance of biblical
authority while making a rational defense of the core of religious
truth.

The development of Turretin's form of enlightened orthodoxy
constitutes an important chapter in the history of the development
of Reformed theology in Geneva. Turretin's thought serves as a
bridge between the period of orthodox Calvinism and the Enlight-

enment era in Geneva, when the dominant theological system was virtually Socinian.

In John T. McNeill's analysis of Calvinism in a changing world of thought, he lists Jean-Alphonse Turretin as someone who "showed the early eighteenth-century trend to more liberal views."[18] However, McNeill discusses this era only in very general terms. This present work on Jean-Alphonse Turretin goes into greater detail to point out Turretin's importance within the context of the history of Reformed thought.

Turretin's theological position is important, not only for the history of Calvinism, but also for the history of English theology. His theological system was remarkably similar to the English Latitudinarian movement of the late seventeenth and early eighteenth centuries. Turretin's belief in the harmony of natural and revealed religion, his emphasis upon the moral and practical aspects of theology, and his contention that the primary importance of the study of God is to promote human welfare in this life, were also important aspects of Latitudinarianism. It is not surprising that Turretin studied in England and was well acquainted with the English Latitudinarian theologians such as John Tillotson (1630–94) and William Wake (1656–1737), both future Archbishops of Canterbury. The correspondence between Turretin and Wake reveals Turretin's inclination toward Wake's theological views.[19]

A study of Reformed theology in this so-called "era of innovation" reveals significant theological development from the foundation of Calvin's *Institutes*. Traditionally, historians argue that this development, referred to as "Reformed scholasticism,"[20] began a century after Calvin's death and stripped his theology of its spiritual vitality and pastoral concern. The Synod of Dort served as a high point for scholastic development, and a study of the debates over the nature of predestination reveals the desire among Reformed theologians to present precise definitions for it. Scholastic Calvinism, however, was not devoid of creative theological thought, as Robert Godfrey points out in his dissertation on the diversity of opinion within the Reformed camp at Dort.[21]

Reformed theologians feared that Arminianism, which greatly relied on an active use of reason, might lead to a denial of the fundamental truths of the faith, namely the deity of Christ and the triune nature of the Godhead. Many Calvinists linked the Remonstrants to the sixteenth-century heretic, Faustus Socinus, who held these same heterodox views. To insure orthodoxy, Reformed theologians promulgated theological formularies that candidates for ordination had to sign in order to enter the ministry. When the French

Academy of Saumur began to popularize a theological position that was, in essence, a compromise between Calvinism and Arminianism, their Reformed colleagues in Switzerland responded with condemnation. Many considered any compromise with Arminianism as the first step toward anti-Trinitarianism and the destruction of the very fabric of the Christian faith.

The Academy of Geneva was a major competitor with Saumur for French-speaking students. Traditionally, the Genevans had sided with their French Reformed brethren on issues in which the French and Swiss Reformed bodies disagreed. On the issue of the compromise doctrines of Saumur, however, Geneva, sided with the Swiss. This clarified the distinction between the type of education that a theology student would receive at Geneva and at Saumur.[22]

The faculty at Geneva formally maintained the distinctives of the Synod of Dort, but the faculty was divided over the necessity of the ordinands to subscribe to the Helvetic Formula Consensus. The advocates of Saumur at Geneva, such as Louis Tronchin, accused their opponents of being "scholastics," since they allowed reason to define the fine points of theology so narrowly that the pastoral aspects of the faith were virtually eliminated. This was obviously a criticism of Reformed orthodoxy and reflected the degree to which theological polemics had divided the academy.

However, it was not Francis Turretin who advocated the use of reason in theology to the extent of removing the internal argument of the work of the Spirit in confirming scriptural authority. Francis Turretin agreed with Calvin's argument on this score. Instead, it was his son, Jean-Alphonse Turretin, who used external arguments based on reason to support the truth of Scripture and who rejected Calvin's argument. The younger Turretin was reacting against what he considered to be the overly defined nature of Reformed, scholastic theology because of its divisiveness and lack of concern for personal piety. He preferred to return to Calvin's pastoral emphasis, as well as that on the salvific nature of Scripture. Absent from Turretin's theological system was any systematic development of the doctrine of predestination, of the specific nature of divine decrees, and the use of specific theological creeds to which ordinands were required to subscribe. He built a theological system that highlighted the clear doctrines that Christ himself taught. His theological system was primarily practical.

Jean-Alphonse Turretin's theological system was, indeed, salvific in focus, but it was not a return to Calvin's. It more closely resembled Socinian-Remonstrant tradition than orthodox Calvinism. By elevating reason as the primary arbiter in theological inquiry, he virtually eliminated the need for the important mysteries of the faith that were central to New Testament theology, e.g., the Trinity and the Incarnation of Christ. Although Turretin accepted these by faith without attempting to explain them, his successors among the theological faculty at Geneva would apply reason to these mysteries. Since they could not explain them, they simply rejected them. The Reformed theologians of Geneva adopted a Socinian position on the Trinity. Ironically, during the second half of the eighteenth century, both Jean-Jacques Rousseau and Voltaire, neither of whom were orthodox Calvinists, mocked the theological faculty for their alleged advocacy of Socinian ideas.[23]

Turretin set the stage for this development with his new theological system and his reliance on rational investigation. His system of natural theology was far more extensive than that of his scholastic predecessors since he attempted to prove as much about God through reason as possible. Concerning special revelation, he used external arguments that relied upon rational proofs to establish the divine origin of Scripture and virtually abandoned the fideistic defense of the witness of the Holy Spirit.

The main purpose of this study is to trace the context and development of Jean-Alphonse Turretin's form of enlightened orthodoxy and to show its significance as a herald of the decline of orthodoxy in the age of the Enlightenment. A secondary goal will show that Jean-Alphonse Turretin, rather than his father, Francis Turretin, diverged from the views of Calvin on the subject of scriptural authority. Jean-Alphonse Turretin's importance as a Reformed theologian lies in his new system of religious authority that rejected the scholastic methodology of his predecessors.

To understand the development of Jean-Alphonse Turretin's theological system, one must describe his views of Reformed scholasticism as well as the theological climate that contributed to his rejection of everything for which his father stood. The first chapter outlines the nature of Reformed scholasticism in Geneva and focuses on the introduction of the most specific theological creed of Swiss Reformed church history, the Formula Consensus Helvetica.

The second chapter delineates the education of Jean-Alphonse Turretin. Included is a discussion of the influence of Cartesian philosophy at the academy, which was introduced by the professor of philosophy, Jean-Robert Chouet. This chapter also has an analysis of the liberal party at the Academy of Geneva that was sympathetic with the compromise doctrines of Saumur and provided Jean-Alphonse Turretin with the basic framework for his theological system. Foremost among the leadership of the liberal party was Louis Tronchin and Philippe Mestrezat, both professors of theology. Lastly, a brief description of Turretin's travels abroad indicates other influences on his thought that gave him a predisposition to form a theological system that Protestants of both Lutheran and Anglican confessions could accept.

The third chapter focuses on Turretin's system of natural theology and specifically, the way that deism, atheism,and Socinianism posed far more fundamental threats to Reformed orthodoxy than the doctrines of Saumur. Turretin's views of natural revelation indicate a desire to convince unbelievers of the reasonableness of the Christian faith.

In the fourth chapter, Turretin's system of special revelation is discussed. Here Turretin stands in contrast with both his father and Calvin with his use of external or evidential proofs for the divinity of Scripture. This, too, was an attempt to show the non-Christian that the Christian faith had a rational basis.

Chapters five and six outline the application of Turretin's views of religious authority in the theological climate of Reformed Switzerland. Turretin worked toward the abolition of the Formula Consensus in Geneva and he was involved in the negotiations over its abrogation in the neighboring city of Lausanne. In addition, chapter six discusses Turretin's simple form of theology that focused on a small core of fundamental doctrines which constituted the basis of his attempts to form a union with the Church of England and the Lutherans of Prussia.

1

The Nature of Reformed Scholasticism and the Debates over the Adoption of the Helvetic Formula Consensus in Geneva

To understand Jean-Alphonse Turretin's concept of enlightened orthodoxy, one must first examine the theological climate at the Academy of Geneva prior to and during the formative years of his education. The second half of the seventeenth century was a troubled period at the academy. It was embroiled in bitter disputes among the faculty over the issues of the Formula Consensus and universal grace. Educated at the academy from 1685–91, Turretin became a strong advocate for toleration among Protestant factions as well as a fervent opponent of Roman Catholicism. His penchant for a tolerant (at least among his Protestant brethren) approach to religion was largely a reaction against Reformed theology as it was epitomized in the Helvetic Formula Consensus. This has generally been viewed by scholars as the high point of the theological development within Calvinism known as "Reformed scholasticism." As an advocate of religious tolerance, one of Turretin's foremost accomplishments was to change this Reformed scholastic movement by working for the abrogation of the Formula Consensus in 1706. His stance against the Formula Consensus was a natural consequence of his system of enlightened orthodoxy.

The Development of the Scholastic Method in the Post-Reformation Era

It is significant to note that the scholastic method, which had primarily been a medieval Roman Catholic approach to theological study, began to penetrate Protestantism in the wake of both Luther and Calvin. Luther was thoroughly trained in the tradition of late-medieval nominalism as can be seen in his stance on the question of universals. He was, however, quite skeptical of the use of scholastic philosophy in theological discourse. For example, in his *Disputation Against Scholastic Theology* (1517), Luther denounced Occamist theology mainly for its semi-Pelagianism and for its application of logic to theological mysteries.[1] Calvin, though trained as a humanist, shared Luther's disdain for scholastic thought.[2]

Catholic scholasticism continued, in spite of opposition from the Protestant Reformation, into the sixteenth and seventeenth centuries. The center for such thought was no longer Paris, but Salamanca in Spain and Coimbra in Portugal where the Society of Jesus and the Reformed Carmelites supported it. This sixteenth-century Catholic scholasticism had a presence in Germany as well through the efforts of the Spanish Jesuit, Gregory of Valencia (d. 1603), who was a professor at Ingolstadt. Its center of influence, however, was in Spain.[3]

The Spanish Jesuit, Francisco Suarez (1548–1617), was the most prominent of the Spanish scholastics and taught philosophy and theology at Segovia, Valladolid, Rome, Alcalá, Salamanca, and Coimbra. The *Disputationes metaphysicae* (1597), his most influential treatise, went through twenty separate editions and was read widely by Protestants and Catholics alike throughout Europe.[4] Martin Grabmann praised it as a monumental achievement in scholastic philosophy for its synthesis of medieval scholastic arguments and for its careful discussion of philosophical problems and solutions.[5]

In order to defend the Catholic faith, Suarez drew upon the arguments of medieval scholastic theologians, such as Durandus, Giles of Rome, Peter Lombard, Duns Scotus, William of Ockham, and especially Aquinas. Suarez used Thomist metaphysical proofs for the existence of God such as the cosmological argument.[6]

In the *Disputationes metaphysicae,* Suarez addressed the fundamental distinction between essence and existence. He differed from Aquinas by holding that objective being has a real existence, rooted in the truth of divine knowledge.[7] In his discussion of the Trinity, Suarez argued that the divine Persons, though distinct, cannot be separated in being because of their necessary connection with one another. He disagreed with Aristotle's argument that things which are the same as a third thing are equal. Rather, he said that this argument cannot apply to the Trinity because of the Infinity of divine essence.[8]

As with the revival of Catholic scholasticism, the growth of Protestant scholasticism began before the deaths of Calvin and Luther. It became the organizing principle of Protestant theology by the end of the sixteenth century and in the next century, it dominated both Lutheran and Reformed camps.

It is very difficult to come to a precise definition of Protestant scholasticism. Two distinct schools of thought have emerged on this issue. The first, espoused principally by Brian Armstrong, views Reformed scholasticism as a marked deviation away from the clear Christocentric emphasis of Calvin and toward a speculative system centered on the doctrine of predestination. Armstrong describes the general tendencies of the movement and provides a framework for more specific discussions of the subject.[9] According to Armstrong, there are four main characteristics in Protestant scholasticism:

(1) Primarily, it will have reference to that theological approach which asserts religious truth on the basis of deductive ratiocination from given assumptions or principles. This provides a logically coherent and defensible system of belief, which generally takes the form of syllogistic reasoning. It seems invariably based upon an Aristotelian philosophical commitment and so related to medieval scholasticism. (2) The term will refer to the employment of reason in religious matters, so that reason has at least equal standing with faith in theology. Thus, some of the authority of revelation is lost. (3) It will comprehend the sentiment that the scriptural record contains a unified, rationally comprehensible account. It may be used as a measuring stick to determine one's orthodoxy. (4) It will include a pronounced interest in metaphysical matters, and abstract, speculative thought, particularly with reference to the doctrine of God. The distinctive Protestant position is made to rest on a speculative formulation of the will of God.[10]

The second position that has gained increasing acceptance in recent years is espoused by Richard A. Muller who notes an essential continuity between Calvin and his successors. He concludes that their major differences were primarily concerned with organizational structure rather than with doctrinal content.

One of Muller's major contributions is his definition of "scholasticism," which stresses the organization of theology rather than its specific content. Muller defines Reformed scholasticism as:

a highly technical and logical approach to theological system, according to which each theological topic or *locus* was divided into its component parts, the parts analyzed and then defined in careful propositional form. In addition, this highly technical approach sought to achieve precise definition by debate with adversaries and by use of the Christian tradition as a whole in arguing its doctrines. The form of theological system was adopted to a didactical and polemical model that could move from biblical definition to traditional development of doctrine, to debate with doctrinal adversaries past and present, to theological resolution of the problem. This method is rightly called scholastic both in view of its roots in medieval scholasticism and in view of its intention to provide an adequate technical theology for schools, seminaries and universities. The goal of this method, the dogmatic or doctrinal intention of this theology was to provide the church with "right teaching," literally, "orthodoxy."[11]

He later expands this definition by referring to scholasticism as a whole as:

a discipline characteristic of theological system from the late twelfth through the seventeenth century. Since scholasticism is primarily a method or approach to academic disciplines it is not necessarily allied to any particular philosophical perspective nor does it represent a systematic attachment to or concentration upon any particular doctrine or concept as a key to theological system.[12]

Having defined the term, Muller argues that its use was essential for defending orthodoxy, especially during the high orthodox era. He asserts that, although the theologians of the post-Reformation period used a scholastic methodology to clarify the Reformed system, they remained in essential agreement with the first generation of Reformed thought in content.

Muller views the antischolastic biases of Luther and Calvin as mere short-term abandonments of the medieval scholastic *locus* method. The followers of Luther and Calvin, who were responsible for systematizing and defending the theology of the first generation of the Reformation, relied on the "schoolmen" as their only model. Their dependence on such a formulation systematic theology does not mean that they agreed with the content of medieval scholasticism; they merely used its organizational structure.

Muller's main contention is that the Reformed scholastics who came after the Reformation were the real codifiers and perpetuators of the Reformation. They were responsible for organizing the theology of such founders as John Calvin, Wolfgang Musculus, Peter Martyr Vermigli, Andreas Hyperius, and Heinrich Bullinger. It is important to note here that Muller advocates the multiple origin of the Reformed faith and dismisses the notion that Calvin was the sole, or even the principal, founder of the movement. One must speak of a Reformed movement rather than of Calvinism per se.[13]

The major difficulty with applying Muller's definition to the entire post-Reformation period is that it assumes that all of the post-Reformation theologians had the same purpose. Certainly, Muller would admit that there were many differences between individual theologians and that some displayed more of a speculative approach than others.

In fairness to Brian Armstrong, some of the post-Reformation scholastic theologians did conform more exactly to his definition than to Muller's. For example, Pierre du Moulin (1568–1658), one of the major leaders of the French Reformed church in the era of the Synod of Dort, was a thorough advocate of the speculative, Aristotelian form of theology that Armstrong's definition finds normative. Armstrong cites du Moulin: "I will boldly state that theology is more contemplative than practical, inasmuch as contemplation is the reason for action, for by good works we aspire to the vision of God." In du Moulin's case, many influences contributed to his scholastic framework, though his privileged class status played the largest role.[14]

Muller's view, however, has gained increasing support in recent years and his thesis is particularly applicable to this discussion because Reformed scholasticism provided the backdrop for the development of Jean-Alphonse Turretin's system of enlightened orthodoxy. Interestingly enough, Turretin viewed the movement along Armstrong's lines and saw his own system as a return to the humanistic emphasis of the magisterial reformers. In light of these two perspectives, it is important to sketch out the development of the Reformed scholastic movement that Jean-Alphonse Turretin disagreed with so ardently.

The Development of Reformed Scholasticism

Richard Muller has provided the best framework for understanding the development of Reformed scholasticism up to the time of Francis Turretin. Muller divides the post-Reformation era into three periods. (1) Early orthodoxy, from 1565 to 1630 or 1640, saw the internationalization of Reformed theology embodied by the Synod of Dort. This was the era of Theodore Beza, William Perkins, Amandus Polandus von Polansdorf, and Girolamo Zanchi. (2) High orthodoxy fully modified and developed the system of theology, It concluded at the end of the seventeenth century and contained the works of such theologians as Francis Turretin, John Owen, and Benedict Pictet. (3) Late orthodoxy, which developed after 1700 was philosophically eclectic and less acrimonious in its attacks on other orthodox Protestant groups than the earlier periods. During this time, rationalist philosophy superseded orthodoxy and dethroned theology as "the queen of the sciences."[15]

Muller disagrees with Armstrong's contention that the scholastics emphasized "a more philosophically and metaphysically oriented theology grounded on a speculative formulation of the will than had been seen in earlier Protestantism." This definition assumes a substantive change from a biblical, christocentric theology to an Aristotelian-based system that focused on the doctrine of predestination.[16]

Reformed scholasticism was not at all a negative development, but a necessary one designed to protect the essence of the Reform. The issue for Muller is not one of comparing Beza or Zanchi's treatment of predestination to Calvin's but rather of analyzing "the influence of Calvin and his contemporaries upon a developing Augustinian theology the roots of which extend into the middle ages, indeed, back to Augustine."[17]

The key point of Muller's analysis is that the Reformed scholastics employed medieval models for systematizing theology, but retained the basic doctrinal content of the Reformation. For Muller, a change in method by no means implies a change in dogma. He admits that the theological systems of the seventeenth century differed markedly from Calvin's 1559 edition of the *Institutes,* but the development of such changes must be analyzed and then the question of why they occurred can be determined. Only at this point can one judge whether or not Reformed scholasticism was really faithful to the heritage of the Reformation.[18]

In his analysis of this issue of continuity, Muller raised two important questions concerning the theology of high orthodoxy: Is it a predestinarian system and is it a form of rationalism? If one answers affirmatively to both, one must admit sharp changes from the Reformation period. Prolegomenon, he argues, serves as a key topic for answering such questions because it was "designed specifically for the purpose of presenting and defining the presuppositions and principles controlling the system of theology as a whole." Muller contends that predestination is never presented as a controlling theme in the Prolegomena of the Reformed scholastics. It serves simply as one among several doctrinal foci.[19]

On the issue of rationalism, Muller asserts that scholars have mistakenly believed that reason and revelation had equal footing in Reformed scholasticism primarily because of the simultaneous development of the Protestant system and philosophical rationalism. This is a false assumption, he argues, because the Reformed scholastics generally opposed both Cartesian deductivism and Baconian inductivism. Eventually, by the mid-eighteenth century, the triumph of reason over revelation succeeded in dismantling of the scholastic method. This, by no means, indicates that the orthodox theologians rejected the use of reason. They used it as a means of understanding revelation. In cases where revelation did not meet the standards of reason, the scholastics followed the example of the Reformers and accepted the revealed mysteries of the faith as suprarational.[20]

On this point, Muller disagrees with the traditional analysis of the "Calvin against the Calvinists" approach of such scholars as Basil Hall, Ernst Bizer, and Hans Emil Weber. These historians argue that rationalism served as the primary principle of explaining the will of God. Bizer, in defense of this approach, redefines rationalism as a "system assuming both the standard of Scriptural revelation and the standard of rational proof to the end that faith rests upon demonstrable evidence and rational necessity." It is not a system that elevates reason as the sole norm of truth.[21] Muller prefers the latter definition and disagrees with Bizer's distinction because it allows for two very different meanings for the same term. In addition, Bizer's definition denies the law of noncontradiction in areas where reason and revelation conflict.[22]

Muller contends, however, that reason was very helpful for the Reformed scholastics. It helped describe the doctrines of Scripture, made the faith understandable to unbelievers and illustrated biblical mysteries such as the Trinity and the Incarnation. In addition, Muller observes that reason cannot properly judge mysteries that are "incomprehensible," but it can judge Lutheran and Roman Catholic doctrines, such as transubstantiation and the ubiquity of Christ, which the Reformed school deemed self-contradictory.[23]

Muller concludes that the Reformed scholastics used reason more freely than either Calvin or Luther. The scholastics needed to use reason in their construction of a carefully defined theological system in order to combat an increasingly sophisticated Roman Catholic apologetic. They were not, however, rationalists.[24]

Having dealt with the relationship between reason and revelation, Muller goes on to assert that the structure of Reformed Prolegomena of this period indicates that Reformed scholastic theology, as a whole, was primarily soteriological rather than speculative.[25] The conclusion is that the similarities between Protestant and medieval scholasticism are mostly in method of presentation. The Protestant variety adopted what they considered the best part of scholasticism: organizational brilliance and precision. It also avoided excessive speculation in epistemology and metaphysics. This allowed for the preservation and protection of the thought of the Reformation.[26]

Of particular importance to Muller's analysis is the work of Theodore Beza. Historians such as Bizer have blamed Beza, in particular, for introducing a "rationalistic spirit" into the faith as well as for moving the doctrine of predestination out of soteriology, where Calvin had put it, and into the doctrine of God, where it became a necessary corollary of divine sovereignty. Muller takes issue with this approach by arguing that Beza's treatment of predestination in the *Tabula praedestinationis* (1555) is primarily pastoral and provides assurance for the elect. Instead of focusing on the specific aspects of reprobation, Beza emphasized an invitation to all individuals to a saving knowledge of Christ.[27]

The second major point that Muller makes is that Beza did not replace a Christological focus in his theology with a "causal structure." Instead, Beza "argues the relationship of Christ and the decree in terms of a formula of limited redemption." Christ's work as the mediator reveals God's love and righteousness in order that the elect might be sanctified.[28]

Furthermore, Beza's *Tabula praedestinationis* was not a systematic theology, but only a short description of "the order of causes in predestination." Historians, he argues, have wrongly treated it as a system. Even so, Muller points out that the work is still primarily Christological in focus. It does include a strong adherence to a double-predestination, supralapsarian position. The deterministic side of Beza's work, however, always exists "in tension with a christocentric piety." Muller concludes that Beza clarified Calvin's thought and enhanced its precision. He did not formulate a "necessitarian system" based solely on predestination, but remained true to the essential nature of Calvin's theology.[29]

Muller goes on to place Ursinus and Zanchi within the same schema. They were more systematic and more clearly defined in their theology, but their scholasticism preserved the orthodoxy of the first generation of the reformers. Polanus and Perkins, for their part, emphasized the causal priorities of predestination, but they did not make predestination the sole controlling principle for systematizing theology. Predestination served merely as one among several such "boundary concepts" as the Trinity, *sola gratia,* the belief that God was not the author of sin, and the role of Christ in salvation. Muller argues that both Polanus and Perkins remained strongly Christological in their discussions of the divine will, which became effective through Christ.[30]

One of the key components of Muller's framework is the scholasticism of Francis Turretin. It is important in this discussion because Francis' son, Jean-Alphonse, reacted against the so-called scholasticism of his father. Francis was also one of the more famous of the so-called scholastics, especially because of the use of his *Institutio theologiae elencticae* as the standard theological text at Princeton Seminary in the nineteenth century until Charles Hodge published his own systematic theology, itself much indebted to Francis Turretin. Turretin is best known in the United States for his influence on the Princetonians, Charles and A. A. Hodge and B. B. Warfield.[31]

Muller's analysis of Francis Turretin shows that he was in agreement with Calvin on many of the essential aspects of his theological system. In fact, Muller concludes that Turretin allowed reason to play only a small part in establishing the divine origin of Scripture. Reason could not serve as the foundation of the faith because it was marred by the Fall. Reason could, however, be used to deduce doctrines that logically follow from clear biblical passages. By using this methodology, Turretin was able to avoid the rationalistic tendencies of the Remonstrants as well as the extreme fideism of the Enthusiasts.

The Introduction of the Helvetic Formula Consensus in Geneva

The major aspect of Francis Turretin's theological system, which his son detested, was epitomized in the theological creed that the elder Turretin introduced in Geneva. The Formula Consensus has generally been seen by historians as the epitome of Reformed scholastic theology. A study of its context and development will provide important insights into the nature of this form of theology. Reformed scholasticism's use of creeds developed out of an attempt to synthesize the theology of Calvin in response to specific theological, philosophical, and political challenges to Reformed orthodoxy. The Helvetic Formula Consensus was a response to the growing popularity of Remonstrant thought and the moderate compromise position of the Saumur Academy.

This form of Reformed thought, which developed after the Synod of Dort, was, in essence, a compromise with the contentions of the Remonstrants. It reflected the humanistic emphasis of the French church. It became known as "Amyraldism" or "Salmurianism" and grew out of the theological system of a professor of theology at the French Academy of Saumur,[32] Moïse Amyraut (1596–1664).[33]

Amyraut formulated the concept of "hypothetical universalism" that moderated, in theory, the Reformed doctrine of limited atonement as defined at the Synod of Dort. He maintained that God's redemptive plan includes all individuals, but cannot be fulfilled unless they believe. Since they cannot believe without the power of the Holy Spirit, a second, limited election is necessary for the elect. The basis for such an election is hidden in the counsel of God. In addition, Amyraut argued that the heathen did not need a specific knowledge of Christ but would be responsible only for the amount of light received. Since his concept of hypothetical universalism provided for the salvation of the elect alone, Amyraut believed that his theory would bridge the gap between Reformed and Remonstrant. The majority of Reformed theologians, however, rejected his system as the first step toward Arminianism.[34]

Josué de la Place (1596–1665), a colleague of Amyraut at Saumur, also proposed a theological concept that aroused shockwaves among most of the theological community of the Reformed church in Switzerland. The Synod of Dort had upheld the concept of the immediate imputation of Adam's guilt and subsequent condemnation. La Place, by contrast, advocated the concept of the mediate imputation of Adam's sin and based the human condemnation on individual depravity, rather than on a depravity resulting from Adam's sin. The underlying thought was that one man should not be responsible for another man's sin.[35]

Another of the professors at Saumur, Louis Cappel (1585–1658),[36] in his works, *Arcanum punctationis revelatum* (1624)[37] and *Critica sacra* (1650),[38] proposed several concepts about textual criticism and punctuation of the Old Testament that challenged the authority of the Masoretic text of the Old Testament. The first work was an anonymous reply to Johann Buxdorf's (1564–1629) argument concerning the authenticity of the vowel pointing of the Hebrew text of the Old Testament.[39]

The question of the punctuation of the Hebrew text of the Old Testament had been an important issue of scholarly concern among Reformed theologians during the first half of the seventeenth century. Johann Buxdorf, professor of Hebrew at the University of Basel, had written as early as 1620 that the vowel points of the Hebrew text were as old as the consonants. This issue was important because the vowel pointing made the meaning of the text more clear. Without the vowels, there could be several different readings for many passages. In addition, if the vowel points were added by the Masoretes five or six centuries after Christ, they would have been added by individuals not under the inspiration of the Holy Spirit. They would, therefore, be subject to error. The vowel points would, in reality, be the Masoretic commentary on the Old Testament and one could not be certain of the meaning of many passages. As a result, the Jesuit argument that the Old Testament meaning was obscure and in need of official church clarification would be strengthened. Buxdorf preferred to argue that the vowel points were added by the prophet Ezra and the rabbis of the Great Synagogue. Such editions would carry the weight of divine inspiration and the clarity of the text would be assured.[40]

Reformed scholars of the mid-seventeenth century, following Buxdorf, considered all other versions of the Old Testament as subordinate to the Masoretic text. When a version had a reading in variance with the Masoretic text, the latter reading would always be preferred. Cappel followed the work of the rabbinic scholar, Elijah Levita, and posited that the vowel points of the Masoretic text were most likely late additions, done perhaps as late as the period of the Babylonian Talmud.[41] In addition to the problem of punctuation, Cappel cited the plethora of textual variants in the Hebrew Text and the many readings of the Masoretic, which made little sense in their context. He advocated a critical approach to textual criticism that would employ other ancient translations and educated guesswork to improve upon these poor readings in the Masoretic text. Cappel was quick to point out, however, that none of these variants involved any important issue of doctrine on morality. He saw his work as an improvement on the Masoretic text.[42]

The Reformed scholastic theologians, who had elevated Scripture over the reasoning of critical scholarship, feared that opening the Masoretic text to critical inquiry would subject the Bible to the dictates of human reason. Francis Turretin feared that Cappel's approach would undermine the authenticity and authority of the text. He argued that the Masoretic text did not differ from the original autographs and cited the work of scholars such as Buxdorf, Arnold Boot, and Bishop Ussher. Textual criticism and punctuation of the Old Testament were reserved as areas that one must accept by faith and in which the dictates of reason should not enter.[43] John Beardslee describes the Reformed response to the subject of the textual criticism of Cappel:

Francis Turretin noted that Cappel's "theories" meant that the best text of the Bible we can possibly have depends on human scholarship;

this seemed to cut ground from under Protestantism. Such admission that there had been "corruption of the text" he regards as human error. Cappel's theories were generally rejected in Reformed circles, although tolerated in France. The inspiration of the vowel points became virtually an article of faith in Switzerland, and dogma retarded the growth of scholarly criticism.[44]

One reason that such ideas were popular at Saumur was the desire of the theological faculty for an effective apologetic argument against Roman Catholicism. Roman Catholic scholars said that Reformed theology minimized the love of God in favor of his decrees. The concepts of the mediate imputation of Adam's sin and hypothetical universalism upheld the Reformed doctrines of human depravity and divine election while emphasizing that God offered each individual the fair opportunity to come to a saving knowledge of Christ. The stress on textual criticism at Saumur pointed to an openness to rational inquiry that made Reformed thought more palatable for the reasonable inquirer.

The Formula Consensus was not approved in the Swiss Confederation until 1675 and not until four years later in Geneva. In its final form, there were twenty-six articles. The first three were directed against the textual criticism of Louis Cappel. The articles defended the literal inspiration of Scripture, the preservation of the vowel points of the Masoretic text, and the lack of any need to resort to the use of ancient translation or conjecture to improve upon doubtful readings in the Masoretic text.

Articles four to nine and thirteen to twenty-two were directed at the teachings of Amyraut. These articles denied that God intended to save all people on the condition of their faith in Christ. They outlined the Reformed position on the limited atonement of Christ and stated that general revelation could never lead the heathen to salvation. Salvation in the Old Testament was limited to the elect of the nation of Israel and, in the New Testament, to the church.

Articles ten to twelve attacked the views of Josué de La Place and stated that one stands condemned before God for one's own sin, for the sin of Adam and for inherited depravity. Articles twenty-two to twenty-six held that only two covenants between God and man existed in the Bible; the covenant of the works between God and Adam and the covenant of grace between God and his people. These articles were directed against Amyraut's concept of three covenants: those of nature (between God and Adam), law (between God and the nation of Israel) and grace (between God and the church).[45]

This Consensus was meant not only to condemn Salmurian theology, but also to unite the evangelical cantons in a common definition of the faith. Such unity was deemed necessary to strengthen Reformed Switzerland against the Counter-Reformation.[46]

The disunity it sought to remedy in the period before its adoption was epitomized in Geneva. The leading theological professors at the Academy of Geneva, including Francis Turretin, had received some theological training at Saumur under the guidance of Cappel, Amyraut, and La Place. Louis Tronchin and his colleague, Philippe Mestrezat, both grew to admire their mentors at Saumur and propounded Salmurian doctrines in their theology classes at the Academy of Geneva. Francis Turretin, however, reacted strongly against the teachings of Saumur and wanted to maintain the tradition of the Synod of Dort, which condemned such innovations.[47]

Geneva was not the only city that debated the controversial doctrines of Saumur. The debate raged throughout the cantons of Switzerland. Geneva, partly because of the theological diversity of the faculty at its academy, would be the last city to ratify the Formula.

One can trace the controversy in Geneva over the disputed doctrines of Saumur back to 1647 when Alexander Morus (1616–70), professor of theology at the Academy of Geneva, expressed sympathy with some of the Salmurian teachings. Morus, French by birth, was gifted with tremendous oratorical abilities. He had studied at Saumur and completed his theological education at Geneva in 1639, when he was named professor of Greek at the academy. He enjoyed strong support from the Council, which recommended him for ordination in 1641. However, the Company of Pastors was suspicious of his theological leanings and attempted to postpone his ordination for one year. They feared, in particular, that Morus supported La Place on the mediate imputation of Adam's sin, Amyraut on universal grace, and Piscator on the passive righteousness of Christ.[48] The Company was not able to delay the process because of pressure from the Council. When Morus denied all charges of heterodoxy, he was duly ordained. In 1642, the Council also strongly urged the Company of Pastors to elect him professor of theology to replace Spanheim, who had left to teach at Leiden. After a three-year hiatus from controversy and with his popularity growing, new rumors began to circulate concerning the content of Morus's lectures as well as his personal conduct. Apparently, many believed that Morus was a womanizer and members of the Company believed that if his personal conduct was suspect, his theology could be also. As a result, the Company summoned him for further questioning, which significantly tarnished his reputation, even though he was able to convince the majority of members that he was not teaching Salmurian theology. Upon request, the Company sent out a testimonial stating that Morus was indeed orthodox. However, he had grown weary of the constant inquiries and rumors and decided that it would be best for all involved if he left Geneva.[49]

Having accepted a call to pastor a church and teach theology in Middelbourg, Holland, Morus asked the Company to provide an honorable letter of dismissal. Having received it, he remained in Geneva for eight more months, while questions concerning his beliefs continued to circulate. At this point, the church in Middelbourg requested further assurances. Part of the problem was that Morus seemed to support Salmurianism in his lectures, but when asked about such statements, he denied any support of the disputed doctrines. He was charged with a host of irregular activities, such as skipping lectures in order to eavesdrop on the meetings of the Council while the representatives of the Company of Pastors were reporting on his orthodoxy.[50]

Although he eventually was able to clear his name, the affair led to the règlement of 1647 and the theses of 1649 to be signed by all candidates for the ministry. The articles were the first step toward the adoption of the Formula Consensus. Beardslee describes the articles as follows:

> They [the theses of 1649] involved the following affirmations regarding original sin; that the sin of Adam is directly imputed to everyone so that we are individually on three counts, Adam's sin, for we sinned in him (directly imputed sin), the corruption of our own nature is the penalty for Adam's sin (mediately imputed sin), and our own sin. . . . The remaining "Articles of Morus' dealt with predestination, redemption and grace in such a way as to exclude any ground for salvation except God's good pleasure toward the elect, and any suggestion that Christ died not for any except those who were eternally elect.[51]

These articles contributed to the basis of the Formula Consensus. They needed to be revised, however, in order to serve as a general formulary for the entire Swiss confederation as well as for Geneva. The Formula Consensus and the debates concerning its scope occupied the majority of theological discussion during Jean-Alphonse Turretin's tenure as a student at the academy.

The Morus affair, being one of the major, preliminary skirmishes leading up to the adoption of the Formula in Geneva, did not at all insure that the conservative party would prevail in doctrinal affairs. Having pressured Morus to leave his post, the Company of Pastors felt that they had rid themselves of the threat of the encroachment of the Salmurian doctrinal position. However, the worst was yet to come. Philippe Mestrezat, elected as Morus's replacement, was as much of an adherent of the teachings of Saumur as was Morus. The Company was understandably concerned and, before 1659, Antoine Léger, a professor of theology, suggested the possibility of a creed for all of the Swiss cantons in a private letter to Antistes Ulrich of Zurich. Upon the death of Léger, however, the Council elected Louis Tronchin as his replacement. Tronchin, yet another advocate of Saumur, would be one of the mentors for Jean-Alphonse Turretin.[52]

The movement toward the formulation of a new Swiss theological creed continued, however, in spite of the addition of these liberal minded, theological faculty at the Genevan Academy. As early as 1667, Lucas Gernler (d. 1675) of Basel wrote to Johann Heinrich Heidegger of Zurich that at least four Swiss towns would support Francis Turretin's efforts to rid the Academy of Geneva of the Salmurian teachings. Francis Turretin himself complained to the Company of Pastors that the teachings of Mestrezat and Tronchin had violated the orthodoxy of the Synod of Dort. The occasion of Turretin's objection was the refusal of Charles Maurice, a graduate of the academy and a candidate for a Reformed pastorate in France, to sign the 1647 and 1649 rules of the Reformed faith. He preferred to sign only the Articles of Dort and the confession of the Reformed church of France. The implication was that Maurice considered the Genevan doctrinal statements to be much more tightly defined than had been the pronouncements of Dort. Mestrezat and Tronchin objected to any attempt to force Maurice to sign the articles, asserting that Maurice, as a French pastor, should not sign the Genevan articles.[53]

Turretin, however, attempted to force Tronchin and Mestrezat to sign the articles as well. They refused to do so and, significantly, four Genevan pastors stood with them. Although they were clearly in a minority within the Company of Pastors, they brought their case to the Small Council, which provided them with a compromise solution. Tronchin and Mestrezat would not have to sign the 1647 and 1649 articles, but they did sign a compromise formula, under pressure from the Small Council and the Company of Pastors, stating that they would not teach anything contrary to the rules of 1647 and 1649. This decision allowed for some measure of toleration for the liberal party. It also aroused suspicion from among the more conservative theological elements in Zurich, Basel, Bern, and Schaffhausen, each of which threatened to withdraw their students from the academy unless the liberal party agreed fully to the articles.[54]

This incident, called the "affaire de la grâce universelle," caused such controversy that the enrollment of theology students dropped significantly after 1669. In addition, Francis Turretin was so alarmed by the growth of the strength of the liberal party within both the academy and the Company of Pastors that he wrote to Heidegger on 6 November 1669, and suggested the formulation of a new creed for all of Switzerland for which subscription would be required. The idea was, therefore, to force the liberal party to submit to a strict anti-Salmurian creed.[55]

The Council hoped to quiet the whole issue by returning to the old subscription of the articles. However, within twelve days of this pronouncement, a significant event took place when the professor of philosophy, Gaspard Wyss, died. His replacement, Jean-Robert Chouet, was an ardent Cartesian and an opponent of such a requirement. The Council ordered him, subsequently, to teach according to the old Reformed creed whenever he commented on theological subjects.[56] It was obvious, therefore, that adherence to the articles would not insure that the doctrines of Saumur would not be taught in Geneva. Members of the conservative party felt that a more formal and more thorough condemnation of the suspected teachings was necessary.

In 1669, several theologians, including Hummel of Basel, Ott of Schaffhausen, and Gernler of Basel, met at Baden and agreed formally upon the necessity of drafting what was to become the Formula Consensus. Heidegger concurred, but significant variations among the major cantons arose concerning the nature of such a creed. The more conservative theologians wanted statements directed against not only the doctrines of Saumur, but against Cocceianism as well.[57] Others, such as John Rudolph Westein of Basel, objected to the very notion of a formulary.[58]

Many of the leading divines at Zurich advocated a thorough rejection of any concept that was the least heterodox, including the covenant theology of Cocceius. Zurich, one of the most conservative of the cantons, had withdrawn its theological students from the Saumur Academy as early as 1636, preferring to send them to Montauban where they would be assured a more conservative approach to theological education. The predisposition in Zurich in favor of the Formula can also be seen in an incident in 1660, when a certain Rev. Michael Zink was suspended from the ministry for disagreeing with the canons of Dort on the issue of reprobation. Although Zurich had not formally subscribed to Dort, this act showed their support for its doctrinal provisions. The main proponent of the Formula Consensus in Zurich was Johann Heinrich Heidegger.[59]

By June of 1674, the Swiss Evangelical diet ordered the creed to be drawn up. Gernler would normally have been the most obvious choice to write the Formula, but he had just died and it was left to Heidegger to compose the initial draft. This insured that the Formula would be drawn along the more moderate line since Heidegger would not countenance a denunciation of his own Cocceian form of Calvinism. Having written the draft, Heidegger allowed the ministers of Zurich to suggest changes. They did so making the condemnations of Saumur sharper and more specific.[60]

The newly drafted Formula faced the difficult prospect of adoption within the various cantons. Basel was the first to sign in 1675 and Zurich quickly followed. The more conservative theologians in Zurich, led by John Müller, Waser, and the Antistes opposed the moderate tone of the Formula and attempted to have the text altered in order to condemn Cocceianism. Müller openly preached against Heidegger and covertly composed an alternate creed. In addition, Müller, leading the high Calvinist party, attempted to have the seventh article of the Formula changed, saying that it attributed to the law what was really fulfilled in Christ. Heidegger protested, by claiming that the Formula never gave the law such a status. He said that the passage in question referred to the law fulfilled in Christ. In any case, the burgomaster would not allow the Formula to be changed, but did allow a clarifying notation to be placed in the city archives.[61]

Bern subscribed to the Formula in June and the other cantons followed in 1676. Neuchâtel usually agreed with their Swiss brethren on theological matters. The opposition in Neuchâtel was led by John Rudolph Ostervald, who objected to the statements in the Formula concerning the Masoretic pointing. Neuchâtel finally signed the document, but individual subscription was not required.[62]

The city of Geneva did not accept the Consensus until 1679. The conservative party in Geneva was similar to the Heidegger party in Zurich and wanted to condemn only the controversial doctrines of Saumur. The faculty of the Academy of Geneva, however, was not uniformly against the teachings of Saumur and some of its members saw no reason to condemn their French Reformed brethren. During two years of debate between Tronchin and Mestrezat, on the one hand, and Turretin on the other, the Academy of Geneva witnessed intense arguments over the issue. The debate drew several prominent French theologians into the fray, including Jean Claude.[63] He despised the mere thought of such a creed for fear that it would divide, rather than unify, the Swiss Reformed church. Claude and Jean Daillé (1594–1670) argued that the rigid, mechanical theory of biblical inspiration advocated in the Consensus would render the entire study of textual criticism and of ancient translations useless because if necessitated the perpetual miracle of the divine preservation of the text.[64]

By September of 1676, the Company of Pastors showed little desire to discuss the Formula Consensus or to make it binding to the academy. They believed that the creed would be too technical for less than the best theological minds to decipher. By February 1678, however, the Company of Pastors favored approval and in January 1679, the Council formally announced that candidates for ordination would have to subscribe to it. Several factors contributed to this change in posture. First, Heidegger had testified that the articles would merely safeguard the authority and authenticity of the Bible and would not regulate on matters of grammar and criticism. Second, the other Swiss cantons applied significant pressure to the Company of Pastors in Geneva to accept the Formula Consensus. Beardslee notes that it took pressure from the civil power of the various Swiss cantons to persuade the authorities in Geneva to go along with the creed. In other words, the theological arguments in favor of the Formula Consensus were not as persuasive as the political arguments. Beardslee concludes that, in Geneva, the Consensus possessed only a tenuous amount of support that would not last long after Francis Turretin's death.[65]

The Helvetic Formula Consensus represents a Reformed scholasticism that was characterized mainly as a thorough definition of orthodoxy along credal lines. Its minute detail was intended to defend Reformed theology against any tint of Remonstrant thought. Theologians such as Francis Turretin refused to countenance any possibility of a repetition, in Geneva or in Switzerland, of the theological diversity in the Low Countries where Arminianism had its stronghold. They saw any compromise, such as the doctrines of Saumur, as the first step toward the dissolution of the heritage of Calvin. The scholasticism of the Formula, thus, had an apologetic purpose as a response to specific philosophical and theological developments in the third quarter of the seventeenth century. As the historical milieu changed even further during the last quarter of the century and the beginning of the eighteenth century, the old patterns of the Consensus were no longer useful in defending Reformed thought. The next generation of theologians at Geneva, led by Jean-Alphonse Turretin, would develop a new system of enlightened orthodoxy that would emphasize a more practical faith, which was far removed form the old, tightly defined theological creeds.

2

Reformed Liberalism at the Academy of Geneva: The Education of Jean-Alphonse Turretin

Even after the Company of Pastors and the Small Council approved the enforcement of adherence to the Formula Consensus as a prerequisite for ordination and admission into the Company, significant differences of opinion continued. Mestrezat and Tronchin signed the Formula, but still objected to it for several reasons. First, they sincerely believed that its articles contradicted both Scripture and good sense. Second, they saw in the Formula a narrowing of the definition of Reformed orthodoxy beyond the views of Calvin and Beza, and the Helvetic Confession. Third, they felt that forcing the theological students to sign the articles would divide, rather than strengthen, the Reformed movement. In this last argument, they were in agreement with their French colleagues. By signing the Formula Consensus, Mestrezat and Tronchin promised that they would not teach Salmurian theology. They had previously reduced their teaching loads following the affair of 1669 and had been teaching private classes where they could employ a critical approach to theological issues that favored Saumur without fear of punishment.[1]

Although Francis Turretin had accomplished his task of enforcing his brand of orthodoxy upon the Academy of Geneva, his opponents, even though they had to assent to the Formula, continued in their opposition to the elder Turretin's views. They wanted to teach their students in a way that ensured the next generation of Reformed pastors and theologians would adhere to a more moderate form of Reformed thought.

When Francis Turretin died in 1687, the reactions of the pastors and theologians in Geneva were understandably mixed. Although the sixteen-year-old Jean-Alphonse Turretin received many letters of condolence from Protestant leaders throughout Europe, others privately exulted in the passing of his father. For example, Daniel Chamier, a Reformed pastor and a graduate of the Academy of Geneva, who had been ordained in neighboring Neuchâtel because he refused to sign the Formula, expressed his delight to his uncle Louis Tronchin. Chamier ridiculed those who eulogized the late Reformed theologian when he wrote: "Good God, to go and spread such foolishness in the flesh is to mock both God and man. If we had only heard the same news [about Francis Turretin's death] some thirty years ago, our Church and your Academy would have been so happy! God has lavished his mercy upon them and has pardoned the excesses that his [Turretin's] passion and lack of charity have caused them to commit."[2] It is significant that this letter was addressed to Tronchin because it indicates that the liberal party in Geneva was more relieved than grieved at Francis Turretin's death. He had been a stumbling block to their efforts to construct a more reasonable form of orthodoxy that could stand firm against the rigors of Socinianism, deism, atheism, and Roman Catholicism. With the death of Turretin, the door swung open for the liberal party to dominate the academy, the Company of Pastors, and the City Council.

Developments at the Academy of Geneva

The chief role of the academy was to prepare young men for the ministry within the Reformed church. The complete course of training lasted four years including two years of philosophy and two years of theology. The subfields of the philosophy curriculum included logic, physics, chemistry, cosmology, and anthropology. Furthermore, students continued their courses in Greek and began elementary lessons in Hebrew during their first two years. Young Jean-Alphonse Turretin listened to six hours of lessons a day during the philosophy phase of his education.

His classmates came from a diverse array of backgrounds. The academy attracted many foreign students, mostly from France, but it experienced a significant drop in native students due to dissatisfaction over the "querelle de la grâce universelle".

The last twenty-five years of the seventeenth century witnessed the growing secularization of the academy, not only in the discipline and academic performance of the student body, but also because of the growing dominance of Cartesian philosophy. During this period, a growing number of students were preparing themselves not for careers as ministers, but as lawyers, public officials, and merchants. Heyd points out that the number of students studying philosophy was growing at the expense of the theology department. From 1655 to 1665, sixty-one percent of the students were studying theology. This figure dropped alarmingly to forty percent from 1675 to 1685. Further, for the same two time periods, the percentage of students studying philosophy increased from thirty-nine percent to fifty-nine percent.[3] Since the number of students from France grew during this period, the change might well have been due to the problems within the French academies caused in turn by the growing royal hostility to the French Reformed church. Understandably, with the prospects of persecution on the horizon, many students decided to complete their education outside of France. Further, the possibility of repression might well have played a role in many deciding not to study theology at all. In addition, the revocation of the Edict of Nantes in 1685 resulted in a significant decline in the number of French students at the academy. Many decided to go to other schools farther away from France than Geneva. Neuchâtel and Vaud contributed at least partially for this decline by sending philosophy students to the academy from their environs. A major reason for the popularity of philosophy at Geneva was the arrival of a new faculty member, who would become one of the mentors for Jean-Alphonse Turretin, Jean-Robert Chouet.[4]

Jean-Robert Chouet

The teaching of Jean-Robert Chouet left a profound imprint upon the young Turretin. It was Chouet's experimental method and use of Cartesian philosophy that was most important. When Turretin entered the academy in 1685, Chouet was at the height of his career and enjoyed an international reputation. Pierre Bayle had been one of his students and had remarked that he was one of the most important and prestigious philosophers of the era.[5] According to Charles Borgeaud, Chouet left a tremendous imprint on the students at the academy because he was totally dedicated to his work while many of his colleagues split their time between teaching and other occupations such as medicine or the ministry.[6]

Chouet has been credited with the introduction of Cartesian philosophy in the academy, a system of thought that Turretin employed in his theological discourses. It seems quite surprising that Chouet, who had taught at the Academy of Saumur for five years, received the chair of philosophy at the Genevan academy precisely during the era of controversy over the theological position of Saumur. During the 1660s, the Salmurian and Arminian ideas were the main targets of both the Company of Pastors and the conservative members of the academy. Chouet, understandably, could never have gained the post if he had openly advocated Salmurian theology. Consequently, the choice of Chouet to succeed Gaspard Wyss was not an easy decision for either the Company or the Council. Chouet's father, Pierre Chouet, was an important printer in the city and his mother, Renée Tronchin, was the daughter of the famous theologian Théodore Tronchin. In addition, his uncle, Louis Tronchin, was his major supporter. In fact, it was Louis Tronchin who first convinced Chouet to seek the post in the first place. Although Chouet was a Cartesian and had taught at Saumur, he was very careful during the proceedings leading up to his appointment not to offend the more conservative members of the academy. His predisposition to avoid controversy led to his request for the Company of Pastors to forego the customary disputation in which he would have to answer questions on controversial topics. The Company, led by Francis Turretin, decided instead to draw up a list of conditions that would prohibit Chouet from teaching the disputed doctrines of Saumur. Heyd observes that the Council applied considerable pressure on the Company to ensure that Chouet, who had already gained a wide reputation, would join the faculty.[7]

Almost immediately after his accession to the chair of philosophy, the Company of Pastors required its members to sign the 1649 articles with the *sic sentio* (thus I believe). Six members refused to sign in this manner and were allowed to sign instead with *sic docebo* (thus I will teach). Chouet, facing the prospect of signing the articles with the *sic sentio* before he would be allowed to join the ranks of the Company, notified them that he would not sign. He reasoned that he was not a professional theologian, but a philosopher who should not have to comment on such technical matters that were beyond his area of expertise. He was, therefore, allowed to sign a special statement that referred directly to the 1647 and 1649 articles with the *sic docebo* and was thereby admitted into the Company.[8] Heyd summarizes the process as follows:

> The opposition to Chouet's nomination in Geneva seems, then, to have been the result of the rivalry between Tronchin and Turretin and the suspicions concerning the theological views of anyone coming from Saumur. Cartesianism was not an ideological issue in Geneva in 1669, but Salmurian theology was. By convincing his colleagues that he was going to stay out of that controversy, Chouet managed to win accep-

tance to the Company of Pastors and to the Academy in a period of tighter orthodox control. As for Tronchin, he could gain the upper hand when it was a question of nominating a philosophy professor, but he was definitely in a minority, both in Company and Council, when it came to theological issues.[9]

Although theologians at the academy continued to view Arminianism, Salmurianism, and Roman Catholicism as the major threats to the Reformed faith, deism and atheism were beginning to be seen as far more dangerous. The works of Spinoza and Hobbes took aim at the heart of the Christian faith by denying the validity of biblical miracles. In addition, by 1678, the French Oratorian priest, Richard Simon, published his famous *Histoire critique du Vieux Testament,* which denied the Mosaic authorship of sections of the Pentateuch such as those passages referring to the death and burial of Moses.[10] This early use of biblical criticism was far more dangerous to the integrity of the biblical text than had been Cappel's position on the inspiration of the vowel points of the Masoretic text. Now biblical criticism was beginning to cast doubts about more basic assumptions.

In such an environment, Chouet introduced his Cartesianism into his physics classes and soon such ideas were finding their way into the theological realm as well. Chouet found in Descartes an ally for the Reformed faith. However, in the process, his methodology would call into question all areas of theology, including those topics which had been labeled as mysteries, namely the Incarnation and the Trinity. Turretin, by employing aspects of Chouet's Cartesianism, constructed a system of religious authority that was even more rationalistic than that of any of his predecessors.

The magnitude of the danger of such new ideas explains in part why Chouet's Cartesianism could be introduced without causing any real furor. The Company of Pastors was far more concerned about the more immediate threats of deism or atheism. Cartesianism, although it represented a departure from Reformed scholasticism, was quite compatible with many aspects of Reformed thought, especially the Reformed argument on the spiritual presence of Christ in the elements of the Lord's Supper.

The threat of these new ideas reached into the academy itself during the period of Chouet's tenure as professor of philosophy. Heyd points to two important examples of this threat. In 1676, one of Chouet's students was suspected of atheism. Chouet was assigned to interview the suspect and warned him not to show any indications of doubt as to the existence of God even though the student denied the charge. In 1678, two other students were suspected of deism. Heyd writes that this incident "illustrates the type of relationship between Cartesian natural philosophy and radical religious views at a time when the new philosophy was not yet integrated into the official orthodox theology." One of the suspected students, François Deschamps, had been a recent convert to Protestantism from Roman Catholicism. He came to Geneva in 1678 and applied for admission for the study of theology. Although it is uncertain whether he was formally admitted, Deschamps did begin to teach private philosophy lessons. Rumors began to spread concerning these lessons. Furthermore, one of his students, Aaron Savignac, had expressed doubts concerning the inspiration of Scripture and the divinity of Christ. During the Company of Pastors' investigation into the incident, both men affirmed adherence to orthodox belief. When Deschamps was asked what he had been doing since his arrival in Geneva, he answered that he was teaching philosophy after the model of Descartes and had not strayed from orthodoxy. Although these men were cleared of all charges of heterodoxy, the investigation by the Company indicates a sensitivity to the possibility of any incursion of heresy into the academy. The Company would investigate all cases in which the possibility of theological error existed.[11]

In spite of the threat of these new ideas, Chouet became firmly entrenched among the theological establishment of Geneva and quickly expanded his influence into the political environment as well. He held the chair of philosophy until 1686, when he was elected to the Small Council, and he maintained the conciliar post until he was elected syndic in 1699.[12]

During the period when he was one of Jean-Alphonse Turretin's teachers, as one of two professors of philosophy at the academy, Chouet taught two-thirds of all the philosophy lessons. His colleague, Daniel Puerari, a physician by training, taught the rest. Chouet's class met two consecutive hours every Monday, Tuesday, Thursday, and Saturday, devoting Wednesday afternoons to experiments.[13]

Chouet gave physics lessons four days a week, alternating between dictating and explaining his lessons to his students. Typically, the professor of philosophy had to adhere closely to the Aristotelian organizational structure. However, by 1668, the philosophy professors began to have their course notes printed, which allowed them greater freedom to diverge from the Aristotelian organizational pattern. Heyd asserts, however, that even though the content of Chouet's teaching did depart from standard Aristotelian practice, he did not depart drastically from scholastic methodology in his teaching style. Heyd cites the practice of public disputations in philosophy as an example. Students would typically defend a series of theses drawn from their philosophy courses, which was the standard scholastic method. Furthermore, in his physics courses, Chouet maintained an Aristotelian organization, but also began to infuse Cartesian categories into it. For example, in his discussion of the concept of the "void," Chouet employed the inductive method of experiment, but coupled it with the use of Aristotelian syllogism. Further, he replaced the Aristotelian dualism of matter and form with the Cartesian identification of matter with extension. Chouet, according to Heyd, "defined matter exclusively in terms of extension and explained in detail why it was the essence of matter. Like Descartes, he chose wax as a 'model' for matter in general, which changes its qualities very easily but remains always extended."[14]

Heyd argues further that Chouet did not introduce Cartesian physics at the expense of a rigid Aristotelianism at the academy. Chouet's predecessor, Gaspard Wyss, was already combining Aristotelianism with new developments in physics. Chouet's contribution was not, therefore, breaking with a pure Aristotelilan philosophical system, but systematizing an eclectic system and presenting an alternative to the old, outdated Aristotelian methodology.[15]

Chouet adopted the Cartesian expression *Ego cogito ergo sum* as the first principle of cognition. Heyd emphasizes, however, that Chouet was a pragmatic Cartesian who used the *Cogito* primarily as an argument against the skeptics.[16] Chouet functioned more as a scholastic and stressed, according to Heyd, "the deductive, systematic, indeed dogmatic aspects of Cartesian philosophy which were quite compatible, methodologically speaking, with scholastic tradition."[17] The duties of a philosophy professor were to present a body of knowledge in a systematic fashion. Usually the professor would spend one class period a day dictating philosophical texts to the students. This methodology carried with it a signifcant element of traditionalism. However, in his informal teachings and in his experimental work, Chouet was freer to use his Cartesian framework.[18] Mme Labrousse agrees that Chouet did not totally abandon the Aristotelian framework in his teaching. She writes that Chouet:

> In his regular teaching assignments, was always as Cartesian as a professor could be. . . . He held, if not always by his explicit regulations,

at least by practice and by the curriculum, to give the Aristotelian system a considerable place in his teaching, and in every case to borrow from him the general categories for his courses. The innovators were not revolutionaries; they restrained themselves from fully exposing the more recent philosophy and from giving them preference on occasion. But the methods of discussion of theses remained unchanged and by that a philosophy like that of Descartes found itself strangely distorted.[19]

An important source for the development of Chouet's Cartesianism can be found in his correspondence with his former mentor at Nîmes, David Derodon. Derodon was very involved in theological polemics in an attempt to present a cogent argument of Christian faith against the atheists. In doing so, he employed philosophy and dialectic reasoning. Heyd comments: "[It] had its basis in the traditional view of philosophy as a useful tool for theology, a view which, under the renewed influence of Thomism, was shared by many of the Protestant 'scholastic' theologians of the seventeenth century. It had the double effect of rationalizing theology and of subjecting philosophy to the exigencies of theological considerations."[20]

The use of such rationalism can be seen in Derodon's stance on creation, which Chouet described in a letter to Tronchin. The question was whether God had the freedom to create or not create the world. Derodon concluded that he did not have the freedom *not* to create since the creation flowed out of God's attributes of wisdom and goodness.[21] This departed from the traditional Calvinistic view, which emphasized that the end of creation was the glorification of God while its cause lay in the divine attribute of goodness. Heyd points out that Derodon limited divine omnipotence because the traditional position did not satisfy the demands of reason. Chouet commented on the issue in a letter to his uncle, Louis Tronchin, saying that God did not have the freedom of indifference in creation but had to create out of the necessity of being consistent with his nature. For Chouet, this necessity was more an example of the perfection of God than of weakness. If God created the world based on reasons that only he in his wisdom could understand, he would still create freely. For God to go against the good reasons of his own judgment would be folly. One could say that God is determined by such reasons, but this is not to say that his decisions are not made freely. He is bound by his own nature and to act otherwise would render him less than God.[22]

Chouet observed further that for God to do something with wisdom, his actions would have to be in accord with reason. A wise decision, therefore, would need to be a reasoned one, even when the actor was God himself.[23] Therefore, if God were to have some reasons to create the world, such an act would not be free but would be dependent on such reasons. Heyd argues that Chouet "assumed that Reason had a binding power over Will. In this intellectualist assumption Chouet clearly belonged to a whole trend of Protestant theology in the seventeenth century which tipped the traditional balance between Reason and Will in favor of the former."[24]

Chouet had a difficult time reconciling dogmatic decrees that denied the necessity for God to act in a manner dependent on reasons or causes. By the 1670s, Chouet had denied the practice of splitting hairs on the issue of God's will and the reasons for creation. Instead he stressed "the absolute simplicity, freedom and omnipotence of God."[25] He denied the practice of evaluating the divine nature based upon human categories of decision making and accepted that the divine nature of God was pure even though it might seem to possess contradictory elements from a human perspective. By adopting such a posture, Chouet could reconcile orthodox Reformed categories in the area of theology proper, while maintaining his intellectual standards of inquiry. Heyd correctly points out that it was Chouet's Cartesian methodology that provided a basis for clarifying his position.[26]

By 1680, Chouet had further clarified his position on this issue. Cartesian philosophy gave him the justification for accepting Calvinistic dogmatics fideistically while maintaining an emphasis on rational inquiry in other areas of thought. Chouet distinguished between the finite and the infinite and admitted that, at times, humans fail to understand the reasons why God does certain things such as to create the world. If it is clear and distinct that God is divinely perfect, his creation of the world must be free. It naturally follows from the postulate of divine perfection that God's free will governs all of his external acts.[27]

Chouet thus adopted a fideistic position toward theological concepts of God that are philosophically impossible to reconcile. He distinguished between the divine need for basing decisions on reason and the human need to do so. Furthermore, on issues such as the Trinity, Chouet recommended tacit acceptance without the need for philosophic justification. In Chouet's letter to Sarrasin dated 1 Sept. 1680, he comments:

> You ask me how this maxim that all that is in God is God could accord with the personal relationship in the godhead. . . . As a philosopher, I

never subject the Trinity to rational inquiry. I consider it as a totally incomprehensible mystery to the human mind and, as a Christian, I believe it to be exactly as it is taught in Scripture without going beyond it.[28]

Chouet was not a fideist in the area of Eucharist theology, however. He still applied Cartesian categories to the problem of the Lord's Supper. Thoroughly rejecting transubstantiation, Chouet argued that the body of Christ located in Rome cannot be the same body located in Paris. This would go against proper reasoning. A physical body could only exist in one place at a time. Therefore, the Roman Catholic view of the Eucharist would have to be false unless there was never more than one mass taking place at a particular time. Chouet continues:

> One asks him further if in the moment of transubstantiation the substance of the material of the bread is annihilated truly and in reality or if it changes only in name in taking on itself the body of the Lord Jesus Christ. If he responds that it is annihilated, I do not see how all the material of nature or all the stuff of the world, which is the same thing, would not be thus at the same time, because otherwise a same thing would be annihilated.[29]

Chouet goes on to say that the body of Christ cannot be of one nature in heaven and another one on earth. Christ's body, in other words, cannot exist as a mere piece of bread. The Roman Catholic distinction between the accidents and the essence in the Eucharist would thereby be an arbitrary one with no validity outside the mind.[30]

Chouet's position on the Eucharist is an excellent example of his use of Cartesianism in the realm of theology. Descartes's equation of matter with extension made belief in the Roman Catholic position on the Lord's Supper virtually impossible. Descartes believed that one substance could not assume the physical and spatial characteristics of another and still maintain its original identity. This was precisely the position of Chouet.[31]

However, Chouet did not exclusively use Cartesian methodology but also employed the principle of *Libertas Philosophandi*, which stated that one should not trust a single authority, such as Aristotle, in the realm of philosophy, but work with an entire spectrum of philosophical systems in the search for truth. Further, Chouet defined philosophy to include only evident discourse and thereby separated the discussion of philosophy from that of theology.

Chouet's limiting of this principle to the realm of philosophy helped him to stay out of controversy.[32]

Although Chouet avoided such controversy in the area of theology, Heyd points out that Chouet was opposed to the "religious utilitarianism" of such philosopher-theologians as LeClerc. Chouet specifically rejected LeClerc's assumption that reason should only be applied to those truths which are "essential for salvation." Chouet preferred, rather, to give reason free reign in all areas of study as well as respecting the fact that man's reason could not enable him to comprehend certain truths about God that are beyond the powers of reason.[33]

Chouet's important innovation was to insist that philosophy was not merely the maidservant of theology. He argued that philosophy should be studied for its own sake and not for the basis that it might give for the study of theology. Chouet's separation of philosophy from theology, coupled with his avoidance of theological debates, kept him from being a controversial figure. However, his emphasis on the principle of *Libertas Philosophandi* left an important mark on his students, including Jean-Alphonse Turretin.[34]

Louis Tronchin (1629–1705)

Chouet was not the only faculty member at the academy that would have an important influence upon Turretin. The second major source for his thought on the subject of religious authority was Louis Tronchin, who was the son of Théodore Tronchin, professor of theology at the academy as well as a delegate to the Synod of Dort. The younger Tronchin studied at Saumur under Amyraut, despite the fact that his father had been a vigorous opponent of the Salmurian doctrines. By 1661, Louis Tronchin had become a professor of theology at the Genevan Academy also.

The importance of Tronchin as a theologian in the Academy of Geneva is usually traced to his role in opposing the introduction of the Helvetic Formula Consensus.[35] It is likely that Tronchin did not publish any of his controversial works as a direct result of his defeat in 1679.[36] Even though Tronchin lost this battle, his views eventually dominated the theological science in Geneva, partly because Francis Turretin died in 1687 and Tronchin lived until 1705. Tronchin exerted his influence on the direction of the Company of Pastors for almost two full decades after the death of his rival. In addition, Tronchin was able to teach his students the theology of Saumur in private classes held in his home. Many of these students would later carry his theological message, not only at the academy, but within the Republic of Letters as well.

J. E. Cellérier refers to Tronchin as the "true mentor" of Jean-Alphonse Turretin. He writes, in addition, that Tronchin "created, by his teaching, this brilliant generation that would later direct a great philosophical and religious movement."[37] Turretin was not the only significant product of Tronchin's pedagogy. The enigmatic Pierre Bayle[38] and the Remonstrant theologian and literary critic, Jean LeClerc, both received their theological training under the watchful eye of Tronchin.[39] LeClerc would, in turn, be an insightful confidant of Turretin. Tronchin's reputed influence on students who would later be so critical of the conservtive and scholastic form of theology taught at the academy makes one wonder about the orthodoxy of Tronchin himself. Was he merely a Salmurian or did he have more heterodox views? What did he teach that made his students abandon the scholastic form of Reformed thought that was so dominant at the Academy of Geneva during the time of their education there? What specific ideas would his students, particularly Jean-Alphonse Turretin, adopt in formulating their own theological positions?

One can gain insight into the "enlightened orthodoxy" of Tronchin through a brief discussion of his position on the religious authority issue. It is important to note that the younger Turretin sided with Tronchin against his own father on most theological issues. One can point to several categories of accord between the theological systems of Tronchin and Jean-Alphonse Turretin. First, Tronchin applied the rigors of reason to virtually every area of theological discussion and believed fully that reason does not contradict, but rather supports the Christian faith. Second, his sytem of natural theology provided an essential basis for his position on special revelation just as Turretin's would. Third, Tronchin's views of special revelation differed in some aspects from those of Turretin, but they were in complete agreement on the nature of the essential revealed doctrines of the faith. Fourth, his objections to Roman Catholic theology, especially the doctrine of transubstantiation, were picked up by Turretin. Lastly, his openness to dialogue with members of rival Protestant denominations, such as the Lutherans and the Anglicans, and his desire for closer relations with them was an important example of Turretin's desire to forge a union among the three groups.

Tronchin's use of reason as the judge of virtually every area of theology was a fundamental aspect of his class lectures.[40] Walter Rex observes that Tronchin's "readiness to re-examine the traditions of the past and reach new conclusions wherever necessary, the sense of standing firm not on human authorities but on truth itself, was perhaps Tronchin's greatest quality as a teacher." Further, Rex writes that Tronchin's method for determining the correctness of religious knowledge was based on the Cartesian principle, which states that if reason does not affirm a concept, it is better not to believe it at all. Tronchin affirmed this concept in his 1671–72 lectures on Marc Freidrich Wendelin's *Christianae Theologiae libri II:* "Nothing should be affirmed that we do not perceive clearly either in nature itself or in that which God has taught."[41] Pitassi comments that Tronchin's combination of Cartesianism and Salmurianism rationalism resulted in a theology that was "orthodox in its major themes, but in its methodology, ready to make use of not only Scripture, but also the new instruments of philosophical reason."[42]

The place of reason in religious matters was an important theme of the Protestant-Roman Catholic polemics of the day, especially when Roman Catholic apologists employed the arguments of the Pyrrhonists to show that the Bible is not clear in its teachings and that one must rely upon the authority of the church for correct dogma. In addition, anti-Catholicism was particularly strong within Reformed circles during this period because of the extent of the persecution of Protestants in France. The revocation of the Edict of Nantes in 1685 caused a wave of French Protestant refugees into Switzerland and Holland, and was the subject of much theological discourse concerning the responsibility of Protestant loyalty to the king in times of religious conflict. Tronchin, for his part, argued that reason was the ally of the Protestant in the religious debates with the Roman Catholics because the Roman Catholic apologetic depended upon the fideistic acceptance of authority. This was the reason why Tronichin saw Pyrrhonism as the greatest enemy of true religious belief.[43]

In his attempts to convince Mme de la Fredonnière, a native Genevan living in France, not to convert to Catholicism, Tronchin repeatedly pointed out the necessity of using reason to evaluate the two rival beliefs. He was confident that the consistent application of such a method would support the Protestant position. This use of reason was also reflected in Tronchin's sermons. After all, he argued in his 16 August 1692 sermon that the Apostles themselves reflected "conformity with the light of natural reason" in their zealous propagation of the gospel.[44] He pointed out further that the Apostle Paul, in his address to the Athenians in Acts 17:30–31, contrasted the uncertainty of pagan ignorance with the certitude of the Christian view of the Last Judgment and the resurrection from the dead.[45] Jacques Solé concludes that Tronchin believed that the misunderstanding of the evidence for the Christian faith was not simply error, but sin.[46]

The fact that many Roman Catholic apologists in France used arguments based on Pyrrhonism against the Protestant position of scriptural authority forced Protestants to establish a defense of the Bible based more on reason than on the traditional, subjective, Calvinistic argument. This states that the Holy Spirit confirms in the heart of the believer that the Bible is of divine origin and therefore, is authoritative. Tronchin, seeing reason as supporting the Protestant position of *sola Scriptura,* used rational defenses to a large extent, without totally abandoning the traditional defense.

Not only did Tronchin hold to an alliance between reason and revelation, he also argued that natural revelation served as an important witness to the truth of the Christian faith and the primacy of scriptural revelation in the quest for religious knowledge. In fact, Tronchin's position on natural revelation provided an important basis for Turretin's own thoughts on the subject. Turretin attempted to prove as much as possible about God through the use of natural theology. This was not an argument against Roman Catholics, but an apologetic against the more insidious claims of the deists and atheists who Turretin believed were a greater threat to the very fabric of the Protestant faith by the early years of the eighteenth century. Turretin's enlarged scope for natural theology followed essentially the same track as Tronchin's.

Relating natural revelation closely to special revelation, Tronchin noted that the former serves as the basis for the latter. He compared the differences between natural and special revelation to that between the Old and New Testaments: "The Old Testament which previously was sufficient, no longer is so according to certain men, but one could say that it is in a mediatorial sense, because if a man reads it with a desire to profit from it, God promises him the full and clear revelation of the Gospel."[47] He further wrote, referring to the important passage on natural revelation, Romans 2:11–16, that "any man who does all that God reveals to him, will be excused of all wrong, the judgment of God being regulated acording to the measure of revelation."[48] He claimed that God is revealed through both natural and special revelation, and followed Amyraut in asserting the possibility of salvation for the individual who had never heard of Christ. God judges according to the measure of revelation that the person receives. Turretin followed this argument closely.[49]

As to his position on special revelation, Tronchin held that the Bible was divinely inspired and without error. He described the biblical authors as amanuenses of the Holy Spirit who were not able to err. In his proofs for the divine origin of Scripture, he agreed with Francis Turretin and Frédéric Spanheim that internal and external marks helped support the idea of the divinity of Scripture. The external marks dealt with proofs not cited in the text of the Bible. Such evidence included the antiquity of Scripture, the testimony of martyrs, the general consensus of Christians about the divine authority of Scripture and the testimony of Jews, pagans, and Muslims. The internal marks rested on the sublimity of the content of Scripture, the fulfillment of prophecy, the consistency of purpose to show God's glory and the salvation of man, and the fact that the Bible maintains such consistency in spite of its plethora of authors over such a long span of time. However, he argued that the "sublime and efficacious truth of Scripture" serves as the best argument for its divine origin.[50]

He emphasized that no one has the ability to identify the scriptural marks of divinity. Only the Spirit of God can give humans the capacity to see such divine marks. Technically, therefore, no proofs for the divine nature of biblical revelation could be brought forward. When one does recognize such marks, it is God who is at work in the individual through the Person of the Holy Spirit.[51]

His position on the marks of Scripture was a sharp deviation from Calvin, who maintained the Bible to be self-authenticating and claimed that the Holy Spirit confirms in the heart of the Christian that Scripture is God's Word. Calvin rejected the scholastic emphasis on natural reason and proofs for establishing scriptural authority and employed external proofs about the consistency, accuracy, and prophetic nature of the Bible. He intended them to be merely helpful additions for those who already regarded it as authoritative.[52] Tronchin, for his part, granted the Holy Spirit a significant role in leading the believer to a proper interpretation of Scripture, but he did not emphasize the subjective defense of the interior witness of the Spirit. He wrote: "It is for this reason that God wishes that we would ask for his spirit of light and wisdom, so that we may see the marvels of his word." Tronchin's expanded use of the external marks of Scripture reveals an important change in emphasis from Calvin.[53]

This is not to say that Tronchin denied the divine origin of Scripture. His point was that Scripture is strong enough to withstand any examination. His careful defense of the truth of Scripture indicated his high view of *sola Scriptura* and of biblical inspiration and authority. In fact, he held to the orthodox position on these topics. He was quite fearful of any misuse of such biblical authority, especially at the hands of Roman Catholic theologians. In his comments on the subject, Tronchin was critical of the Roman Catholic misuse of Scripture and used this opportunity to explain his own position on biblical inspiration. He argued that the church treats Scripture as if it were a dangerous book. He explained:

> In Spain and in Italy, all one needs is a New Testament to be led to torture. Judge if this is not contrary to what David says in Psalm 89: Your word is a lamp to my feet and a light to my path: and what St. Paul says in 2 Timothy 3: You have learned since your youth the holy writings, which have rendered you wise unto salvation: because all Scripture is divinely inspired and profitable for teaching, for convincing, for reproof, for instruction and for training in righteousness, to render the man of God accomplished in every good work.[54]

Tronchin's position on the inspiration and authority of Scripture was actually quite orthodox, although he did not go to the extreme of adopting the position of the Formula Consensus concerning the inspiration of the vowel points of the Masoretic text.

Not only was his position on biblical inspiration orthodox, but his position on the subject of biblical mysteries shows that he had not employed rationalism to the extent that he would reject such basic "mysterious" doctrines. It was the traditional practice of Reformed theologians, beginning with Calvin, to label passages dealing with the Incarnation or with the Trinity as mysterious, meaning that they could find no adequate philosophical explanation for such biblical doctrines. The more rationalistic approaches of the late seventeenth century, such as that of the British deists, attempted to remove the element of "mystery" from such passages.[55] Tronchin, for his part, maintained the traditional position. In his sermon notes on a prominent passage concerning the incarnation, 1 Timothy 3:16, he argued that one can only receive biblical mysteries with the aid of the Holy Spirit.[56] He also wrote that one cannot understand the Incarnation; only the Holy Spirit can. All that the Christian needs to know on the subject is revealed to the believer by God.[57]

In the area of biblical interpretation, Tronchin held to the perspicuity of the text as a central defense against the Roman Catholic charge of biblical obscurity. However, Tronchin did not allow for various interpretations of a biblical passage all to be correct. He firmly advocated the single meaning of the text, the one that the biblical author intended to convey. He believed it was perfectly possible for a theologian to be mistaken in certain fine points of a theological concept and yet grasp its essential qualities. This point does not erase the concept that there is one correct meaning. He pointed out that many conflicting philosophical systems have existed throughout the centuries, but they were not all correct. This would require a denial of the law of noncontradiction. The same would be true in biblical hermeneutics. If an interpretation contained the main idea and yet had some error in certain details, one could correct it with careful study and meditation upon both Scripture and the "nature of things."[58] Concerning the conflicting ideas of the Reformers on the doctrine of the Lord's Supper, he wrote:

> This is why when even the reformers did not understand or explain clearly enough the manner of our union with Christ in the Eucharist. I would not abandon their communion because the foundation of their sentiment is by itself true and because I can clarify that which was obscure to them by using the light that I am able to use myself or take from those who have gone before us and explain certain issues in a clearer fashion, the nature of things and the meaning of the word of God.[59]

The point that Tronchin made is that the neutral seeker who possesses the illuminating power of the Holy Spirit would find the correct interpretation of Scripture if he meditated carefully. Without careful meditation coupled with the power of the Spirit, he wrote, every individual would be able to read into Scripture what he wanted. Some interpretations might be pure while others would be corrupt. One must examine difficult passages carefully and accept only what is clear and distinct. Anything that obviously contradicts Scripture should be rejected. Tronchin continues: "I say to you frankly that those who follow the doctrine of a Church . . . without examination, on pretence that they do not have enough light to understand the true sense of Scripture, do not appear to me to be reasonable."[60] He reasoned further that since Scripture is the standard by which one determines religious truth, no one should fear open examination of it: "It is not necessary to believe that it is a commendable modesty to not dare to judge the true sense of Scripture to discern if there is any error [in the teaching of a particular church]. . . . It is rather a blindness and an unworthy proposition and contrary to the duty of a good Christian."[61] This was one of the major reasons why he opposed the concept of narrow religious creeds. Tronchin was so confident about the clear teachings of Scripture that he felt that such creeds were unnecessary.

Tronchin, in another letter to Mme de la Fredonnière, attempted to assure her that God's Word is sure and dependable. Referring to Psalm 119, where David wrote that God's Word is like a lamp, he pointed out that a lamp's purpose is to light the pathway to insure safe travel. Referring to 1 Timothy 3:16, he wrote:

> According to your way of thinking, Madam, that which can make wise for salvation, can it not suffice in order to be saved? And that which is inspired by God to convince, can it not decide issues of controversy? Can you believe that it is right to teach a book made by God expressly in order to be the source and the rule of religion? And to discern the truth that it wishes to establish against the errors which man has introduced?[62]

He then advised her to follow the "torch" of Scripture, which would lead her through the maze of false doctrines. It is important to note here that he was advising a layperson and, more importantly, a woman. He was not addressing an individual with scholarly training in biblical studies. Obviously, Tronchin believed the Bible was perspicuous enough for a laywoman to read and understand and be able to recognize the differences between true and false doctrines essential for salvation.

In addition to Tronchin's views on the doctrine of revelation, his polemics against Roman Catholic theology provide an important insight into his use of Cartesianism in theological discourse. He attacked the Roman Catholic system on several teachings, including the tyranny of its goverment, the doctrines of the mass and purgatory, the supremacy of the papacy, and the misinterpretations of Scripture, especially of those passages supporting doctrines essential to salvation. This last issue is significant because Tronchin regarded the Remonstrants as fellow Christians even though he did not agree with several aspects of their views of personal response to the Atonement of Christ. However, he could not accept Roman Catholics into such fellowship because of differences on "matters essential for salvation." For J. A. Turretin, the idea of matters essential for salvation would serve as a test to determine whether or not he could form a common base for Christian union. The issue was not to separate over secondary theological issues, as the advocates of the Formula Consensus had done, but only to separate on areas of disagreement on doctrines essential to salvation. This was exactly the position of Tronchin.

Tronchin's openness to dialogue with the Remonstrants is evidence of his attitude toward freely discussing any area of theology as well as his desire to unify over essential doctrines. Although Tronchin did not agree with Arminian theology, he was sympathetic toward it because of his Salmurian position and was willing to discuss the philosophical problems of the consistency of the Reformed doctrine of predestination. Roger Stauffenegger argues that Tronchin's subtle reasoning in his arguments against Remonstrant theology shows a sympathy to the Arminian position and provided Jean-Alphonse Turretin with an important lesson. Turretin would later engage the Remonstrant Jean LeClerc in a significant correspondence over many years in which Turretin would quite openly discuss the most intimate details of his personal life as well as his theological beliefs.[63]

It is important to note that Tronchin's emphasis upon Christian union based on the essentials of the faith would become one of the hallmarks of Jean-Alphonse Turretin's theological system. The reason that Turretin desired union with the German Lutherans and the Anglicans was precisely because all these groups shared a common set of core beliefs. Separation for Turretin would come when such agreement was lacking. Union with the Roman Catholics, or even the Gallican church, which had its own problems with Rome, "could not be approved of by God."[64] In fact Tronchin advised some of the French refugees to leave France after the Revocation of the Edict of Nantes, rather than to adopt a Nicodemite stance and pay lip service to the idolatry of "Babylon."[65] The only way Tronchin would agree to an accord with the Roman Catholic church would be if they accepted the Protestant positions on all the "essential" issues; in other words, if they converted to Protestantism.

In his arguments against the authority of Rome, Tronchin was aware of the common counterargument that the multiplicity of Protestant sects proved that one could not arrive at religious truth through the study of Scripture alone. If the Bible were the sole authority in religion, it would naturally follow that biblical scholars would all be in agreement and there would be no need for such a splintering of the faith. This was a very persuasive argument that left a profound impact on both Tronchin and Turretin. It was a central motivation in Turretin's attempt to unify the Protestant sects. The popularity of the Socinian and Anabaptist movements, both of which claimed the sole authority of Scripture, was an embarrassment to such Reformed scholars. Tronchin was eager to condemn such sects and, in a letter to Mme de La Fredonnière, he expressed his opinion that such groups so obviously opposed the clear teaching of Scripture that it was easy to dismiss them "with certainty."[66]

While noting the spread of many sects, Tronchin blamed their proliferation on human ignorance. In the midst of such a diversity of religious opinion, he posited the need to achieve certainty in the area of religious truth. One can gain such assurance, he wrote, through careful meditation and study of Scripture. Tronchin defended the use of reason and found basic Cartesian methodology absolutely essential in discovering clear and simple truths in Scripture. He claimed that any rational inquirer can find the doctrines essential for salvation in the Bible without any cause for disagreement at all. The biblical truths are that clear: "Anyone who with a truly pious spirit, and devoted to the truth, reads Scripture in order to find the necessary truths for salvation, is capable of understanding it for himself; and this is the duty of each individual."[67]

Tronchin did not totally disparage the use of tradition as an aid in determining religious truth. The church fathers and the ecumenical councils were valuable, but he cautioned that one should never accept them as infallible guides.[68] He noted that Roman Catholic apologists had argued that Scripture was unclear and that the traditions of the church, which included the writings of the church fathers, could adjudicate between disputed interpretations. Tronchin reasoned that the views of the fathers were much more difficult to interpret than was Scripture.[69] In addition, he argued that such traditions were the product of fallible man, while the Bible was the very Word of God: "Our faith is founded solely on the Word of God and not on the authority of men who are subject to error."[70] Christ and the Apostles, as the authors of the New Testament, would never have countenanced some of the traditions of the Roman Catholic hierarchy. Tronchin wrote: "J. Christ, the author of our faith, and the Apostles, the wisest of ministers, have not commanded such traditions, and have established only a simple religion accompanied by the word to instruct men."[71]

One of Tronchin's main objections to Roman Catholic dogma centered upon the nature of the Eucharist. He believed that an idolatrous position on the Lord's Supper was indeed grounds for separation. He argued strenuously that the Roman Catholic position advocated the worship of the common elements, rather than Christ himself. He claimed that, physically, Christ could only be present in one place at a time. His position on the Eucharist was essentially Cartesian. He claimed that transubstantiation is "contrary to right reason" and that it destroys the light of reason"

because it contradicted Descartes's definition of matter as extension and that a physical object could not be in more than one
place at one time.[72] The Catholic position that Christ is physically
present in the Eucharist wherever it is celebrated is contrary to
the dictates of reason and common sense.[73] He would accept fellowship with both Anglicans and Lutherans, though, because their
views on the Eucharist did not include the adoration of the host
and the resacrifice of Christ.[74] In fact, he praised the Lutheran
position on the subject precisely because Lutherans did not worship the elements.[75] However, he disagreed with the Lutheran conception of the ubiquity of Christ because it also contradicted the
Cartesian doctrine of matter as extension.[76]

Rex concludes that Tronchin's theological system can be characterized as one of questioning all points of dogma, even the very
base of theology itself, the Bible.[77] However, Tronchin was confident of Scripture's ability to meet such a test. Further, he used
natural light as the basis for analyzing one of the most important
mysteries of the faith, the nature of the Lord's Supper. He was
willing to use Cartesianism here primarily because it supported
the Reformed position. In areas where natural light would not be an
ally, he reverted back to the traditional defense that such essential
doctrines as the Incarnation and the Trinity were mysteries of the
faith. These basic approaches to the study of Scripture served as
an essential foundation for Jean-Alphonse Turretin's approach to
the subject of religious authority.

An important issue that Turretin would face was the possibility
of the union of the Reformed, Anglican, and Lutheran confessions.
Tronchin provided an early basis for this union with his open attitude toward the Church of England. He argued that the main differences between the Reformed churches and the Anglican church
were merely ceremonial and therefore, not substantial. He would
not countenance union with such sects as Anabaptists, Enthusiasts, or Socinians. Although such groups held that the Bible was
the sole authority for religious faith, Tronchin believed that their
interpretations of Scripture were so far-fetched that one could not
take their claims seriously. Tronchin pointed out that any neutral
individual, reading the Bible with an unbiased eye, would immediately recognize the errors of these sects. Tronchin explained that
each individual Christian has the spirit of discretion and can examine the dogmas of the Roman Catholic church according to the
rigors of biblical truth. He considered it almost criminal negligence
to accept such doctrines without examining them.[78]

One of Tronchin's main objections to Protestant sects such as the

Anabaptists was the emphasis upon personal revelation. Tronchin maintained that the Christian church had no need for any further revelation beyond what was already in the Bible. In addition, the emphasis of such groups upon contemporary miracles was grounds for caution, since the Bible taught that the Antichrist would perform miracles in order to fool the masses. He saw no need for prophets or miracles and pointed to 1 Corinthians 13, which referred to the passing away of miraculous gifts because God never intended miraculous events to last forever. In fact, he argued that one should reject even miracles, if they turned someone away from scriptural truth. The authority of the Bible was preeminent over any contemporary experience. In addition, he minimized the use of prophecy fulfillment to fortify personal belief, writing that God did not give it as a foundation for our faith, but as a buttress to the faith that the believer already possesses. In interpreting prophetic books of Scripture, he cautioned the reader of Scripture to cling to the ethical nature of the writings rather than attempt to interpret current events in light of such prophecies. "The style of the prophets, and the interconnectedness of their discourses are different from other divine writings, that one does not know how to determine which prophecies have significance in regard to several circumstances."[79]

Turretin would pick up on Tronchin's arguments against the enthusiasts and other such sects. Turretin was likewise quite suspicious of contemporary miracles. Biblical miracles were acceptable and served as important proofs for scriptural authority, but Turretin could see no purpose in nonbiblical, supernatural events. This view would prove to be quite consistent with his use of rationalism and is further evidence of his agreement with the teachings of his mentor, Louis Tronchin.

One cannot overemphasize the importance of the education that Turretin received from his mentor at the Academy of Geneva. He sided with Tronchin rather than with his own father on the crucial theological issues that ultimately led to the demise of the Helvetic Formula Consensus. It was in Tronchin's classroom that the young Turretin would learn and adopt his mentor's theological system and methodology. Tronchin's use of Cartesianism in theological discourse helped to break the stronghold of scholastic methodology over the theological curriculum, which was based on the organizational structure of the Aristotelian corpus. When Turretin taught theology to the next generation of students at the academy, he would not organize his lectures according to the categories of Aristotle, but would employ an eclectic method drawing from a number of philosophical sources including Descartes. This new framework, which he drew to a large degree from Tronchin as well as Jean-Robert Chouet, would enable him to change several aspects of the old form of Reformed scholasticism, especially in his elimination of credalism as epitomized in the Formula Consensus. From Tronchin, he gained most of the specifics of his theological program, beginning with a methodology of questioning all points of dogma. He derived his theory on toleration and unification from Tronchin and the liberal party at the academy. In addition, as colleagues on the theological faculty, they had ample opportunity to work together toward the elimination of the Formula as well as the union of the Reformed, Lutheran, and Anglican churches. This would be based on a common core of fundamental theological articles that they all held in common.

It was Turretin who delivered the oration at Tronchin's death in 1705. In a stirring eulogy, he praised Tronchin for his love for God, his defense of the church and of the Academy of Geneva, for his labors for uniting the various strands of Protestantism, for his scholarship and critical method of examination, and lastly, for his passion for truth.[80]

Turretin's Post-Graduate Studies

Having completed his course of studies at the academy, Turretin wanted to polish his academic skills in preparation for a career as a professor. He needed some of the international experience that most of the faculty at the academy had.

From 1691–93, he traveled and studied abroad and met the most renowned theologians and philsophers of the age. He received such attention mainly on the strength of the international reputation of his father. In February 1691, he arrived in Holland and received a warm reception from the Protestant intellectual elite. Historically, there had been a close connection between the Academies of Geneva and of Leiden where Frédéric Spanheim (1632–1701) was the professor of church history. Spanheim was a native Genevan who had followed the controversial Cocceius as professor of theology at Leiden a half-century after Cocceius's death. He later ascended to the church history post in 1671. Spanheim was a champion of orthodox Calvinism, especially against the Remonstrants, and strongly defended the canons of the Synod of Dort. By 1677, in his defense of the faith against the philosophies of Hobbes, Spinoza, and Lord Herbert of Cherbury, he adopted the distinction between essential and nonessential Christian doctrines, a distinction that Jean-Alphonse Turretin used extensively in his attempt to form a union of Protestant confessions.[81]

While studying at Leiden, Turretin developed several friendships that would lead to life-long correspondences. For example, he met the famous Remonstrant Jean LeClerc, who was also a native Genevan and a graduate of the Academy of Geneva. LeClerc had rejected the Reformed faith and found refuge at Amsterdam where he taught at the Remonstrant seminary. He adopted a very critical view of Scripture that reduced the locus of divine inspiration to those texts which explicitly stated that God himself was speaking. In addition, LeClerc became a journalist of renown in the Republic of Letters. In his *Bibliothèque universelle,* he published articles on theology, science, history, and philosophy. Turretin's correspondence with LeClerc provides historians with important insights into Turretin's opinions on sensitive theological topics.

In addition, he met Pierre du Bosc (1623–92), a graduate of the Saumur Academy, who is best known for his disdain for doctrinal controversies and for his emphasis upon personal response and practical application to scriptural truth. Jacques Basnage (1653–1723) was another theologian of note that Turretin was able to meet. Basnage had studied at both Saumur and Geneva under the elder Turretin and Louis Tronchin. He served as pastor of the Walloon congregation at Rotterdam, where he wrote polemical treatises against Bossuet and worked as a diplomat for Prime Minister Heinsius.[82]

Turretin also met the famed Pierre Jurieu (1637–1713) who was perhaps the most important representative of the French Calvinists. Hermann Roell (1653–1718) was another of Turretin's acquaintances in Holland. Roell was professor of theology at Franeker and was a follower of Cocceius and Descartes. He attempted to harmonize reason and revelation, holding that revelation was given to supplement the inadequacies of reason. He was a controversial figure because of his emphasis upon the use of reason and his position on the eternal generation of the Son.[83]

Elie Saurin (1659–1737) was another controversial figure whom Turretin encountered in Holland. Saurin, pastor of French congregations at Utrecht and Amsterdam, was an ardent opponent of Pierre Jurieu and in 1691, composed a major treatise condemning the theology of Jurieu as being against the best interests of the French Reformed church of the refuge. Their disagreements were very personal in nature and although the synod of Leuwarden attempted to reconcile them, they continued to carry on their virulent disagreements publicly.[84]

Lastly, during his tenure at Leiden, Turretin also met Pierre Bayle, who was the subject of much controversy concerning the nature of his true religious sympathies. At the end of Turretin's tenure in Leiden, he composed a treatise attacking the Roman Catholic use of Pyrrhonism. Bayle read the work and marveled at Turretin's brilliance as well as his personal character. He commented: "You have seen the theses that he defended on Pyrrhonism and the Roman Catholic Church and that he has dedicated to you, the pastors of Geneva. His work has gained him a singular greatness here with a reputation rare among men his age."[85]

Turretin left Holland and traveled to England in 1693. He would write later in his life that he had profited more from his interaction with the British theological community than from any other. He first met with Gilbert Burnet, who had formerly been the recipient of the hospitality of the Turretin family in Geneva.[86] Soon he was introduced to the major theological figures in the Anglican church, most of whom were adamantly opposed to the Formula Consensus. Turretin quickly established a common ground with these Anglican divines by pointing out that many of the differences between Reformed and Anglican religion were not as significant as had been previously thought. For example, differnces of church polity posed no real problem since Calvin himself had never condemned it, nor had Calvin condemned indifferent ceremonies. Turretin said that the episcopate was a pragmatic rather than a divine institution and that each national church had the right to legislate concerning it. Turretin felt perfectly justified in his opinion that he could be a Presbyterian while in Geneva and an Anglican while in England.[87]

While in England he began a life-long friendship with William Wake, canon of Christ's Church, Oxford, and rector of St. James, Westminster, who would later become the archbishop of Canterbury. Their correspondence centers upon the subject of the unification of various Protestant faiths: Anglican, Reformed, and Lutheran. Wake was a product of the Latitudinarian movement, a movement that advocated a philosophy of religious tolerance that was to become central to Turretin's conception of religious authority. Wake, in fact, entered into a long correspondence with Louis Ellies Du Pin for the purpose of investigating the possibility of a union between the Anglican church and the Gallican church. He never dreamed of submission to Rome, but his spirit of toleration formed an important common ground with Turretin who was able to confide quite freely to the future archibishop.

At the end of his several months sojourn to London, Turretin visited the famous universities of Cambridge and Oxford, where he met numerous scholars. While at Oxford, he met Isaac Newton and he was very impressed not only with Newton's great knowledge of mathematics, history, and chronology, but also with his tremendous personal piety. Comments Turretin: "One must be very skilled in mathematics to appreciate his genius, but I brought from my encounters with him the most beautiful ideas of the grandeur of God, of the profound veneration that one must maintain for this supreme being, of the immortality of the soul, and of the excellence of the Christian faith."[88]

Later in 1693, Turretin journeyed to Paris where he met even more notable intellectual figures. He saw Jacques Bénigue Bossuet (1627–1704), the famed Bishop of Meaux whose writings against the Protestants had aroused such furor among Huguenots of the Refuge. He also met the Jesuit church historian, Jean Hardouin, who taught rhetoric and theology at the College Louis Le Grand in Paris and wrote extensive articles on Scripture, numismatics, and history. He encountered Nicholas Malebranche (1638–1715), an ardent Cartesian as well as an advocate of occasionalism. In addition, he met Bignon, Mabillon, Commire, Baillet, Fontenelle, and Pavillon.[89]

In Paris, Turretin had two goals. First, he continued his personal writing and research. Second, he make it a point to interact with the literary figures of the Parisian salons.[90]

By the time of the completion of his journeys abroad, Turretin had accumulated a notable array of contacts throughout the Republic of Letters. He had also gained invaluable experience in his interaction with such a broad spectrum of theologians and philosophers. Undoubtedly, this experience confirmed his predisposition toward the formulation of a more broad-minded theological system, which would be palatable to a far wider range of thinkers than had been the scholasticism of his father.

3

Jean-Alphonse Turretin on Natural Theology

Having returned from his travels abroad in 1693, Turretin was ordained and admitted into the Company of Pastors. He served as pastor of the Italian congregation in Geneva and then joined the faculty of the academy as professor of church history, which was created specifically for him. He later served as rector from 1701 to 1711 until ill-health forced him to resign these additional duties. In 1705, his trusted mentor Louis Tronchin died and Turretin succeeded him as professor of theology.

By the time of Turretin's ascendancy to the faculty, the issue of the hypothetical universalism of the Academy of Saumur was no longer the primary challenge to the orthodoxy of the Reformed church in the Swiss confederation. Since the Saumur Academy had been closed by order of Louis XIV in January 1685, many of the pastors and professors in Geneva were working hard at housing and relocating the French reformed refugees. Furthermore, by the early eighteenth century, three religious or philosophical movements that had long plagued the church were gaining popularity: deism, atheism, and Socinianism. In fact, the major reason that the Reformed orthodox had feared Salmurianism was because it could lead to Socinianism, which could lead, in turn to deism and finally to atheism.

As rector of the academy and as a major spokesman in the Company of Pastors, Turretin was well positioned to defend the faith against these onslaughts. As professor of theology, he was able to instruct future pastors and teachers with an approach that he deemed adequate to defend the faith. In order to establish the truths of Reformed theology on firmer ground, he employed the Remonstrant method of proving the truth of the faith through the external marks of Scripture. In doing so, he virtually abandoned the traditional Reformed doctrine that the Holy Spirit confirms the divine origin of Scripture in the heart of the believer. John W. Beardslee comments that in Turretin's system, "'reason,' not the

Holy Spirit; man, not God, certifies the truth of the claims of revelation."[1] Turretin realized that times had changed and that the traditional approach was no longer viable. In his attempt to prove as much as possible about the nature of God through the use of reason, he advocated a system of natural theology that was so extensive that it served as almost an independent source of religious knowledge. Although Turretin did not completely replace Scripture with natural religion, he gave rational arguments equality with biblical revelation, stating that both are in complete harmony.

Jean-Alphonse Turretin's system of natural theology was a direct response to what he considered to be the most formidable challenges to the faith. Deism gained much popularity in England during mid-seventeenth century and philosophers such as John Toland, Charles Blount, and Anthony Collins wrote treatises that advocated the removal of all aspects of mystery and the miraculous from the Christian faith.[2] Their works were quite popular and, considering the close relationship between Turretin and many important English prelates such as Archbishops William Wake and Tillotson, and Bishop Burnet, it is not surprising that he was well versed in such arguments. In addition, by the mid-seventeenth century the English church had already seen the development of a more independent form of natural theology as a response to deism in the works of such scholars as Walter Charleton and John Wilkins.[3] Turretin corresponded often with his English colleagues and kept abreast of international developments through his communication with scholars throughout the Republic of Letters. In fact, Wake wrote to him on 13 May 1719, and complained about the incursion of such heterodoxy into the Anglican church.[4] It is not surprising that Turretin himself would develop a system of natural theology that closely resembled that of his English counterparts. The major difference was that the threat of deism and atheism came much later in Geneva than it had in England.

Turretin considered atheism a more direct challenge to orthodoxy than deism. In atheism, the world would function strictly according to natural law. More specifically, the term *atheist* was an epithet applied to such philosophers as Spinoza whose writings, primarily his *Ethics* and his *Tractatus Theologico-Politicus,* were widely circulated throughout the major intellectual centers of Europe. This is in spite of the fact that local authorities attempted to suppress both publication and dissemination of Spinoza's writings.[5]

The correspondence between Turretin and his closest confidants reveals this genuine fear of both deism and atheism. The first of these correspondents was Jean LeClerc who was a noted biblical critic himself and was often accused of Socinianism by his opponents, even though his Christology was quite orthodox.[6]

In a letter to Turretin, dated 25 March 1718, LeClerc wrote that his nephew had claimed that there were numerous deists and atheists active not only in Paris but in Geneva as well. LeClerc impugned his nephew, however, as an unreliable source, especially since the nephew could not name a single deist or atheist in Geneva. LeClerc said that his nephew had probably met one or two individuals in Geneva who were predisposed toward some libertine ideas and who were probably half drunk when they expressed such sentiments.[7] These exchanges indicate that the Genevans were quite fearful of the incursion of such individuals in their midst. Any accusation of deism or atheism would be taken quite seriously.

In another letter to Turretin dated 29 November 1726, LeClerc complained about certain libertine writings that rejected the validity of the Old Testament Messianic prophecies as the fabrication of the first-century Jewish followers of Christ. LeClerc saw such attacks as destructive to the basic Christian faith. LeClerc also wrote that there were those libertines in Geneva whose predisposition to atheism wounded not only the faith but also common sense. It is interesting to note that it is LeClerc who is complaining about the libertines. Furthermore, the letter indicates substantial agreement between LeClerc and Turretin concerning their fears of libertine attacks upon the Christian faith. In another letter between the two theologians dated 29 November 1726, LeClerc praised Turretin for his treatises that defended the supernatural elements of the Christian faith, particularly the "mysteries" of the Incarnation and the Trinity, against the threats of the Libertines.[8]

Turretin and LeClerc were agreed in their opposition to antitrinitarian and antisupernatural critiques of the faith. Turretin's concept of religious tolerance extended only to the those believers who held to the essentials of the Protestant faith. He was quite intolerant of those who fell outside that circle. He wanted to convert such individuals and what better way to do so than to construct a rational basis for Christian belief, an apologetic system based not on fideistic adherence of credal conformity, but on rational and historic proof.

Another close confidant of Turretin, Jean-Frédéric Ostervald,[9] the professor of theology at Neuchâtel who joined Turretin in his efforts to rid Switzerland of the Formula Consensus, echoed LeClerc's fears of heterodox thought. In a letter to Turretin, Ostervald described the era as an "angry" time when Christianity was being so "violently and so generally attacked."[10] Further, Ostervald related to Turretin that candidates for the ministry at the Lausanne Academy were becoming more and more predisposed toward "des sentimens extrêmement libres" on several essential aspects of the Christian faith, including the resurrection and divinity of Christ as well as the validity of Old Testament prophecies. Ostervald wrote that these candidates probably gained such ideas in Geneva where Socinianism was becoming more and more popular. He added that many candidates for the ministry in Geneva were beginning to accept a Socinian position on the deity of Christ.[11] One can see reflected in this correspondence between Turretin and two of his closest confidants, LeClerc and Ostervald, that "libertine" ideas that contradicted such central Christian teachings as the deity of Christ were still greatly feared in Geneva. This is significant because Geneva had the reputation of being far too tolerant during this period among more conservative cities such as Bern, which still adhered to the Formula Consensus. Geneva was still a long way from heterodoxy, but the liberal party was gaining such dominance that their focus was not to combat their traditional targets such as the Remonstrants, but the more dangerous forms of thought that could well threaten the very fabric of the Christian faith.

Turretin employed both a disciplinary and an academic approach for combating such heterodoxy. First, he joined forces with the civil authorities to have those individuals who strayed from the basic essentials of the faith banished from the city limits. Second, he composed academic treatises designed to combat deism and atheism. These consisted of direct attacks as well as his own system of natural theology designed to convert those who had strayed from the faith. Most of the material of his published works were drawn from his class lecture notes for his systematic theology course, which have been preserved in the Archives Tronchin. He also supervised the theses of several students who used natural theology as a direct refutation of aspects of deism and atheism.[12]

The Vaudenet affair served as the most visible example of Turretin's disciplinary response to heterodoxy. In this case, he was a participant in a process that included both the Small Council and the Company of Pastors. Turretin's role indicated his own fears of such thought as well as the need to combat it not only theologically, but also politically.

The affair began when André-Robert Vaudenet, a soldier and a vineyard owner, insulted the former syndic, Pierre Gautier. A formal trial ensued before the Council of Two Hundred, with Vaudenet being defended successfully by Pierre Fatio. He was the popular leader who would be executed the following year for leading an insurrection against the dominance of certain elite patristic families within the governing body of Geneva. During the trial, the Consistory found out that Vaudenet had previously expressed doubts about his religious beliefs to a notary when drawing up his will during a period of severe illness.[13]

Two weeks later, Vaudenet was summoned before the Consistory and was questioned concerning his religious beliefs. He admitted that he had doubts about the divinity of Christ and the truth of the Bible but he asserted his belief in one God, who was the creator of the world. Vaudenet expressed surprise that he would be questioned about his faith because he had not even discussed religious matters for over a year.[14]

A special commission of theologians was formed to attempt to convince him of the truth of Christianity. Included in this commission were Calandrini, Pictet, and Turretin, professors of theology, Léger of philosophy, and several former pastors now serving in bureaucratic posts. This distinguished group was sent to convince Vaudenet of the error of his thought as well as to conduct a detailed inquiry into the exact nature of Vaudenet's heresy.[15]

The commission of theologians summoned Vaudenet to a conference on 19 May and attempted to convince him of the divinity of Scripture and of Christ. After Vaudenet requested some time to think about their arguments, the group responded that they would be available to confer with him at any time.[16]

The efforts of the commission failed to convince Vaudenet, who remained steadfast in his deistic beliefs. The Consistory, therefore, decided to use the method of repression and referred the case to the Small Council, which banished him from the city. Vaudenet maintained that the reasons for his banishment were only a pretext because his opinions had been known for a long time. Heyd notes that this pretext was significant because it pointed to the possibility of a relationship between heterodoxy and political and social subversion. Vaudenet suggested in these proceedings that deistic and atheistic ideas were not unknown in certain circles in Geneva, but they were kept quiet to preserve the peace of the general public.[17]

Turretin's role as a member of the commission indicates that he, along with the political and theological leaders, desired to defend the Reformed faith against heterodoxy. In the case of Vaudenet, this defense assumed the form of disciplinary repression. What was also needed, however, was a theological defense against these forms of thought.

Turretin's second method in combating heterodoxy was by direct attacks as well as with his own system of natural theology. The most important direct target of attack was Spinoza, who had long been the archenemy of orthodoxy at the academy. Pitassi argues that the scholars at the Genevan Academy did not attack Spinoza when his works were first published in the 1670s, partly out of fear that any direct public confrontation might arouse more curiosity than disdain.[18] By the beginning of the eighteenth century, however, the theological faculty decided to take a more direct route. Both Turretin and Benedict Pictet, his colleague in the theology department, took specific action against Spinoza. Pictet did so in his *Théologie chrétienne* (1702) in which he criticized Spinoza's positions on miracles, human freedom, and natural determinism. Pitassi points out that Pictet, ironically, drew much of his presentation directly from Pierre Bayle's article on Spinoza in his famous *Dictionnaire*.[19]

J. A. Turretin responded to Spinoza's philosophical system in a series of lectures partly entitled "Réfutation du système de Spinosa."[20] The focus of Turretin's critique was on natural theology and more specifically, on the attributes of God and the freedom of man. Here Turretin explained that his purpose was to "combat his [Spinoza's] ideas on the concept of God, and on the necessity of all events, because such ideas threatened the foundations of natural religion." Pitassi argues that Turretin did not possess a very sophisticated understanding of Spinoza's metaphysics, as was also the case with many attacks on Spinoza in this period. Exaggerations in Bayle's treatment of Spinoza were to blame. Turretin tended to follow Pictet's line of argumentation almost point by point.[21]

Following Pictet's basic methodology, Turretin listed several major theses of Spinoza that he intended to refute, including the concept that there is only one substance in the world that exists necessarily. In addition, Turretin took issue with Spinoza's argument that this substance is infinite and eternal. This must be God and all particular things are modifications of this unique substance. Finally, Turretin disagreed with Spinoza's emphasis on determinism.[22]

On the first point, Turretin declared that many substances do exist because they possess different attributes. For example, a circle is different from a square and two substances that think differently are not really the same substance. Further, the being that formed all the substances in the world is different from its creation. Turretin accused Spinoza of atheism, primarily because of his failure to distinguish between God and matter, which is changeable and divisible. In addition, Turretin argued that because all the beings in the world are modifications of a single substance, that substance would be filled with all the contradictions inherent in the differences among beings.[23]

Turretin went on to argue that spirit and matter are inherently different. He wanted to establish the possibility of the immortality of the soul, which he deemed essential to the Christian faith. He asserted further that matter cannot be the subject of all thought because one can conceive of thought without matter. He wrote: "Since all the properties that I perceive in the body have a necessary connection with matter and that the properties of thought do not have such a connection, thought does not belong to matter or to the body but to a substance that is totally different."[24] Pitassi points out that Turretin wrongly assumed that Spinoza treated matter and extended substance as synonyms. Spinoza, in fact, argued that matter is not identified with extension but implies reference to modes that could be affected by change without the substance itself being modified.[25]

Lastly, Turretin commented on the freedom of both God and man and stated that without freedom there would be no justice, virtue, vice, or anger. After presenting his arguments on behalf of freedom, Turretin listed several objections, which include several made by the British deist Anthony Collins. Pitassi points out that, although Turretin did not mention Collins by name in this case, he did so in his *Dissertatio de libertate Humana*.[26]

In spite of Turretin's lack of originality, his comments about Spinoza revealed his own attitude toward atheism in general, as well as his sense of mission for defending what he considered to be the essential elements of the Christian faith. For example, Turretin commented: "Spinoza was a true atheist. He was not stupid enough to believe all these foolish things, but being an atheist and believing that atheism was being universally condemned, he constructed his impious system under the terms of God, Liberty, and Virtue, etc., to fool men, and to insinuate his atheism with more certainty."[27]

Not only did Turretin attack the major opponents of heterodoxy directly, he also constructed a system of natural theology that he considered a form of knowledge about God independent from Scripture that any true seeker would find compelling. Turretin hoped to form a theological system that employed reason as its modus operandi, yet maintained the distinctive elements of the Christian faith. In doing so, he eliminated many of the distinctive elements of the Reformed tradition in favor of a rational faith that any reasonable individual would accept without the need for the role of the Holy Spirit. Like the Socinians, Turretin held that the Fall had not marred man's rational capacities. This strong reliance upon rationalism to establish the historic probability of the Christian faith was one of the hallmarks of Arminian and Socinian thought. Turretin also maintained that it had its limits in the area of biblical mystery, which included only the Trinity and the Incarnation. Turretin's system of natural theology attempted to prove as much of orthodoxy as possible without the aid of biblical revelation. In addition, he not only responded in his system of natural theology to deism and atheism, but also answered the specific arguments of several prominent theologians and philosophers who had challenged aspects of the Christian faith that Turretin considered "fundamental" truths.

In constructing his system of natural theology, Jean-Alphonse Turretin reacted not only to libertine ideas, but also against the theological system of the conservative party as epitomized in the Formula Consensus. In addition, he incorporated an approach to theology that included the Cartesian methodology of Chouet and the rationalism of Tronchin. He saw Reformed scholasticism as too "rigid" to serve as an adequate defense for the Reformed faith against a new wave of threats to its dominance in Geneva. He condemned the scholastic methodology because it did not lead to an emphasis upon the personal piety of the believer.[28] Further, Turretin traced the history of the use of scholastic methodology from Aquinas to his own era and recognized the Protestant Reformation as a rejection of scholasticism, when what he considered the true spirit of the faith was preached. Scholasticism was, therefore, lifeless and unprofitable for the Christian. He also condemned the use of scholastic terminology because it rendered theology too difficult for the layman to understand. Instead, Turretin preferred to emphasize what the Bible clearly teaches. This, he wrote, would be far more convincing to the unbeliever that the "conjectures" of scholasticism.[29] It is interesting to note here that he did not condemn scholasticism for its Aristotelian roots. His main concern was for personal piety and a religious faith purged from schism and discord.[30]

Turretin hoped to form a theological system that employed reason as its modus operandi, that still maintained the distinctive elements of Reformed thought. He attempted to prove as much of orthodoxy as possible through natural revelation and thereby formulate a defense of the faith based upon the same category of reason to which the deists, atheists, and Socinians ascribed.

One must realize that Turretin represented a middle ground between the detailed dogmatism of the Reformed scholastics on one hand and the libertines on the other. Although Turretin did use rationalism extensively in theology and apologetics, he attacked the libertines for denying the supernatural aspects of religion. He recognized the problem of the complete reign of rationalism in the theological approach of Socinianism, but he held that a rational approach to theology should lead to an acceptance of biblical revelation, which supports the doctrines of the Trinity and the Incarnation.[31]

Essential to a discussion of natural theology is the ability of the individual to employ reason to come to a knowledge of religious truth. Turretin disparaged the arguments of Roman Catholic skeptics who advocated fideistic belief in dogmatics, as well as the views of the enthusiasts who relied upon internal light. Turretin thoroughly depended upon the ability of the redeemed reason of man to serve as an adequate basis for religious knowledge. Natural theology provided an essential foundation for all other aspects of theology.

Prior to analyzing Turretin's arguments on the subject of natural theology, a discussion of several points of *prolegomena* is in order. First, Turretin's use of rationalism served as a measuring rod for his entire system of natural theology. Like the Socinians, he held that the Fall had not marred man's rational capacities. The excessive reliance upon rationalism to establish the probability of the Christian faith was one of the hallmarks of both Arminian and Socinian thought. Turretin employed this methodology, but maintained that it had its limits in the area of biblical mystery. In Turretin's system of natural theology, he attempted to prove as much of Reformed orthodoxy as possible without the aid of biblical revelation. Second, he was not only responding, in his system of natural theology, to deism and atheism, he was also answering the specific arguments of several prominent theologians and philosophers who had challenged aspects of the Christian faith that Turretin deemed to be "fundamental" truths. He directed his arguments directly to the deists and atheists to indicate that they had misused reason, the true ally of the believer. Fideistic acceptance of Calvinism was, therefore, no longer necessary. One could establish a surer foundation for such belief with the aid of reason.

Turretin's use of reason served as the independent arbiter of knowledge in his system of natural theology. He followed a methodology that possessed almost a mathematical simplicity and certainty. Turretin admired the precision of geometry and kept that level of clarity in his theology.[32] He built his arguments upon axioms that he had already established, but he did not believe that one can rationally prove every aspect of divine truth through such an approach. Furthermore, he argued that all of natural theology falls under the rubric of reason. He did allow for some elements of mystery in special revelation, but limited it to the Incarnation and the Trinity. Further, although he acknowledged that the knowledge of God must be imperfect by necessity, he asserted that the rational inquirer can, indeed, come to a real understanding of the nature of God.[33] Turretin's use of reason extended to the area of biblical mysteries. Although Turretin did not reject the necessity of such mysterious elements of theology that reason cannot fully explain, his emphasis upon natural theology as virtually a separate discipline elevated reason to a level that makes such mystery seem contrary to his total system. If Turretin were to deny such elements of mystery in theology, he would be guilty of the very Socinianism that he tried so hard to refute.

Turretin admitted that natural revelation does have limits. He pointed to areas where many essential Christian truths cannot be known apart from special revelation. For example, only special revelation could have allowed the Apostle Peter to recognize the Lord's true identity in Matthew 11:27. Peter could never have recognized Jesus as the true Messiah through the use of natural revelation alone. Turretin, however, carefully limited the extent of personal revelation to New Testament times. He cautioned his readers against the excesses of the "Enthusiasts," who claimed such special knowledge, especially since there was no way to examine their claims. He pointed out that one should not accept such claims without submitting them to the test of reason. It is important to note here that Turretin relied upon the New Testament in support of his argument of the use of reason in examining religious concepts. He saw no possible way of converting non-believers apart from the use of reason.[34] So, in spite of his admission of the mysterious element of special revelation, he held to a closed canon as well as an admittance of the presence of a "mystery" only after a doctrine has been thoroughly examined by reason.

Not only did Turretin hold to some aspects of theological mystery, he believed that the Holy Spirit can use "internal" means to bring individuals to a knowledge of Christ. Foremost among such internal means would be the light of conscience, which provides man with a sense of justice. He pointed out that natural revelation has significant limits since it cannot bring specific knowledge of Christ, but can only provide a predisposition to respond to the Savior. However, Turretin believed that God can use unusual means, such as visions, to reveal himself to the heathens. Turretin held that God does promise to reveal himself to all who seek him, whether he provides the Scriptures to them or not. He was quick to assert, however, that God's natural revelation always acts in accord with reason.[35]

For Turretin, abstract reason was sufficient to prove the existence and attributes of God. His system of natural theology included many areas that traditionally Reformed theologians would not have included under that rubric. Turretin would not think, however, of excluding special revelation from his discussion of theology. The Christian needs both natural and special revelation. He did not fear a thorough investigation into all areas of religious knowledge. In fact, he wrote that other disciplines such as physics, anatomy, and astronomy, contribute to the knowledge that one can gain about God without resorting to special revelation. These disciplines contribute to natural theology. In allowing reason so much authority in religious matters, Turretin opened the door for the possibility of rejecting all religious concepts that do not square with the dictates of reason. Although he himself would not apply his method to its logical conclusion, his successors in Geneva did, resulting in the triumph of Socinianism over Turretin's system of the "essentials" of Christianity within a generation after his death.[36]

In addition to his emphasis upon the use of reason in constructing a system of natural theology, Turretin examined the various philosophical systems of his day. He thoroughly rejected the pantheistic system of Spinoza and, for the most part, condemned Hobbes. Although he did receive a thorough exposure to Cartesianism from Chouet and Tronchin, he did not totally subscribe to it. Turretin was a philosophical eclectic, drawing not only from Descartes but also from Locke and the English Latitudinarians as well. The most important aspect of his philosophical system is its rejection of Aristotelianism. His very eclecticism differed markedly from the organization of his father's theological system and it allowed the younger Turretin to change several aspects of it.

Turretin learned several lessons of Cartesianism from his mentors at the academy. First, his emphasis upon employing a mathematical type system of investigation followed directly from the physical experiments of Chouet's classes. Second, Turretin submitted all areas of theology to the scrutiny of inquiry, even those subjects which had been hitherto restricted. Third, Turretin employed a Cartesian disdain for excessive dogmatism. He did not use Descartes's *cogito,* but preferred to assume the basic axioms of reason and existence without going through any crisis of skepticism. Turretin commented on the issue of doubt: "concerning their objects outside ourselves, doubt is possible. Whether they exist, and are existents of the highest degree of reality, cannot be doubted."[37] Beardslee writes that Turretin based his thought "on the premise that knowledge is possible."[38] Turretin wrote:

> If anyone would undermine the truth of natural theology on the ground that there is no certainty in human affairs, or that it is possible to distinguish that which is certain from that which is uncertain, this is not the place to refute such foolishness, nor will we here demonstrate the principles of human knowledge, but assume them; let any who are afflicted by the disease of this universal doubt go to the metaphysicians—I would almost say, to the physicians.[39]

At the heart of his philosophical system, Turretin selectively employed Cartesianism. In fact, his theistic proofs resemble those of Aquinas more than Descartes.

Turretin was not entirely indiscriminate in his use of Cartesian philosophy. In his *De Saeculo XVII. Erudito,* Turretin spent more time praising Descartes than any other philosopher. Turretin commended the Cartesian system of philosophy.[40] However, he did, at times, criticize Descartes. Beardslee writes:

> On the question of the relation of God to "first principles," he thinks Descartes to be self-contradictory. He does not give details of his argument. Descartes is merely mentioned as one of a number of "theologians and philosophers of highest reputation." One sentence in the passage indicates its motivation: "It would be a cause of amazement that there are philosophers and theologians, among others Cartesians, who say that the essence of things, or first principles, can be changed by God, . . . were there not grave suspicion that, by this nonsensical hypothesis, which confuses all ideas, and overthrows all thinking, they sought support for a very absurd dogma of the church."[41]

This was Turretin's only real criticism of Descartes and it came in an area that related not to philosophy, but to theological polemics.[42] In his discussion of the theory of knowledge, he did not follow Cartesianism in a strict sense but "he is interested in the analysis of ideas rather than in the thinker; he is 'objective' rather than 'subjective.'"[43] Beardslee, again, observes: "It might be mentioned that not only is his philosophy 'Lockean' rather than 'Cartesian,' in its reliance on sense data interpreted by reason, but that, in a very general way, it has a 'Lockean' effect in practical life. . . . Error at the root of religion is simply error not sin."[44]

Turretin, indeed, held much of the philosophical system of Locke. As well as quoting Locke in several instances, he employed the Lockean concept of rejecting innate ideas and stated that truth needs to be discovered through experience and investigation. Turretin wrote concerning innate ideas:

> When we speak of natural ideas concerning justice and injustice, it must be understood, as if ideas and propositions about morals, actually and properly speaking, were imprinted and engraved in the souls of all men, in the way that a seal is impressed on wax, . . . which, if it were the case, would mean that all nations and even all individuals would everywhere and always of necessity have the same ideas and even the same opinions. The celebrated Locke has shown that this hypothesis, concerning innate ideas and principles, clearly does not agree either with human nature or with history and experience. We only mean this, when we say that natural laws, or ideas written on all souls: that, if reason is rightly used, and due attention shown, no one can fail to recognize the equity and wisdom of these duties.[45]

Turretin treated natural theology as the necessary prerequisite for special revelation. Theology therefore needs philosophy. Turretin observed that the role of self-evident principles is foundational to natural theology. Such principles include: the same thing cannot both exist and not exist at the same time; what has been done cannot be undone; and the whole is greater than the part. Other self-evident principles are moral in character and include: each is to be rendered his due; faith is to be kept; and gratitude should be shown for gifts received.[46] Turretin, like Locke, assumed no innate ideas, and preferred to demonstrate distinctive Christian truths by reason.

In addition to advocating a philosophical system based upon Descartes and Locke, Turretin took issue with two of the most important philosophers of his generation, Hobbes and Spinoza. He noted several problems with the ideas of Hobbes as expressed in the *Leviathan* and the *De Cive*.[47] Hobbes had said that natural law is nothing but the "conservation of life and limb" and that "the dictates of reason are not properly called 'law.'" Turretin also objected that Hobbes had said that the root of justice lies in the government; it was more mere societal pragmatism than a divine ethic. Beardslee comments on Turretin's response to Hobbes on these points: "It would seem that he had a clear conception of the difference between Hobbes and typical Christian ethics. He, however, referred rarely to specifically Christian ideas in these sections, for he wrote on natural theology. In fact, the idea of a personal God barely figured in his argument. He wrote more on the incompatibility between the teaching of Hobbes and that of the Roman moralists, than between that of Hobbes and Christianity."[48]

In the oration *Votum pro Pace* (1710),[49] he contrasted Hobbes specifically with the ancient philosophers and did not criticize Hobbes for anti-Christian views. Turretin argued here that the state of nature is not a war of all against all as Hobbes believed. "That political writer of the past century—I might well call him an atheist—who declared that men are by nature enemies, seeking first another's harm, and that the state of nature is a state of war, is rightly accused of describing not a human state of nature, but one for the brutes; the pagan philosophers are much better and more human."[50]

It is important to note that Turretin did not dismiss all the ideas of Hobbes as he did with Spinoza. He explained: "In these statements which we have cited from Hobbes, we do not deny that there is some good."[51]

Turretin found some amount of accord with Hobbes in the area of natural law. However, the area of agreement is quite narrow since Turretin generally deemed Hobbes an atheist who needed to be refuted. Beardslee speculates that both Hobbes and Turretin had an interest in maintaining social order. For Turretin, as one can observe through the Vaudenet affair, theological heterodoxy on essential matters of doctrine threatened the social stability of Geneva.[52] Although Hobbes supported the concept of social order, his very philosophical system was, for Turretin, a threat to the concept of the state as a divinely ordained institution.

Turretin quoted Hobbes's *Leviathan* at this point and repeats the description of the state of nature of the "war of all against all, where life is nasty, brutish, and short." Turretin responded that men possess an important aspect of self-defense in time of danger. Such a desire for protection is natural and correct. However, "these affections are only natural, when indulged within certain bounds; when they exceed these, they are stamped with the characters of vice, not of nature."[53] He claimed that self-love is important and quite acceptable unless it leads us to injure others. Hobbes also qualified his argument about the state of nature, admitting that right reason does have a role in human nature. The dictates of reason, according to Hobbes, led man to seek peace and harmony and to keep his contractual agreements with others. Hobbes defined injury as a violation of right reason which does not have the authority of law. He called these laws "theorems" which pertain to the preservation of the human race.[54]

Turretin has two main objections to Hobbes's qualifications. First, he objected to the statement that the laws of nature pertain only to the preservation of our lives. Turretin claimed that reason extends also to the areas of wisdom and virtue. Second, Turretin disagreed with Hobbes's contention that the dictates of reason do not have the force of law. He believed, rather, that the dictates of reason are really a declaration of God's will, which has the binding force of law. Hobbes's position, therefore, was that of the atheist.[55]

In his discussion of human liberty, Turretin opposed Spinoza who had written that there is no absolute or free will in the human mind. The mind, according to Spinoza, is determined in its decision-making power by external causes. In response, Turretin asked whether the light of nature indicates the duties that men must perform. If this is so, he then asked if men can perform such responsibilities freely. This must be the case, because if it were not so, men would be relegated to the status of mere machines, like a clock. If men were only machines, there would be no possibility of virtue or vice. Spinoza defined virtue as obedience to the laws of nature. If this were true, argued Turretin, then all men would be virtuous since they would all be determined in their obedience to the laws of nature. Further, if there is no freedom of choice, men have to right to be angry if they are offended. In addition, if no freedom of choice exists, all events take place necessarily and there would be no place for conscience, repentance, justice, or punishment. If Spinoza's argument holds, God would necessarily be the author of all evil. Turretin argued further that most of the ancient philosophers sided with the position of freedom of choice.[56]

Beardslee writes that Turretin's criticism of Spinoza on this point is inadequate and raises the question of whether or not Turretin really understood the philosophical implications of Spinoza's thought on the issues of freedom and mechanistic determinism. Beardslee bases his observation on Turretin's statement that Gassendi was really an Epicurean with the irreligious elements removed.[57]

Turretin was careful, throughout his discussion of natural theology, to criticize deists and atheists such as Spinoza and Hobbes. He also had a more positive motivation in constructing such a system, the construction of a reasonable faith that can be greatly supported through natural revelation.

While defining theology as "that discipline which deals with God and divine things," Turretin made a sharp distinction between natural and special revelation. He did not rely at all upon special revelation in his theistic proofs, but defined natural theology as those doctrines which can be established through the use of reason. Dividing his system of natural theology into several sections, he first established the existence of God and the divine attributes. His purpose was to show that one can, indeed, construct a theistic position without depending on fideistic arguments that assume the divine nature of Scripture. Not only did he neglect the use of biblical references to prove his arguments, but he cited a plethora of pagan philosophers of antiquity as his authoritative texts. He did this in order to argue from common ground with the deist or the atheist. Upon establishing the nature of God, Turretin continued by proving the existence and operation of divine providence. He wanted to combat the deistic belief that God is not involved in the governance of his creation. Next, he discussed the free will of man in order to refute both the mechanistic view of human nature as well as any charge that God might be the author of sin. Lastly, he described the functioning of natural law that God has implanted among human societies. This law provided the predisposition to respond to special revelation.[58]

The main source for Turretin's views on the subject of natural theology comes from his major published treatise on the subject entitled, *Theses de theologia naturali*,[59] which makes up the first volume of his *Opera*. This work is divided into several sections: the existence of God, the attributes of God, the providence of God, human freedom, natural law, and the immortality of the soul. In addition, he added to his discussion of natural theology in his commentary on the book of Romans.

One of the most striking aspects of his treatise on natural theology is his citation of classical, rather than Christian, authorities. His favorite authors were the great rhetoricians of Rome, Cicero (thirty-six citations) and Seneca (twenty-six citations). His choice of these writers reflected his bias against the scholastics and his desire to return to a practical and humanistic emphasis of the faith. By contrast, he cited Aristotle only once and the only church fathers that he referred to are Ambrose (two citations) and Tertullian (one citation). He wanted to establish common ground with the deist or atheist by referring to common authorities.

The Existence of God

Turretin's evidence for the existence of God centered on the traditional cosmological and teleological arguments. He did not assume any innate knowledge of God, but maintained that such knowledge must be demonstrated so that different rational inquirers would independently come to the same conclusions. As long as one examines the evidence while using reason, one will come to the conclusion that God does exist.

In his proofs for the existence of God, which Turretin calls the "first truth of religion," he argued in the following manner. "First, there always have been beings, because there now are. Nothing makes itself, but some cause greater than any of the beings of this world would be necessary to bring this world into existence. The second argument is the necessity of the eternal being, inasmuch as there are thinking beings today, while the third argument, from the origin of the world, somewhat overlaps the first, but is based on the assumption that the noneternity of the universe can be independently proved." These and a "fifth argument," from the origin of motion may all be classed as cosmological, and in the traditional pattern.[60]

One of Turretin's main proofs for God's existence was the traditional cosmological argument. The argument pointed out that the "uncaused cause" or the "necessary being" must be God. Since an infinite regress of contingent beings cannot exist in reality, an original, noncontingent cause must have started the process. Turretin argued from natural theology that the world was created in time, which is a denial of both Aristotle and Aquinas. He referred to David Derodon's *La Lumière de la raison opposé aux ténèbres de l'impiété*[61] who argued in a similar manner. Turretin's use of the cosmological argument was not original.

One of his most important proofs for God's existence was the teleological argument. He wrote that the primary truth of religion is the existence of a perfect, infinite being. Since he presumed that God reveals himself clearly in nature, Turretin interacted with the arguments of the skeptics and atheists against the self-evidence of God's existence. Through observing the creation of God, one can recognize the handiwork as that of a wise mastercraftsman.[62]

The very fact that the libertines questioned the existence of God led Turretin to ask how it was possible for one not to recognize the creation as the work of God. He began his argument by comparing the creation to an intricate clock. As one observes the clock, one immediately notices the movement of the hands of the clock and the ringing of the bell at regular intervals. Inspecting the inner workings, the observer has to ask himself whether the machine always existed or was created through mere chance. Turretin posited that the possibility of such a complicated machine arising accidentally without any wise creator would be remote. Therefore, a rational being must have created it. Interestingly enough, Turretin employed this argument of the clock in proving the nature of God as well as his existence.[63]

Turretin asserted that the arguments of the atheists and libertines would lead one to the ridiculous conclusion that works of art do not exist. If all the great creations of the world were the work of chance, one could never recognize beauty. In fact, there would be no such concept as beauty. Turretin was mocking the skeptics here because the concept of beauty is universally accepted.[64]

Turretin next turned to the intricateness of the creation of plants and animals. Both depend on certain conditions in the environment for their survival. A sudden change in temperature could wipe out entire species.[65]

In addition, Turretin wrote that animals perform many duties necessary for survival without any form of deliberation or reasoning. He cited the example of a lioness instinctively defending her young. Turretin admitted, at this point, that he has not proven that an intelligent being did create the world, but he has shown the extreme unlikeliness that creation resulted from mere chance.[66]

Moving from the argument from design, Turretin advocated an argument for the existence of God based on causality. He posited that it is clear that an intelligent being created the world because the face of the universe is filled with a series of essential causes that seemingly bear no relationship to one another. However, the result of such causes is a system that reflects the necessity of design. He concluded that it is therefore certain that the universe is the work of an intelligent master craftsman. Turretin condemned the arguments of the libertines and atheists as pure folly when they point to imperfection within the universe as proof that there could not have been an intelligent creator.[67]

The subject of divine creation of the world in time is an essential topic for establishing the existence of the Christian God. Aristotle's emphasis upon the eternity of the world posed serious problems for medieval scholastic theologians in their attempts to harmonize Aristotelian categories with orthodox theology. Turretin, not being tied to Aristotelianism, argued forcefully for the noneternity of the world. He cited the fact that the earth is relatively new with recorded history going back only a few thousand years.[68] He used the teleological argument to prove the noneternity of the cosmos as well. The evidence of design in the world, its order and regularity points to a creation in time. Turretin wrote:

When we see a beautiful building, who believes that building to have been made by chance motion? When we see a watch, who imagines all those wheels and parts, by which the hours are measured and indicated to have come together by chance motion? When we see a magnificent poem, for example the *Aenead* of Virgil, who dreams that the drops of ink, or the printed characters, have by chance motion so impressed themselves on the paper, as to make that poem?[69]

Although there is some evidence of Cartesianism in these arguments, his proofs for the existence of God are generally traditional scholastic arguments. He employed, for example, the Cartesian argument of the power of God to explain the design of the world. However, Turretin's use of the cosmological and teleological arguments are scholastic rather than Cartesian. This is evidence that he was neither a Cartesian nor a scholastic, but used whatever arguments suited his purpose, regardless of their philosophical origin.

The next important argument in favor of the existence of God comes from universal consent. The growing awareness of travel literature, which revealed significant differences in religious assumptions among pagan cultures, posed theological problems for seventeenth-century theologians. Turretin, however, merely admitted that not all of the world's cultures advocated the existence of a divine being when they were first discovered by the West. He observes that the vast majority of pagan cultures did believe in God. Turretin states: "We will pass by the fact, proved by the famous theologian John Ludwig Fabricus, that the atheism of these people has not been completely demonstrated, and here we argue, not the consent of all without exception, but of nearly all. No great exception can be made of a very few, and these very savage."[70] Beardslee comments of Turretin's argument from universal consent:

> J. A. Turretin does more than to quote one authority against another. A wider acquaintance with the world, and the beginnings of the "science" of comparative religion, force some re-thinking of his case, and contribute to the abandonment of the doctrine of an innate idea of God. J. A. Turretin does not hold that the argument from universal consent, by itself, has less force than the theoretical ones.[71]

An important component of Turretin's arguments against the atheists who object to his proofs for God's existence, lay in a comparison of systems. Turretin asserted that the beliefs of the atheists fail to answer the most basic questions of life and thus serve as an

inadequate explanation for the nature of creation and the maintenance of the world order. Turretin responded:

> When we agree with the system of the atheists, we know nothing, we
> see nothing; the smallest matters are incalculable puzzles. We do not
> know why there are these or those beings, why there is matter, or
> motion, or why we ourselves exist, or whence, or for what purpose,
> we have come into this light of life. . . . Not only are we left in
> darkness, but the most serious absurdities must be granted. It must be
> said, according to this system, that this most beautiful and orderly
> arrangement of things, which we call the world, was produced by brute
> necessity or blind chance. It must be said that this rude mass, which
> we call matter, is furnished with most excellent attributes; that it exists
> by its own nature, that it always has existed, and cannot be destroyed
> by anyone, and not only that, but this brute mass can think, decide,
> investigate, know itself, despise itself, remember the past, foretell the
> future, contain within itself and produce out of itself all thinking, wis-
> dom and excellencies.[72]

Turretin does not fear asking difficult theological questions because he is confident that the position of the atheist is ultimately
self-defeating.

The Attributes of God

Having established the existence of God, Turretin dismissed the
arguments of the atheists. He next directed his attention to another
target, the deists. Turretin's method, in disproving deism, is to
establish the nature of God and then to show that this divine being
actively participates in the affairs of his creation.

Turretin employed the same arguments to prove God's attributes
that he used to prove God's existence. He established common
ground in his arguments with the heathen philosophers of antiquity.
His purpose, in showing such an accord, was to indicate the common ground that the deist can have with the Christian in religious
epistemology.

The first concept concerning the nature of deity is the eternal
existence of God. Having already shown that some eternal being
must have existed in order to generate existence to all other creatures, he argues that if a being had existed before God, that being
would be a necessary cause and would itself be God. The first
cause would have to be supreme and would, therefore, be God.
Heathen religions, as Turretin pointed out, had long adhered to

this concept when they believed in an entire pantheon of gods, and yet acknowledged the existence of a supreme being that existed prior to the panoply of deities.[73]

It logically follows, Turretin argued, that since God had existed from eternity, he must also exist to eternity. It is inconceivable that he could ever cease to exist. Cicero himself had agreed with this concept. Further, God does not owe his existence to any outside cause and must be a necessary being whose nonexistence is impossible.[74]

Furthermore, a being who must, by necessity, exist, would not be capable of change. He reasoned that for a being to change, the change would either come about through another agent or by the eternal being itself. Both of these options would not be possible, however, since God is independent and has no reason to change himself. For him to do so would imply that he either lacked something or possessed an unnecessary attribute. Turretin supported this argument concerning divine immutability by appealing to the authority of Plato and Seneca.[75]

The next argument of Turretin concerning the nature of the divine being asserts that God is a thinking being. This quality is the result of the other attributes that have already been established. Further, since thinking beings exist in the world, it would make sense that a thinking being created them. The intricateness of the creation points to a God capable of design. Thought would be a necessary prerequisite of such a creation. Again, Turretin invoked the views of the ancient philosophers to support his point. Both Cicero and Plato taught that creation was the result of divine reason.[76]

Not only is God a thinking being, he argued, he must concomitantly be an intelligent being. In addition, he must be the most intelligent being and have complete intelligence, or omniscience. he argued that since God has given to man the faculty of intelligence, he himself must have the power of understanding as well.[77]

In defining the extent of this divine omniscience, Turretin held that God is prescient. He wrote that it is absurd to imagine that God would not know in advance what would occur in the lives of the beings that he had created. Otherwise, their lives would be filled with uncertainty and God would, therefore, learn new things, which would be impossible. God would know what will occur in the future. Turretin used analogical proofs to support his argument. He pointed out human examples of judgment of the future such as the politician and the judge who can employ human wisdom to surmise the nature of future events. However, the use of analogy

fails to prove his point adequately. He did claim that divine fore-
knowledge accords with the dictates of reason even though humans
cannot properly understand it. He then appealed to revelation and
prophecy as the crowning proofs of divine prescience. Seneca invoked his blessing upon this argument as Turretin quoted him:
"The whole series of their works is known to the Gods. All the
various affairs conducted by their agency, lie open before them.
But they are concealed from us. And those events which appear
to us sudden and unexpected, were foreknown and quite familiar
to them."[78]

The freedom of God is a necessary corollary to his omniscience.
Turretin called this the absolute freedom of the will. He derived
this statement from the concept that humans possess free will and
their creator must as well. One can also establish this postulate
through observing the cosmos, which contains the marks of a creator who was not driven by necessity. Turretin summarized that
the various nations are agreed in their acknowledgement of the
freedom of God. It would be foolish to worship a God who did not
have control over his own actions.[79]

Postulating that God must always will in accordance with his
nature, Turretin argued that this is not a contradiction of his freedom. For God to act out of moral perfection is for him to act freely.
Seneca had said: "There is a necessity that the same things should
be always agreeable to him, whom nothing can please but what is
most excellent. And he is not on this account less free and powerful, for the only necessity to which he is subject depends on his
own will."[80]

Turretin next proceeded to a discussion of the omnipotence of
the divine being by asserting that a being who created *ex nihilo*
must be all-powerful. He did point out, however, that this power
does not include the ability to perform acts that are contradictory.
God cannot produce a square circle, for example. The manner of
God's power lies beyond man's comprehension. Cicero himself,
Turretin argued, concurred with the concept of God's omnipotence
when he stated that God can accomplish anything. Homer, as well,
had said that Jupiter could accomplish all things.[81]

Next, Turretin explained that the works of God demonstrate
divine wisdom. He defined wisdom as consisting of "pursuing the
best ends by the fittest means."[82] The attribute of wisdom is the
corollary of his other attributes. The God who knows all things
and who cannot err must be all-knowing. Further, since all human
wisdom derives its origin from deity, God must be all-wise. Again,
Turretin agreed with the ancient philosophers on this point. Cicero,

Seneca, Epictetus, and Marcus Aurelius all related God's wisdom to the proper governance of the world.

Turretin went on to explain that "wisdom is the source of holiness."[83] The wise being esteems virtue and condemns vice. Natural law, which points man to perform duties, supports the idea of God's holiness as well. He wrote: "For to the being who so particularly has practiced virtue, and laid before us so many inducements to engage us in the pursuit of it, it must be an object of the highest esteem."[84] In addition, the ancient philosophers related the concept of God's governance of human affairs to his holiness.[85]

Several virtues, including justice, exist under the rubric of holiness. The all-wise God who is holy must also be all-just. Further, man has an inherent consciousness of the concept of justice even though human inclination often points away from the performance of the just action. Not only does man have this inherent sense of justice, the principle is necessary for the maintenance of an orderly society. Many passages in the ancient philosophical writings point to the divine attribute of justice.[86]

Concomitant to justice stands the attribute of truthfulness. Turretin pointed out that truthfulness serves as a branch of the subject of divine justice. God has given man an inherent sense of truth as well and Turretin can conceive of no logical reason for God to lie. Deceit, by its very nature, necessitates that the lying person promote either self-interest or revenge, which God would have no reason to do. Plato had written in support of this concept when he stated that there is no reason for God to lie.[87]

Goodness and beneficence follow next in Turretin's accounting of the attributes of God. The works of God point to these qualities, the creation being foremost. God, lacking nothing, did not need to create, but did so out of kindness. In addition, the nature of creation in its intricacy and beauty points to the goodness of God. Turretin wrote:

> For why were such a multitude of objects provided for the use and enjoyment of man? Why was man himself created capable of happiness? When we partake of those things provided for the supply of our necessities, why do they give us pleasure? Why are we furnished with such a variety of most agreeable fruits? Why is the face of Nature so pleasing? Why is the human body so wonderfully formed, and preserved in safety amidst the multitude of dangers to which it is exposed? What was the cause of these and innumerable other phenomena in the world, but the infinite goodness of God, and his desire to make others happy?[88]

Turretin pointed to Seneca as the supreme example of an ancient philosopher who supported the concept of divine beneficence. Seneca had attributed human benefits, necessities as well as luxuries, to the goodness of God.

Turretin ascribed several other attributes to God including patience, clemency, and mercy, which are self-evident to Turretin based upon God's forbearance with sinful men.[89] So Turretin ended his listing of divine attributes.

Having completed his proofs for the attributes of God, Turretin proceeded to defend his arguments. The problem of the presence of evil in the world was an essential objection to divine goodness that he thoroughly discusses. Pointing to two types of evil, natural and moral, he blames the latter on mankind because men commit sins freely. The sinfulness of man directly results from his freewill. For God to have created men without such volition would have been unworthy of him, but with such a creation comes the possibility of evil moral actions. Natural evil, on the other hand, he defines as a lesser degree of perfection, "which the great disposer of all things may communicate at pleasure; or it is the just punishment of our offenses, a fatherly chastisement, intended to cure the internal diseases of the mind."[90]

Next Turretin discussed his proofs for the incorporeality of the divine being. Given the attributes of God's intelligence, will, and freedom, Turretin concluded that God could not be corporeal. He says: "And indeed we can perceive no connection between extension, divisibility, mobility, etc. and the properties of the mind, such as a power of understanding, judging, choosing, to which may be added, a capacity for wisdom, benevolence, etc. As therefore these latter are the properties of the Supreme Being, it follows, that the former are inconsistent with his Nature."[91] God's infinite qualities, cannot be contained in corporeal form since the body is subject to decay and to change. This would contradict the attribute of immutability. Further, if God were corporeal, he would thereby be divisible and would be limited to individual points in space, which would all imply change. It would not be possible to so confine an immutable being. Turretin conceded that many of the heathen philosophers held to corporeal gods, but he claimed that several did not, including Aristotle and Cicero.[92] Since God is incorporeal, the attribute of omnipresence is possible and ultimately necessary. Turretin asked how it could be possible for such a being to be absent from any place. Both Plotinus and Xenophon agreed with this premise as did Seneca who wrote: "'Wherever you turn yourself you are surrounded with the presence of the Divinity. He is everywhere, his works are full of him.'"[93]

An important issue that Turretin addressed are the proofs for monotheism in natural theology. Since he could not conceive of any arguments in favor of a plurality of gods, Turretin dismissed the possibility. He wrote: "The formation of the world, and the several parts that compose it, which we behold with so much admiration, require indeed an artist, and one infinitely powerful and wise; but, in order to create these productions, a multiplicity of such artists is by no means necessary."[94]

Although he admitted that his argument in favor of monotheism is a negative one, he held that it is nonetheless valid. The burden of proof lay with the polytheists to establish the plurality of divinities. In addition, he argued that since God is a necessary being, a plurality of gods could not be possible. If this were so, none of the divinities could be a necessary being. They could either exist or not exist, and therefore would not be gods at all. He postulated further that a multitude of gods would either have to act in concert or else separately. If the former were the case they would be dependent on each other and if the latter were true none of them could be omniscient. Lastly, Turretin's examination of the nature of creation pointed to a single divine being. The intricateness of the world reflects the workmanship of a single architect. he noted as well what he calls the "folly" of pagan polytheists who revere deities who were harmful to nature and who reproach decency. He cited Richard Cudworth on this point who, in his *Intellectual System of the World,* collected quotations from the ancient philosophers in favor of monotheism.[95]

Turretin discussed several polytheistic religious groups such as the Persians, the Marcionites, the Manicheans, all who misapplied the issue of the origin of evil. These groups ascribed it to an "evil principle" that must have been the opposite of the benevolent deity, but possessed the same measure of power and authority. Turretin asserted that such a concept is contrary to reason because it would ascribe the same attributes to the most perfect of all beings and to the most evil, or imperfect of all beings.[96] In addition, if one granted the validity of such dualism, other contradictions would arise such as the problem of cooperation between the two powers. Since the deities oppose each other, it would be impossible for one to allow the other to perform acts such as creation. The evil power would surely have opposed the creation of the world that contains so much good. It would prefer instead to create a world of chaos, confusion, deformity, and destruction. Turretin considered the arguments in favor of dualism to be self-defeating.[97]

As to the relation of the biblical concept of the Trinity to the idea of the unity of God, Turretin posited that no contradiction exists. Claiming that the Trinity is a "mystery, with respect to which, reason is altogether silent," Turretin did not think it possible for Christian and Jewish writings to deny the unity of God.[98]

In addition to his discussion of the attributes of God, Turretin listed several corollaries that help to clarify his position. First, he criticized those who claim that the divine attributes apply to "senseless matter" or an imperfect being, saying that they do not understand the necessity that these attributes be applied to the infinite-personal God. He also denied the Aristotelian categories of "substance" and "accidents," saying that a thing either exists of itself or is dependent on another thing for its existence. He also denied the necessity of matter saying that God has the power to create or destroy matter. He rejected the existence of uncreated space that could be eternal and independent of God. It is not only impossible to prove the existence of such space, but its independence from God would also limit divine power and dominion.[99]

Divine Providence

Turretin devoted the next section in his treatise on natural theology to the study of divine providence. In establishing the correctness of God's interaction and direction of human affairs, Turretin directly attacked deistic philosophy, which denies such a relationship between the creator and the creation.

He divided his discussion into four sections: the meaning of providence, the proof of providence, the objections to providence, and the manner of operations of providence. When Turretin asked whether or not providence is operational, he was really positing whether or not God actively governs the world. Providence, he wrote, consists of two particular facets: preservation and governance. Preservation relates to God's control of nature, while governance has to do with God's relationship to human society.[100]

He argued that the attributes of God, which he has already established, point to the necessity of providence. God's infinite wisdom makes it necessary for him to take care of his creation. His benevolence was revealed in creation and it would seem unlikely that a benevolent God would ignore his handiwork. Since God is omniscient, he is very well acquainted with all human events. His holiness necessitates his reckoning of the goodness or evil of the actions of men. Because of divine immutability, God can never withdraw his attention from his creation.[101]

The only reason Turretin can envision for God ignoring his creation would be either a lack of desire, power, or knowledge. But divine ignorance goes against the attribute of omniscience and a lack of power against omnipotence. As to a lack of desire, he wrote that "the guardianship of the world is an object most worthy of his wisdom and equity."[102]

Turretin listed several other bases for divine providence. First, he compares God to a wise artist who could not ignore the management of his creation. Even the animals care for their young. Therefore, Turretin, reasoned, since God is the most excellent being who sets the example for all others, he could not neglect his "offspring."[103]

At this point, Turretin referred back to his second argument in favor of God's existence. He wrote that a necessary being does not require assistance from any source, but created beings depend on their creator for their existence. He concluded: "Abstracted from the will and the power of the Deity, created Beings are mere nothing; and therefore they must of necessity be preserved by the same good pleasure, to which they were at first indebted for their existence."[104] The implication here is that created beings would cease to exist if God did not sustain them. Turretin, having completed his arguments in favor of divine providence, listed several objections followed by his responses. The problem of evil is an important philosophical issue that Turretin raised in this regard. If creation were continuous, then God would be the author of evil, the argument goes. Turretin responded by arguing that God bestows upon man faculties such as intelligence and freedom in such a way that his creatures may use them as they wish and then deserve either praise or blame for their actions.[105]

Turretin's third argument in favor of providence dealt with the order and beauty of the cosmos. The creation is too intricate and excellent to be the product of mere chance. He explained:

When we contemplate the most beautiful construction of the Universe, in which we perceive such a diversity of objects, such a variety of ornaments, so much stability, in which, if it is considered with proper attention, we see everything excellently fitted to its particular use; finally, in which we perceive that nothing had departed from its situation or lost any part of its beauty in the space, not of a short period, but many thousand years; when I say we contemplate all these appearances, no man, not quite destitute of reason, can possibly imagine, that they are produced without any conducting hand, without counsel or understanding.[106]

He cited the intricacies of the stars and of created beings such as the animals as examples of such providence. It is interesting to note that he notices the work of selection in nature where certain species are prevented from multiplying too rapidly or are prevented from extinction. He then discusses the nature of the human body and was amazed at its intricate detail. He noted its ability to withstand disease, its delicate organs, and the manner in which infants are formed in the mother's womb.[107]

Turretin explained that one must ascribe the origin of the intricacy of nature to blind necessity, chance, or to a wise creator. The last option makes the most sense. Seneca had written: "so great a work could not continue, independent of the care of some guardian; that such excellent order cannot be the work of undesigning matter, nor can the fixed revolutions of the stars be owing to any blind force; that the motion produced by chance is often disturbed, and immediately vanishes into nothing; that such a regular velocity is the effect of an eternal law."[108]

An important objection to the notion of providence that Turretin here addressed is the concept that God created the world and endowed it with the power to sustain itself without the need for divine intervention. He said that such an argument is a confirmation of providence. He wrote:

For he who says that the world is governed by laws, fixed originally by the power of God, and that these laws invariably perform their office, understands by these words the very same thing which we understand by the term Providence.[109]

Second, since God is immutable, once he began to will something, he must continue to will it. Third, those natural laws which govern creation constitute the manner in which divine providence operates. Fourth, he pointed to the presence of human moral principles and attributes their origin to God. Fifth, he pointed out that the results of providence are located in the enjoyment and permanent order of society in the face of so much wickedness and vice. Such a state would be impossible, he wrote, "unless a Being, friendly to the happiness of mankind presided at the helm."[110] The inclinations of infants toward imitation, the care of offspring, the need to live in society are all propensities that God provides. In addition, the fact that man can live a happy life in spite of the presence of so many evil individuals is evidence of the care of God.

Sixth, Turretin argued that the histories of all peoples contain examples of divine judgment that are remarkably similar to those recorded in Scripture. He noted the tragic ends of many notorious sinners, the detection and punishment of secret crimes and conspiracies, the prosperity of virtuous nations, and the condemnations of those nations which fall into sin. These are, for Turretin, evidences of providence.[111]

The seventh argument states that without providence religion and justice would cease. There would be no need to worship a deity that does not interact with his creation. He pointed out that the Epicureans, who had denied providence, had worshipped God because of his excellent nature, but then Cicero criticized the Epicureans for inconsistency on this point. Cicero asked, "Do you owe any piety to the Being from whom you have received no obligation?"[112] Turretin pointed out that the Epicureans are the only exception among the ancient philosophical movements to deny providence. He said: "every one must perceive, that all their supplications, their devout praises, their ceremonies, their fears, their hopes, their confidence, in a word that every sort of religion whatever, has supposed a Providence and been founded on this truth as a radical principle."[113] In concluding his argument, Turretin asserted that special revelation adds other important arguments in favor of providence such as miracles and prophecy.

At this point, in Turretin's fifth dissertation on the subject of natural theology, he defended the doctrine of providence against possible objections. He discussed several general principles as a basis for his defense of providence. First, he asserted that in the area of philosophy, it is often difficult for one to grasp the meaning of some arguments. Second, many aspects of providence are mysteries, and lie, therefore, beyond the reaches of man's wisdom and understanding. He wrote: "Now who will dare to assert, that he clearly understands what is agreeable to, and what is inconsistent with the Divine Perfections, that all the works of God, that things past, present and to come with their whole series and connections, and that all the circumstances of his future Being, evidently lie open to his view?"[114] Thus, most of the objections to providence relate not to providence proper but to the manner of its operation. The problem is not with providence itself but with a misunderstanding of its nature. Most objections, therefore, are easily refuted and contribute to the proof of its operation.

The first objection is that everything in nature has a natural cause and nature works without the necessity of a divine mover. Turretin agreed with part of this assertion by stating that God's manner of working in the world is to employ the natural order that he has set up. God, furthermore, almost always acts in accordance with natural law, and miracles, therefore, would occur very rarely. He concluded that nature is nothing else but God's wise governance of his creation.[115]

The second objection states that many aspects of life do not point to the ordered governance of the universe, but rather to disorder and to chance. Examples of such disorder would include storms, earthquakes, poisons, and other aspects of nature that destroy the "fruits of the earth."[116] Turretin answered that God has indeed created a world system with general laws that allow for instances of destruction but that overall accomplish "the most valuable and salutary ends."[117] He claimed that it is the practice of God not to infringe on the natural operation of such laws on a perpetual basis. In addition, such events as storms or falling rocks may appear irregular and yet serve an important and useful purpose. The problem here lies in a lack of human understanding, a deficiency that can perhaps find its cure through scientific discovery. For example, prior to the discovery of the circulation of the blood, the progress of medicine was quite limited. After its discovery, however, medicine advanced rapidly. The study of God's providence is much the same, but some truths will never be fully known until man sees God face to face in the afterlife.[118]

Thirdly, many aspects of nature that, at first, seem disagreeable can be quite beneficial. For example, antidotes can be extracted from poisons.[119] Turretin writes: "in this state of darkness, in which our faculties are circumscribed within narrow limits, it is impossible for us to judge with propriety concerning the works of God, concerning their utility and inconveniences, their beauty and deformity."[120]

The third objection relates to the role of chance in human affairs. It appears to the casual observer that many events occur haphazardly rather than as the result of divine guidance. Turretin replied that one may well be unaware of the reasons behind a certain event. Though one might well attribute its causation to luck, in fact, providence is the author. Part of the problem here lies in the difference between the perception of man in comparison with that of God. He wrote: "we do not know the particular reasons why God should choose one number of leaves, or of grains of sand, rather than another: But all these things arise from general Laws, established by the Deity, and therefore are all the objects of his providential appointment. God knows them, he presides over them, for they are the consequences of Laws which he himself has constituted."[121]

The fourth objection states that certain events find their cause in man's freedom rather than in God's providence.[122] Turretin responded to this objection by relating man's freedom to God's design. God directs the world through the use of individual freedom. Humans are subject to God's direction, but their freedom is not impeded. Events that occur as a result of human effort find their ultimate source in divine direction.[123]

The fifth objection states that the argument for providence forces God toward unworthy humiliation in lowering himself to human affairs. Turretin countered with the assertion that this objection misunderstands the nature of divine majesty. God's governance of the cosmos is one of the main components of his majesty and points to his greatness. God's actions, he explained, are perfectly voluntary and do not at all disturb God's tranquillity. One should, rather, marvel, at the inconceivable greatness of his administration of the affairs of the universe and offer praise to God for it.[124]

The next objection declares that if one assumes the operation of providence then one would also have to assume that God is sometimes angry with his creation and, at times, is appeased. Both qualities, the objection continues, are inconsistent with the nature of God. Turretin wrote that the Epicureans raised this objection. He answered it with the explanation that when men describe emotions such as anger in God, they are speaking in anthropomorphic terms. When God either approves or disapproves of the actions of men, he reflects his holiness and justice.[125]

Turretin deemed the next section of objections to divine providence more challenging than the previous group. He responded to the argument that pious men all too often live in poor and unhappy circumstances. It would make sense for a just God to reward those people who are most godly in their lifestyles. Turretin answered this objection by stating, first, that not all men who appear to be pious are really religious. Second, even pious individuals are still sinful, and third many circumstances such as poverty are deemed unfortunate from a human perspective yet God might have some higher purpose in allowing a pious man to live in humble circumstances. Further, the peace of mind that pious men enjoy has far greater value than earthly riches.[126]

The next objection is similar. The fact that the wicked often prosper is evidence against providence. Turretin replied that wicked men are often unhappy and are tormented by pangs of conscience. Secondly, their wickedness might well lead to riches, but often it leads to the destruction of such wealth or in their committing of such crimes they are apprehended and punished by the civil authorities. Finally, Turretin speculated that if the wicked do escape all troubles, God still is responsible to practice forbearance in order to lead such people to repentance. The judgment belongs, rather, to the future state where the wicked will surely receive their proper punishment. An additional argument that he advanced is that temporal gains are not the chief good of man.[127]

At this point, Turretin asserted that God normally will not intervene in the affairs of nature through the use of miracles. In order to reward continually the pious and punish the wicked he would have to perform miracles on a regular basis. This would be unworthy of God. Physical laws are fixed. Turretin wrote: "Physical laws are therefore fixed except by the rare case of divine intervention."[128] Turretin emphasized the inherent freedom of God over the power of natural law.

The last objection to the operation of divine providence is the most difficult of all, according to Turretin. The argument says that a benevolent deity would not allow sin to enter the world since sin contradicts God's holiness. In his response, Turretin assumed that God cannot be the author of sin but it is rather the fault of man. In fact, God has given men an innate abhorrence of sin and has provided conscience to enable man to determine the difference between just and unjust actions. He wrote that God has done everything possible to prevent man from committing sin while not violating the sanctity of human nature.[129] The problem lies with man and especially with his free will. Inherent in this freedom is the possibility of sin and rebellion against God. Further, he argued, neither virtue nor piety would be possible without freedom.[130] There would be no concepts such as freedom, reproof, blame, reward, punishment, or judgment without it. Without freedom, God would not be the judge of humanity and there would be no need for religion or providence.[131]

An additional objection to Turretin's argument arises in the form of the possibility that God might have created man free but without the possibility of sinning such as is the case with angels. Turretin replied that God, indeed, could have immediately placed man within the angelic world without the possibility of sin, but the greater good for man was for him to pass through a state of trial and of discipline. Trials serve to improve the virtues of the pious and noble man and render the individual worthy of divine reward.[132]

He cited several authorities to support his arguments, including Leibniz, who wrote in his *Essays of Theodicy* that God, who could have created any number of possible worlds, created the one that contained the presence of evil in order to make possible all the virtues of life.[133]

Lastly, if any objection remains, Turretin pointed out that there are times when we cannot fully understand the ways of God and are too ignorant to judge his counsels. Even though some aspects of his governance might appear unjust to the human observer, God's ways are so much higher than man's that we must assume that he governs in a just manner. Man must wait for the final judgment in order to witness the resolution of the tension between good and evil.[134]

In the next section of Turretin's work on natural revelation, he discussed the manner of divine providence. He pointed out that providence extends to the entirety of nature and referred to the objections of Aquinas and Jerome, who said it was ridiculous to believe that God bothers himself with a knowledge of the minutia of the natural world, such as the number of flies in the world. Turretin disagreed by referring to the biblical passage that says that God knows whenever a sparrow falls to the ground and knows the number of hairs on our heads. The human body, he wrote, is so incredibly intricate that the malfunction of a very small organ can end a life. The entire body, therefore, must be under the power of divine preservation.[135] Pliny had written similarly "Nature . . . is no where more complex than in her smallest productions; for in larger bodies, where the matter is so copious, the workmanship is easy; but in forming so small and almost imperceptible objects, what reason, what power, what inexplicable perfection are discernible."[136]

The error of such objections as Jerome lay in their misunderstanding of the nature of God and in their mistaken idea that God cannot be concerned about individual things. Turretin continued to say that God is in control of his creation that nothing can occur by chance. If one were to remove from God the control over individual entities, God would effectively lose his direction over the whole of creation because the whole is composed of particulars. One cannot help but notice the nominalist argument here.[137]

In his description of the manner of the operation of providence, Turretin explained that providence includes those events which result directly from human free acts. He wrote that man, endowed with liberty, occupies the highest position in the order of creation and could not conceivably be excluded from the care of such a wise and loving God.[138]

Next, Turretin remarked on the differences between preservation and government. He used the term *conservatio* to refer to the maintenance of creation by the sheer will of God. Only God can prevent all creation from annihilation. God created *ex nihilo* and he sustains his creation by the same power.[139] God's immutability is evidence of this continuation of the same mode of operation. Once God begins to will something, he must continue to do so since he does not change. One can, therefore, conceive of preservation as a continual creation. Divine preservation extends to the maintenance of living creatures, with their powers and faculties.

As to divine governance, God governs substances in accord with their nature. For example, he governs animals, who do not have the power of reason, in a mechanical way. He governs, man, by contrast, in a more personal fashion. Since man has been enlightened with the power of reason, God allows man to choose a manner of action freely. God's omniscience means that he knows all aspects of human thought and conduct. God does approve or disapprove of the free acts of humans in accordance with his attributes of justice, truth, and holiness.[140]

Turretin contended that there should be a human response to divine providence. Humans should be thankful for God's work and should submit to his will at all times. He also serves as a source of aid and we should take advantage of it in times of need. Further, man should attempt to become virtuous and pious.[141] Lastly, he wrote, "as the ways of God are frequently concealed from us, we should be instructed by wisdom to judge with caution and modesty, with respect to both persons and things, and to restrain our opinion of matters involved in obscurity and perplexity, until the day comes, when every thing, relating to which we are at present in the dark, shall be placed before us in a clear point of view."[142]

Natural Law

Turretin included a thorough discussion of the subject of natural law in his treatise on natural theology as an apologetic device to combat the deistic position on this topic. He denied Hobbes's contention that positive religion is the creation of the state preferring to attribute natural law to an ultimate, divine source.

In his defense of natural laws, Turretin asserted that they are self-evident and it would be ridiculous to deny them. Further, the laws of nature have roots deeper than mere education. In other words, natural law is not simply a product of an educational system in a learned society. He wrote that philosophers, by contrast, are influenced by opinions based upon human prejudice.[143]

Turretin admitted that not all cultures agree perfectly on these laws, but he does not see this as necessary to his argument. Turretin concluded:

Wherefore if there are any individuals of mankind, or if there are whole nations, who neglect utterly to cultivate the faculty of reason, or who are diverted from attending to its dictates, either by a false education, the strength of passion, or any other similar obstruction; it is not at all surprising that they should be ignorant, with respect to the true and genuine principles of morality, implanted in their nature.[144]

No matter how barbarous a people seem to be, they could not possibly be devoid of ideas of morality and justice. Their application of such morality may be wrong, but they do admit general moralistic principles. The more barbarous a people are, the more they misapply the morality that they possess.

It is important to note here that much of the weight of Turretin's argument stems from observation of human behavior. When Turretin was able to base his arguments upon the observation of various cultures rather than upon God, natural revelation takes on more of an independent form. Although he stated that natural revelation is the mere maidservant of special revelation, in practice it can virtually stand on its own.[145]

Turretin related the concept of the freedom of the will to the necessity for natural law. In his discussion of free will, Turretin pointed out two types of causes for human action, free and necessary causes. He observes that necessary causes always produce an effect when they possess the necessary power. Free causes have the option, by contrast, to choose to produce an effect or not.[146] True freedom of the will comes from comparing motives and deciding between them. Understanding and will are both part of the mind and the judgment of the understanding is the determination of the will. He pointed out that the fact that men do have such choice does not mean that men always make the correct or best choices. On the contrary, poor decisions are not a result of the lack of liberty but of poor usage of it.

One of the essential proofs of free will, according to Turretin, lies in the use of conscience. God had the power to create beings that do not exist in and of themselves, but can employ power over their own actions. Since man is created in God's image, he has conscience. Further, this liberty cannot be destroyed by the passions of man, but men are susceptible to moral weakness. Man has freedom of choice but often makes wrong choices. He is responsible for such choices because of his liberty.[147]

Turretin observes also not only that man has freedom of the will, but that there are certain laws of nature that one can employ to judge the correctness of man's choices. He asks whether man is independent of such natural law. Turretin answered that it is inconceivable to believe that man would not be subject to any such law. Given the nature of God, it naturally follows that God has given men the bond of morality. Man, therefore, possesses both intelligence and liberty as well as ideas of duty, order, justice, and some kind of internal concept of God. Turretin concluded:

> Finally, man is endued with every power necessary to religion, and to the civil and social life. Who can believe that almost all these advantages were given to him in vain? And yet they would be in vain, if no law was provided to subject mankind to its authority and direct them to the proper exercise of these excellent faculties.[148]

Since man is subject to natural law, the breaking of such law would be considered a vice. If this tendency to break the natural law is unrestrained, he argued, man would possess no dignity. Turretin called the result of unrestrained license, "wickedness, discord, and misery."[149] He compared the moral nature of man to that of animals and asserts that man could not survive alone in the wild. He needed society, which provides him with security and protection. The laws of nature are manifested to man within these societal groupings. These moral axioms are self-evident in such communal environments. He listed several basic moral axioms such as "we should give everyone his due; we should not violate our faith; we should be grateful for benefits received."[150] But such ideas have been common to all men in all societies. Turretin argued that if such ideas are universal they must have a common source, God himself. God has provided man with such principles to help man to direct his conduct.[151]

He defined the laws of nature in the following fashion: "The laws of nature then, are the dictates of reason, which derive, as it were, their origin from the order and harmony of the universe, and carry along with them their own confirmation and demonstrative evidence."[152] Turretin saw prudence as the key to being obedient to such laws. Wicked men do not obey such principles, he wrote, but when they themselves suffer wrongs, they are the first to complain. Turretin claimed that this is evidence that the wicked are appealing to some implanted sense of justice. The only people who would not have such a sense would be those living in a very primitive, barbarous culture. Turretin did not go as far as to say that man is endowed with innate ideas, but he did believe that social norms of morality are inbred in the nature of human society.

A further argument of Hobbes states that although the civil leaders of the state construct legislation and make the laws of the state, there is no law antecedent to the laws of the state. There would, therefore, be no natural law that would be self-evident to man. All laws are mere social conventions. Ideas of justice and virtue possess no prior existence to the growth of civil authority. Turretin responded that Hobbes's arguments go against the dictates of reason. A civil leader does not have the power to alter truth or change the nature of evil action such as murder into just, moral activities. He argued that man has no basis for judging between good and evil unless he possesses the law of nature. There is a "common principle of intelligence" for all men that shows them what is evil and wrong. To say that such common knowledge of good and evil is only a matter of opinion is "sheer madness."[153]

Turretin admitted that human legislation is, indeed, based upon compacts between people, but he pointed out that it is natural law that gives man the sense of obligation to obey his compacts. Some bond must have existed before all other contracts that provides man with the very concept of forming and obeying the provisions of agreements. This bond is nothing else but the law of nature.[154] He added that it is God himself who implants in us this sense of obligation because he is the author of the natural order and exists antecedent to all agreements between people.

Turretin argued, further, that there are aspects of law that are derived, in part, from self-love and utility. However, the duties that God requires us to perform are not against our own self-interest. These natural laws are, therefore, quite practical. If these laws of nature did not work in real life, human society would not function properly and they would have to be rejected in favor of rules that would be more applicable to the human condition. Without the bond that unites society, the human condition would sink to the depths of misery and there could be no mutual performance of obligations.[155] Utility would, therefore, be an excellent motivation for us to obey the natural law. It not only works, but it is in our best self-interest to obey.

Beardslee comments that Turretin's system of natural law portrays God in an impersonal light. Turretin saw God as "the lawgiver and judge as a matter of emphasis, rather than the author of salvation or even the author of the decrees of predestination, by which some of fallen mankind are conducted to bliss. This resulted from the increased emphasis on natural reason. Sound reason, or clear thinking, if not allowed to use Scriptural, or specifically Christian data, ought not to be expected to reach Christian conclusions."[156]

This is not surprising, however, since Turretin's purpose in discussing natural law is to combat specific deistic arguments that are in conflict with orthodox theology. Natural theology, for Turretin, cannot prove all aspects of Christian religion such as the details of soteriology. Natural theology prepares the way for special revelation to define the doctrines of the faith in a specific manner. The fact that Turretin did not emphasize the nature of predestination in his discussion of natural theology is because it belongs in a discussion of special revelation. He minimized his definition of predestination in his biblical theological system because of the divisive tendencies of the subject.

Turretin distinguished between justice and utility. Utility shows us that a certain action is prudent and easily applicable to real-life situations. He wrote that utility alone may spur man to a certain action, but ultimately, unless man lies under the sovereignty of a God who requires obedience, there is no real obligation on the part of man to behave in a certain fashion.[157]

He concluded that if Hobbes is correct in his arguments, humans owe no duty to a divine being. Such an idea was unthinkable for Turretin. For him, the very good of society is rooted on the foundation of the performance of duties before God. He wrote that man does not worship and obey God based upon the benefits that society gains from such activity. The real reasons for worshipping God are his attributes and authority. God's very nature demands our worship.[158]

Turretin continued to discuss the concept of duty and especially those duties which relate directly to the self. These duties do not include any sense of obligation to society as a whole. Any man stranded on an island devoid of human life would have the same duties toward the self as any man living in the midst of society. In order to perform such duties toward the self, one must preserve his mental faculties in such a state that is agreeable to the direction of wisdom and the dictates of nature. Turretin admitted that there are certain actions that are advantageous to the self that are disadvantageous to society such as stealing. In addition, there are other actions that are advantageous to society that are equally unjust. An example of this would be stealing from the rich and giving to the poor.[159]

The next section of Turretin's discussion of human responsibility focused on the duties that man owes to God. He began his discussion by assuming that God is the creator of man and, by virtue of that fact, man naturally owes his allegiance to his Maker. Further, man should have as clear an understanding of the nature of God as possible. As a result of such knowledge, man will show respect and reverence toward God. He will love his Creator and show gratitude for the gift of existence as well as God's work of preserving life. The concept of "fearing" God has also to do with God's attribute of holiness. He defined such fear as pious reverence. Since God is omniscient, man should obey his instructions. Since God is benevolent, man should ask God for help in times of trouble. Asking for such help would be equivalent to prayer. He wrote that when one prays, one acknowledges God's power, wisdom, and goodness.[160] In addition, prayer is natural to men in all nations. In times of crisis, especially, man has the tendency to turn to God for assistance. Further, prayer is important because it allows man to express his thanks to God. He wrote: "As God is most benevolent, and at the same time infinite in wisdom and power, we ought to commit all our affairs to his management, and repose an unbounded confidence in him. For as he is supremely wise, he knows perfectly what is best for us."[161]

Responding to the objection that God does not need the prayers of man, he argued that since God is omniscient, God knows the future as well as human desires. The objection states that given such omniscience, prayer would be an unnecessary ritual. However, Turretin countered that the soul in prayer contemplates the excellent nature of God and helps man to imitate his holy qualities. Further, "petition inspires us with humility and a lively conviction of our absolute and entire dependence on God."[162]

Turretin pointed out that God's sovereignty has practical benefits. It provides comfort for man, especially when he encounters the inevitable difficulties of life. Since God is omniscient, he observes human conduct through such trials and he, in fact, allows these situations to occur. This should provide great comfort since God loves his creatures and has their best interests in mind. God must, therefore, have some higher good in mind for man. In addition, all the good things in life are gifts from God and are given to advance his glory. Any true excellence found in man is gained through imitation of the moral excellence of God. The chief goal of man is seeking fellowship with God. Turretin wrote: "But the man who enjoys the friendship of God, is always in possession of the truest and most permanent, and consequently, his chief good."[163]

Next, Turretin discussed the subject of the worship that is due God. Such worship flows naturally out of reverence for him and is based upon his creation of mankind. Further, man has the responsibility to inspire others to worship God. Worship has its proper forms, however. One needs to exercise caution in such activity lest he contradict the nature of God in his worship. For example, there should be no aspects of worship that are unworthy of God such as the exaltation of created beings used as a visible substitution for the invisible God. There should be no oath taking before God because man does not have the ability to guarantee fulfillment. Such promise making before God is unworthy of him because it implies that man has the power to fulfill that which only God himself can guarantee. Turretin observes: "If the deity has at any time, condescended to reveal himself to mankind, and prescribed any form, according to which he desires to be worshipped; faith and obedience, with respect to such a revelation and manner of worship, is a duty required of us."[164]

The next section of Turretin's discussion relates to the duties that man owes to both his neighbors and to himself. The foundation of such duties is the fact that man is a societal being and could not exist for very long in isolation. The need to relate to other human beings is an inherent quality of man, one that God gave to him in creating the human race. This societal quality leads to propensities toward mercy, gratitude, friendship, marriage, and care for children. The improvement of arts and science are also results of this desire of men to live in concert. Such studies are necessary to improve the collective lot of mankind and are natural results of his nature as a social animal.[165]

To prove that man, indeed, possesses this quality, Turretin noted that the use of speech and emotional reactions such as tears and laughter have little significance outside of a social setting. The laws of nature dictate that man should cultivate relationships for the betterment of society. Since God created man to live in society, it makes perfect sense that he should act in such a way as to improve it.

At this point, Turretin cited the golden rule as a fundamental axiom of human relationships: "The negative part is, not to do to another what we would not wish another should do to us; the positive, to do to others as we would desire that others should do to us."[166] This rule has three aspects. First, men are equal in the particulars of their existence. They are further equal in their nature as God has created them. No one man has a higher standing than another before God. Lastly, by means of application one should view actions from the perspective of his neighbor.[167]

Another important natural law states that one should do injury to no one. This is proved by the approbation of conscience and is also a natural consequence of the first two laws. Further, restitution should be made for any injuries that are committed. He wrote that man has the responsibility to make restitution for any wrongs committed to another. It naturally follows that one should act with sincerity in the fulfillment of his promises and commitments. Fidelity is essential for the survival of a society. One should also help others in times of need when such assistance is needed, regardless of the difficulty of providing help. He wrote; "This law derives its origin from the same sources, from humanity, which powerfully excites us to be kind to others, and also from a regard to the good of society, which can only be advanced by mutual discharge of benevolent and good natured offices."[168]

Gratitude is another important natural law that men should practice. Retaliation is allowed in Turretin's system of natural law, but only in cases of moderation where it can transpire with little or no prejudice. Lastly, one should practice those acts which contribute to the overall happiness of mankind.[169]

Turretin listed, in addition to duties that man owes to his neighbor, the responsibilities that he has toward himself. We have, furthermore, such fundamental natural rights as self-defense. Suicide is a crime, according to this argument, since only God has given life, he alone can take it away. For our part, we should grow in wisdom and cultivate our intellect. The need to seek after truth overrides the deceit of the passions and in this pursuit after truth, men need to study branches of knowledge that have valuable purposes as opposed to those which lead to vain speculations. In the pursuit of knowledge, Turretin advocated the life of an active participant in society as opposed to the "ivory tower" approach to learning. Turretin concluded: "To which end, we should choose some active kind of life, or, which is the same thing, some honest and useful profession, suitable to our capacity and circumstances. After we have entered into such a profession we are to exert ourselves in it, with firmness, diligence and the greatest attention."[170]

Immortality

The last section of Turretin's treatise on natural theology is devoted to the subject of the immortality of the soul. His arguments on the topic are not original. He stated that the difference between the nature of the mind and the nature of the body is evidence that when the body dies, the soul does not necessarily die with it.[171]

Second, Turretin claimed that the nature and perfections of God point to an afterlife. Since God is the all-just, wise, and benevolent being and is also all-powerful, it naturally follows that he would provide an ultimate judgment upon each individual according to his works.[172]

The third argument is similar. Since God is absolutely perfect, he must contemplate himself with great pleasure and he must love those who attempt to follow after his attributes and detest those who oppose him. It follows that he must render a final judgment because, in this life, many of the wicked prosper while many of the righteous suffer.[173]

The last argument in favor of human immortality stems from human conscience. Man universally receives a favorable inner feeling from performing good deeds and self-condemnation from evil ones. Furthermore, since many pious men live miserable lives here on earth, the promise of a future reward serves as a great consolation.[174]

The promise of eternal rewards and condemnation for the wicked characterizes Turretin's practical and simple approach to theology. He attempted to construct a theological system that was both applicable to Christian living and defensible for the rational inquirer. His treatise on the subject of natural theology was not a mere series of theoretical statements. It was, rather, a response to specific challenges to Reformed orthodoxy, a response intended to diffuse the atheism of Spinoza and the deism of Hobbes. In addition, it laid the foundation for an acceptance of special revelation that could counteract the Socinian position on the Trinity.

In his treatise, Turretin attempted to establish a nonfideistic apologetic based on reason. It was a theological system intended to support scriptural revelation, but that proved as much about God as possible without the necessity of resorting to the Bible. In his defense of the divine origin of Scripture, Turretin would again rely upon nonfideistic proofs. Such an argument was far different from Calvin's approach of assuming the divine origin of the Bible based upon the interior witness of the Spirit of God.

4

Jean-Alphonse Turretin on Special Revelation

Jean-Alphonse Turretin's teaching on special revelation is central to his entire position on religious authority. In an effort to defend the Reformed faith against the papists on one hand, and the deists and atheists on the other, he constructed a new form of Reformed theology that emphasized the fundamental articles of the faith. This did not mean that he was returning to the so-called purity of Calvin, but rather to what he considered to be the purity of the New Testament. Although he agreed with Calvin that Scripture was primarily salvific in focus, he defended the integrity of Scripture on the grounds of reason rather than on the grounds of the internal witness of the Spirit. Turretin's approach was common among the Remonstrants as well as the Socinians and it prepared the way for the next generation of Genevan theologians to reduce the fundamental articles still further, to the point that the Reformed faith was barely recognizable. Such doctrines as the Trinity and the deity of Christ would virtually disappear. Turretin, therefore, bridged the gap between the scholastics of the seventeenth century and the Enlightenment rationalists of the eighteenth century.

The main source for his ideas on special revelation and biblical accommodation can be found in the second volume of his *Opera* (Basel edition of 1748) and is a series of essays included in the *De Veritate Religionis Judicae* and *De Veritate Religionis Christianae*. In addition, Turretin outlined his exegetical methodology in his 1728 treatise entitled, *De Sacrae Scripturae interpretandae methodo tractatus bipartus, in quo Falsae Multorum Interpretum Hypothes Refellentur, Veraque Interpretandae Sacrae Scripturae Methodus Adstruitur.*

The *De Sacrae Scripturae* was foundational for his entire treatment of special revelation and, as the title suggests, it first rejects false methods and false principles of biblical exegesis. Turretin took issue with four separate methodologies. First, he condemned the Roman Catholic idea that the true meaning of Scripture should be determined through the decrees of the church such as conciliar decisions, papal pronouncements, and the statements of the church fathers. Second, he ridiculed the idea of the Enthusiasts that one determines the meaning of the Bible through internal voices with no real need for careful study in the original languages. Third, he rejected the use of allegorical interpretation and preferred to use the literal sense of such books as the Song of Solomon. Fourth, he decried the lack of biblical study aids and called for careful, scholarly study of Scripture using biblical languages and references to the secular literature of biblical times, rabbinical commentaries, and biblical versions in other oriental languages.[1]

In the place of these methods, which he considered false, Turretin posited his own approach to exegesis, based on reason and an interpretation of the text according the author's intent. Arguing that one should interpret Scripture in the same manner as any other book of antiquity, he asserted that "one must keep in mind the sense of the words and the customs of speech, the purpose [scopus] of the author, what goes on before and what follows." Since Scripture is addressed to men, it must be assumed that one should use reason in exegesis without fear that one's conclusion might be offensive to God. As a result, the Bible never contradicts the light of nature and any proposed interpretation that contradicts reason, such as transubstantiation, must be rejected.[2]

One of the most important aspects of his methodology that bears striking resemblance to Jean LeClerc's approach, is his insistence on the use of proper historical context. Turretin explained:

> No judgment on the basis of the axioms and systems of our day is to be passed on the meaning of the sacred writers, but one must put oneself into the times and into the surroundings in which they wrote, and one must see what [concepts] could arise in the souls of those who lived at that time. . . . For when they [contemporary theologians] impose their meaning on the interpretation of Scripture, they have already in mind a definite system of doctrine that they seek [to discover]. . . . An empty head, if I may so express myself, must be brought to Scripture; one's head must be, as it were, a *tabula rasa* ["a blank slate"] if it is to comprehend the true and original meaning of Scripture.[3]

The meaning of the Bible is not dependent on any oral tradition or opinion of experts. If this were not true, it would be easy for them to adulterate the sense of Scripture because there would be few people capable enough to hold them accountable.

In addition, he wrote that the Bible clearly commands believers to read and meditate upon Scripture. The Bible is not reserved, therefore, for the theological elite. The key principle of exegesis is to test every theory and proposition and retain only what is good and reasonable.

Turretin's approach to biblical interpretation is clearly an attempt to free exegesis from dogmatic and sectarian bounds. It also reflects his confidence in the accord between natural and special revelation. Should the two conflict, the error is not in the text itself but with the interpreter. Lastly, it shows his predisposition in favor of the practical application of Scripture to personal piety and his aversion to scholastic abstraction. He was prepared to follow a reasoned interpretation wherever it would lead, even if it resulted in the denial of a doctrine that his forbears considered an integral or even a fundamental aspect of the faith.

The significance of Turretin's method in the history of exegesis has been made clear by Hans-Joachim Kraus, who attributes the inroads of deistic and Remonstrant biblical criticism to this particular treatise. The comment is well supported by a comparison of Turretin's approach to that of the biblical critics of the era.[4]

The Necessity of Revelation

In his *De Veritate Religionis Judaicae et Christianae,* Turretin recognized the limits of reason in discovering religious truth and posited that man needs additional assistance to come to a saving knowledge of God. As he showed in his discussion of natural theology, Turretin recognized the value of what man can discover about God through the proper use of God-given reason. Natural theology cannot, however, discover such essential Christian truths as the nature of the triune Godhead, the Incarnation of Christ, the means of salvation, the origin of the world, or the nature of the end times. For knowledge of these truths, one needs divine revelation.[5]

In his recognition of the limits of reason, Turretin noted that philosophy itself mixes truth with error. On this score, he criticized ancient philosophy and took issue with several aspects of Aristotelian thought, citing Aristotle's failure to allow for the separation of soul and body and making immortality impossible within his philosophical system. While not denying the value of Aristotelian thought, he simply pointed out its limited utility. Turretin admired Plato for his distinction between spirit and matter, but noted the many errors of Plato, such as his attribution of divinity to stars, the earth, and demons. In addition, he questioned the preponderance of the concept of fatalism in ancient thought that virtually eliminated human freedom, virtue, and vice.[6]

Turretin wrote that not only were the ideas of ancient philosophy in error in many of its precepts, but they lacked practical value. Aristotle, Plato, and Seneca were not clear enough in their writings for the average man to understand. Their reasoning was so complicated and their grammar so difficult to grasp that their value in leading man to a virtuous life was insufficient in comparison with the revelation of the Christian faith.[7]

Turretin found it interesting, however, that the ancient philosophers acknowledged their own limitations in discovering truth and saw a need for divine revelation. Furthermore, he wrote that even the contemporary philosophers like Montaigne admitted their need for divine aid to help them in their quest for metaphysical knowledge.[8] Turretin explained that philosophy is valuable mainly for those who already have a cultivated spirit. However, for the vast majority of people who are concerned with the daily cares and worries of life, philosophy is largely irrelevant.He wrote that these people need special revelation to provide them with a surer, more practical direction than reason alone would provide.[9]

Turretin concluded that without revelation, man would be left in darkness and could easily be fooled by any imposter or fanatic. Further, he found that the Christian faith has two great advantages over deism. First, it is more conformed to right reason and more useful to society. Second, it is more authoritative, since it is grounded on revelation and founded on sure evidences. He saw no reason why deists should reject a faith that is so reasonable. Further, if God has spoken, all men have the responsibility to listen to and obey his words.[10]

Biblical Accommodation and the Marks of Revelation

For Jean-Alphonse Turretin, the concept of biblical accommodation[11] was closely related to the use of rationalistic proofs to support biblical authority. These proofs, commonly referred to as the external marks of Scripture, had been an important argument in favor of scriptural authority since the time of Calvin. Turretin, having left the Calvinist concept of the interior witness of the Holy Spirit almost totally undeveloped, listed the standard Reformed external marks of Scripture, including miracles, fulfilled prophecy, and the eyewitness testimony of the biblical authors.[12]

Although he mentioned Calvin's argument that these marks merely support biblical authority rather than prove it, he devoted so much attention to them that he practically ignored the role of the Holy Spirit in authenticating Scripture. He directed his arguments almost exclusively toward the nonbeliever or the deist, who would require more objective proof for the truth of Scripture and of the Christian faith. The proofs are so incontestable for Turretin that any reasonable individual should be convinced of the divine origin of Scripture. His insistence on such proofs follows the Socinian approach quite closely. Remonstrant theologians such as Philippe van Limborch and Jean LeClerc also employed similar defenses of the Christian faith.

Turretin used such an evidential approach in his *De Veritate Religionis Judaicae et Christianae*. He reiterated the importance of the concept that the Christian can accept the divine origin of the Bible based upon the testimony of Christ. Unbelievers, however, might not be so easily convinced. Turretin responded to the growing tide of deism and atheism, whose adherents evaluated Scripture based upon the dictates of reason.[13] Turretin countered by demystifying as much of Scripture as possible without eliminating those doctrines which he considered essential to the faith in order to show that Scripture did fulfill the demands of rational inquiry. Turretin also advocated the Cartesian approach that emphasized clarity and preciseness as a test of truth. Turretin believed that the New Testament met this test, while the Old Testament was much more obscure.[14]

The concept of accommodation is important for Turretin because it describes how the Old Testament could be inferior in terms of its ability to meet the Cartesian standard and yet still be inspired by God. Furthermore, accommodation defines the very nature of biblical revelation. Turretin did not employ the verbs *accommodare* or *attemperare* with the Latin noun *error,* but with the verb *concedo* (to give up, relinquish) plus the dative *captui* (to the blind mental capacity). In other words, God accommodated his revelation to the mental capacity of mankind, which he described with the word *rudis* (rude, rough, undeveloped). In spite of this, the revelation was not necessarily errant, but accommodated to the limited state of the Hebrew people. God must reveal himself in this way to combat the religious errors that man would certainly commit if he did not possess revelation. This does not mean that man cannot discover truth in science, only that he cannot obtain true knowledge about God apart from revelation.[15] However, such religious truth came in accommodated terms. It is contained in written

form and can thereby be examined and understood. It also comple-
mented natural revelation by providing specific information about
God and his relationship to man, such as divine promises, warn-
ings, and guidance.[16]

Turretin argued further that God transmitted his revelation to
man by progressive degrees of illumination. The older the revelation, the dimmer the light. The most undeveloped aspects of biblical revelation that possessed biblical marks, therefore, would be
the Mosaic eyewitness accounts of the Exodus and the provision
of the Mosaic Law. God provided these accounts in accordance
with man's mental capacity, which was blind in comparison with
the light of New Testament revelation. As God increased his revelation gradually, he increased the light of revelation and made it
"more perfect." It culminated in the revelation of Christ. Turretin
here related the doctrine of accommodation closely with his position on Christian "essentials." He argued that God only holds individuals responsible for knowledge by virtue of their mental
capacity. If God accords less light, fewer essentials are necessary
for salvation. God would require less of the patriarchs of the Old
Testament, therefore, than of those who possess the revelation of
the New Testament, thus allowing for the possibility of salvation
for those individuals without sufficient light to accept Christ. It
should be noted that Calvin did hold to a form of progressive revelation, but not in the rationalistic manner espoused by Turretin.[17]

The Characters of Revelation

The question of the marks of Scripture had been an important
argument in favor of scriptural authority since the time of Calvin.
Turretin's mentor, Louis Tronchin, as previously indicated, used
greatly of the marks of Scripture in his own system of religious authority.

For Turretin, the internal marks consisted of the beauty of the
doctrines of Scripture, the Bible's accord with reason and conscience, its utility, and the consolation that it provides for believers.
The external marks, consisting primarily of miracles and prophecy,
received the bulk of Turretin's attention. In addition to miracles
and prophecy, Turretin included the excellence and beauty of the
gospel, the characteristics of its teaching, and the propagation of
the gospel. Turretin claimed that since both internal and external
proofs have their own value, one should not regard one as more
valuable than the other. For the person who is already a believer

and is predisposed toward doing the will of God, the internal proofs alone would be sufficient to convince him of scriptural authority. For the nonbeliever or the deist, however, more objective proof would be of great assistance in establishing a rational basis for the truth of Scripture and of the Christian faith. In this regard, Turretin cites John 10:38, where Christ tells Jews that if they do not believe his words, they should believe his works. The same lesson should apply to the deist or the unbeliever. The external proofs are so incontestable for Turretin that any reasonable individual should be convinced of the divine origin of Scripture.[18]

The obvious reason for this is that he directed his arguments not toward the believer, but toward the deist and the atheist. His apologetic system was not, therefore, a total repudiation of Calvin's since it is directed to a different audience, but it minimized Calvin's arguments to an almost unrecognizable degree. His insistence on such external proofs followed the arguments of Socinus and Grotius quite closely. The Remonstrants in Amsterdam, LeClerc and Limborch, also employed similar defenses of the Christian faith.

The Extent of Revelation

A common criticism leveled against revealed religions such as Christianity has been that the extent of its revelation has been limited to a chosen few with the vast bulk of humanity never having the opportunity to respond to it. Although Turretin responded to this criticism in his discussion of natural theology, he pointed out in his treatise on special revelation that a surprising number of heathen nations have had access to God's specific actions through history. For example, he carefully noted that both in Creation and in the Flood, God did reveal himself to all creation. The miracles of Moses were known by the Egyptians and by all the neighboring peoples. Jonah was sent to Ninevah, Daniel and Ezekiel to the Babylonians. The Greek version of the Old Testament, the Septuagint, facilitated the study of the Old Testament to non-Jews since Greek was the spoken language of most of the known world. When the message of Christianity was dispersed, it was able to be received by most of humanity.[19]

Although he asserted that most of the world had access to some aspect of special revelation, Turretin commented that both general and special revelation were not equally propagated throughout the entire world. The capacity of each person to understand general revelation is proportional to the individual's intelligence, education, age, social status, and many other factors. There are a myriad of levels of understanding of general revelation, and the disparity of talents is great among individuals. He saw no reason why the dispersion of spiritual grace should be any different. Some people receive a greater measure of special revelation than do others. It is the same way in natural revelation. The philosopher has access to more of it than does the peasant. God is not obligated to provide the exact measure of special revelation to each person. Correspondingly, he saw no reason why there should not be various degrees of reception of special revelation. Further, each person is judged according to the light that God has provided. The pagan, with no knowledge of Christ, will be judged according to the natural law written on his heart and not by the Mosaic Law or by the message of Christ. In this regard, he cited Romans 2:12 and Luke 12:48, which are two standard passages on the subjects of natural law and of the degrees of talents.[20] Turretin did not say here that the pagan can be saved without a knowledge of Christ, but he did leave that possibility open.

The Evidence of Revelation

Having established the widespread dispersion of divine revelation, Turretin moved to a discussion of the evidence that must accompany it. In this section, Turretin declared that one cannot prove religion in the same way that one can prove mathematics. One can, however, employ historical proofs to establish the reasonableness of the Christian faith.[21]

His first principle was that faith should never be opposed to reason. Since both are sources of truth they should not contradict each other. In addition, since God himself is the author of both the light of reason and the light of revelation, one should use them both in concert. Revelation can provide knowledge of areas that reason could never hope to discover. At times, there may be an obscurity or an apparent contradiction between reason and revelation, but that would be due to an incomplete understanding of the real meaning of the revelation. He noted, in this regard, that reason is an essential tool in helping man to understand divine revelation. If one does not have the use of reason, it would be impossible to distinguish between true and false revelation. Furthermore, one could not understand Scripture without reason. It is not necessary, however, for revelation merely to repeat what one can discern through reason. Reason and revelation do not have to provide exactly the same content.[22]

The Divine Origin of the Old Testament

Proceeding to a more direct discussion of the evidence that must accompany revelation, Turretin began with an evaluation of the divine nature of the Old Testament. Elevating the Old Testament to an exalted position in the communication of divine revelation, he saw it as less complete than the revelation of Christ and the Apostles in the New Testament because it does not provide a full knowledge of the gospel. The Hebrew Bible, however, contains much essential special revelation. It provides a detailed account of God's working throughout history, an essential witness to the divine nature, and important predictions concerning the Messiah. Furthermore, the Jewish law served as an important preparation for the more perfect dispensation of grace. In the Old Testament, pious believers did not know specific information about the afterlife, but it was sufficient for them to know, in general terms, that a certain reward awaited those who placed their hope in God.[23]

Turretin reiterated the importance of the concept that the Christian can accept the divine origin of the Old Testament based upon the testimony of Christ. Unbelievers, however, might not be so easily convinced. Turretin directed his arguments toward the deist or atheist who needs to evaluate Scripture based upon its marks. The Old Testament, he argued, possesses such marks and can be deemed to have a divine origin.[24]

Accommodation in the Old Testament

In his defense of the divine origin of the Old Testament, Turretin carefully upheld the historical accuracy of only those passages bearing the marks of eyewitness accounts, fulfilled prophecy, or miracles. Since Old Testament Messianic prophecies are one of the two most important marks of biblical authority, he went to great lengths to preserve their validity. He did not, however, go into great detail in defending the historicity of the early portions of Genesis against any of the notable biblical critics of his generation such as Richard Simon. Rather, he spoke in general terms that centered mainly upon the historical accuracy of the rest of the Pentateuch. The reason for this was that Turretin considered the early patriarchal accounts an inferior form of revelation to rest of the Old Testament and the Old Testament as a whole as inferior to the New Testament. The main value of the Old Testament lay in pointing toward Christ. It gave a detailed account of God's working throughout history, provided an essential witness to the divine nature, and recorded important Messianic prophecies. Turretin explained: "The Law was given by Moses, but grace and truth come through Jesus Christ (John 1:17). It is, then, not in the rudimentary teachings of Moses, or in the weakness of the Prophets, but in the fullness of Christ that we ought to find truth and grace." Turretin went on to say that the Old Testament authors were limited in their understanding of God's redemptive plan for mankind as well as about the natural world.[25]

The historical accuracy of the first few chapters of Genesis was the most difficult of the entire corpus of the Old Testament for Turretin to defend. In his later discussions of the historicity of other parts of Scripture, he relied heavily upon the validity of the testimony of eyewitnesses. In the Genesis accounts of Creation, the Flood, or the Tower of Babel, the author of the Pentateuch (Moses, according to Turretin) was not an eyewitness. Turretin, therefore, did not defend a literal space-time interpretation of these passages, but preferred to protect their dogmatic content, arguing that the author composed these passages in a figurative and mysterious prose that was not meant to be literally accurate. These accounts were sufficient to teach the basic sequence of events without providing precise details. One should, therefore, concentrate on learning the moral lessons from such passages rather than attempt to garner scientific knowledge. This approach would be in harmony with the intent of the biblical author.[26]

Turretin's treatment of the early portions of Genesis provided an important point of departure for a discussion of his position on the relationship between Scripture and science, an issue that is intricately intertwined with the doctrine of biblical accommodation. Since Scripture is accommodated to the level of man's understanding, it would make sense that it would not provide more advanced scientific knowledge than was generally available at the time when it was written. In the period after the acceptance of the Copernican view of the cosmos, Reformed theologians attempted to reconcile apparent contradictions between Scripture and science in order to preserve the inerrancy of the text. Michael Heyd comments that Turretin did not attempt such a harmonization. Turretin represented, rather, the more traditional approach that did not attempt to read Scripture as a scientific textbook. Heyd points out that Turretin saw no insufficiency in the theological teachings of Scripture even though he accepted a "mechanistic-Cartesian" view of the cosmos.[27] Turretin argued that the purpose of Scripture is to lead man to pious and virtuous living, not to provide specific, technical information about the cosmos. Furthermore, since the Old Testament authors were quite ignorant about the natural world, they spoke in phenomenological terms about natural events. It was not necessary for the biblical authors to know, for example, that the sun does not revolve around the earth, and thus they could be technically quite mistaken when they said that God made the sun stand still for Joshua so that he could defeat his enemies in battle. Such language is accommodated to man's limited knowledge at that point in history. God is not fallible, but rather man's understanding is limited. Technical discussions about cosmology, Turretin pointed out, properly belong to the realm of philosophy rather than to that of theology.[28]

Turretin's use of accommodation allowed him to argue that neither scientific nor historical accuracy are important in light of the clear spiritual lessons that one can gain from Scripture, especially from its more primitive forms. For example, he did not defend a literal reading of the biblical account of the Creation or of the Fall, and listed a series of religious lessons that these stories teach. He had serious problems with the biblical account of the Creation and the Fall of man and does not attempt to defend their historicity. In fact, he argued that if God were to reveal an accurate scientific account of Creation, the Hebrew audience would not have been able to understand it.

Similarly, the biblical account of the Fall does not have to be literally accurate, but must reveal the essential religious truth of man's alienation from God and his need for a Savior. Several other stories in the book of Genesis pose problems for Turretin, including the Tower of Babel, the Flood, and the appearances of angels. He defended the possibility that these stories might have occurred, but admitted that their literal veracity could not be proven. Nor would it be profitable to go to great lengths to establish their accuracy, which is irrelevant compared to their religious teachings. He instead provided some arguments that indicate that these accounts are not unreasonable.[29]

Turretin's questioning of the literal accuracy of the account of the struggle between Jacob and God is an important example of Turretin's approach to the early portions of Genesis. Turretin argued that the story contradicts the Mosaic conception of God. Moses had such a noble and lofty view of God, he argued, that it would be inconceivable that God would participate in a literal fight in which he would lose to a mere man. Turretin preferred to defend the moral aspects of this story, especially the idea that believers must persevere in their prayers until God relents to answer. One should not, therefore, take this event as a literal, historical occurrence. This type of argument was in line with Turretin's evidential approach to Scripture in which he defended the historicity of events where the author was an eyewitness. It also reflected Turretin's exegetical emphasis on interpreting biblical passages based upon their historical and grammatical context. He argued that passages convey spiritual meaning because he believed that the context demands it. Furthermore, these early pericopes are accommodated to the simplest level of mankind's ability to understand.[30] The use of this kind of anthropomorphism was for Turretin the most primitive form of accommodated revelation. Such revelation does not insult the majesty of God, but emphasizes the primitive level of man's understanding.[31]

A possible objection to such accommodated revelation was that God could well have changed the mental capacity of man so that man could perceive God directly without the need for God to come down to the level of man. Turretin responded that God prefers not to change the order of nature and holds each man responsible for the level of light that he is able to comprehend. Each man is judged individually according to the amount of light received.[32]

Turretin also employed the concept of accommodation for the more advanced period of the Exodus and the giving of the Mosaic Law. The historical nature of the accounts is not in question here because the author was an eyewitness. However, the Mosaic Law itself was quite archaic, according to Turretin, compared to the clear teaching of the gospel. He attempted to explain these "archaisms" in several ways. For example, the strict dietary provisions and the various rituals of the early Hebrews were intended to prevent them from intermarrying with the Canaanites and from falling into idolatry. Such a rigid code was necessary for a primitive people who were not ready for the gospel of grace. He also argued that many aspects of these provisions were "obscure and imperfect" even though they contained the "characters of truth, holiness and divinity." In addition, Turretin considered the majority of the Mosaic ritual to be of "little value." Without the clear revelation of the New Testament, he asserted that one could well question the "wisdom, equity, goodness, and other perfections" of a God who would command men to follow such rules. With the coming of Christ, however, "everything obscure is unravelled, and all deficiencies stamped with perfection." He continued: "We know the cause and the mystery of the legal rites; we know that they were the rudiments of a puerile age; we know that they were shadows of good things to come, whose body is Christ, and we are blessed with more complete and with more solid principles of wisdom, with the wisdom of men, or, of the perfect, which succeeded in the place of the former rude dispensation."[33] The more archaic aspects of the Law could, therefore, be correct for the purpose of preventing the Hebrews from intermarrying pagans or following the idolatry of their neighbors, but would be wrong for New Testament believers to follow.

The major problem with the rest of the Old Testament for Turretin lay in the area of apparent errors in chronologies and genealogies. Since the rest of the Old Testament possessed the external marks of eyewitnesses and fulfilled prophecy, its historical accuracy was not in doubt. Turretin did not bind himself to defend such apparent errors because they do not affect any major biblical doctrine. He did posit that such conflicting chronologies might be only apparent contradictions such as the different methods of dating the reigns of the Israelite kings. His suggestions followed the standard Reformed system. Any errors that he cannot explain, he attributed to the copyists. It is important to note that Turretin did not insist on absolute accuracy in Old Testament chronologies and historical accounts because the Old Testament authors intended to convey religious truth rather than precise historical detail.[34]

Old Testament Prophecy

For Turretin, the purpose of Old Testament prophets was to remind the people of their duties through their public exhortations. Their testimony was validated by excellent moral character and zeal to reveal the glory of God. In addition, he posited that their testimonies were inspired by God. He supported this by emphasizing the nobility of their ideas, the majesty of the writing style, and a wisdom that paganism could not approach. It is important to note that, in spite of Turretin's insistence on the predictive character of the prophets, he did not think that prediction was their primary function.

The predictive capacity of the prophets was, however, for Turretin one of the main marks of the divine origin of their messages. He listed three aspects of the true prophet. First, his prophecies must be published before the event. Second, they must take place at a stated time. Third, they must be such that human wisdom could not have predicted them. The more ancient, clear, and detailed these prophecies were, the easier it was to recognize the hand of God in them. In addition, Turretin distinguished between prophecies that were fulfilled within the scope of the Old Testament and those which were fulfilled in Christ as the Messiah. In defending the authority of the Old Testament, he limited his discussion to those prophecies fulfilled within the context of that body of writings.[35]

Turretin cited several examples of such prophecies. In Leviticus 26 and Deuteronomy 27, Moses predicted that the Jews would be led into captivity, that they would be subjected to a horrible famine, that they would be led into Egypt, and that a great many of them would finally repent. These prophecies were fulfilled in the captivity in Assyria, in the destruction of Jerusalem, and in the captivity in Babylonia. Isaiah's prophecies were likewise quite accurate. In Isaiah 44 and 45, the prophet predicted that the nation of Israel would be restored to their land and that the temple would be rebuilt. In addition, the prophet named Cyrus as the person who would be instrumental in accomplishing this. Turretin pointed out that this was written two hundred years before Cyrus. It is certain that this prophecy was written before the Babylonian Captivity since Micah, Nahum, and Jeremiah alluded to it and copied it in several places.[36]

The predictions of Jeremiah were also quite substantial as were those of Elijah on the destruction of the house of Ahab. Further, the prophecies of Daniel touching the four great kingdoms were fulfilled. The author of the book of Daniel, in the eighth chapter, predicted the destruction of the Persian Empire by Alexander the Great. In chapter 11, the prophet said that the fourth king of Persia would surpass all of his predecessors in riches and would form an alliance against Javan. This referred to Xerxes who fought a great war against Greece. At the end of the chapter, Daniel mentioned the kings of Egypt and Syria, their wars and marriages up until Antiochus Epiphanes. His prophecy was so compelling that the third-century critic Porphyrus wrote that it had to have been written after the reign of Antiochus Epiphanes.[37]

Turretin upheld the integrity of these prophecies and stood for an old date for the book of Daniel. He posited that the Jews held their canon in high regard and would not have received books without authority or known author. In addition, the Hebrew canon was closed at the time of Artaxerxes and no other book was admitted because they believed that the gift of prophecy had ceased.

Second, he said that Ezekiel exalted the prophetic gift of Daniel while Josephus wrote that the prophet's predictions were fulfilled in Alexander the Great at his entrance into Jerusalem. In addition, the book of Maccabbees referred to Daniel as a true prophet of God. Christ and the Apostles also saw Daniel as a prophet. Lastly, all of Christian tradition revered the book of Daniel as authentic.[38]

Turretin had a profound respect for the Old Testament prophets. Although they did not possess full revelation about Christ, their prophecies pointed to his messianic office. This respect toward the prophets reflected Turretin's emphasis upon the external marks of prophecy and miracles. The predictive realities of Old Testament prophecy served as a foundation for Turretin's defense of the truth of the Christian faith. Prophecy, for Turretin, went beyond man's capacity and indicated the very handiwork of God himself.[39]

Old Testament Miracles

In defense of the miraculous, Turretin proposed that eyewitness testimony establishes such events as historically reliable. Although contemporary readers of Scripture do not view the miraculous directly, they do possess the written records of the eyewitnesses. Turretin explained that such testimony is trustworthy primarily because of the moral stature of its authors. One should not, therefore, doubt the accuracy of their writings. Since scholars generally accepted the accuracy of other writings of antiquity such as those of Plato and Aristotle, there is no reason to doubt those of the Hebrew authors of the Old Testament.[40]

Turretin defended the historical accuracy of the miracles of the Old Testament. Biblical miracles, he argued, serve to validate divine revelation. He, therefore, limited the extent of miracles to the biblical canon and allowed for no possibility of contemporary miracles because the canon had been closed. In addition, the devil possessed no power to perform miracles because such power would render ineffective the use of miracles to confirm the divine nature of biblical revelation.

The most important passage that Turretin discussed in regard to Satanic ability to perform miracles was one that had been the subject of much controversy. In 1 Samuel 28, the alleged conjuring of the spirit of Samuel by the medium of Endor raised the question of whether or not the agents of Satan could perform valid miracles. Was this spirit really the spirit of the prophet or was it a mere forgery or a demon? If it was a valid miracle, it would elevate the power of Satan to perform miracles to the same level as God himself.[41] Turretin proposed three possible solutions to the passage. First, citing the authority of Martyr, Origen, and Ambrose, it was possible that, before the Incarnation, Satan exercised dominion over the spirits of the deceased who languished in purgatory. This would make it possible for the woman to have truly conjured up Samuel's spirit. Second, the medium might have raised up a spirit that was not Samuel but only pretended to be Samuel. The argument here was that since Samuel was a prophet he would not have been in purgatory or under Satan's power. Third, the incident might well have been brought about through the work of the medium who took advantage of Saul's superstitious tendencies. Turretin sided with the last option mainly because he did not want to attribute to Satan the ability to intervene in the natural law. The miraculous, according to Turretin, only served to confirm the work of God. If Satan could likewise perform miracles, there would be no way to verify the handiwork of God. One of the most important sources of evidence for the operation of God in the human realm would thereby be lost.[42]

Turretin's treatment of the subject of miracles aroused some opposition. His treatment of the witch of Endor was the subject of a response by Jean-François Buddeus (1667–1729), a pietist and a professor at Jena, who held that the devil had assumed the figure of the prophet Samuel. Therefore, Buddeus believed that Satan can, indeed, perform incredible feats, but that these acts are not true miracles. Satan's acts do not alter natural law, but he possesses more power than does man. Such power would include the ability to create ghosts, to understand certain secrets and other forms of knowledge that are beyond human capacity. Buddeus wrote that his views did not lessen Turretin's arguments in favor of the use of miracles to prove the divine nature of the Christian faith. Only God himself can change the laws of nature.[43]

Turretin responded to Buddeus's comments in a letter to Auguste-Gotthelf Graf, a councilor in the court of the duke of Gotha. He wrote that although he respected Buddeus and held no animosity toward him for his criticisms, he did not agree with them. Turretin admitted, however, that evil spirits do have some powers, but they cannot perform true miracles. He said that stories about ghosts inhabiting houses for centuries, spirits rising from the dead, or about the power of witches are all superstitious falsehoods. In addition, he noted during the previous forty or fifty years, the number of recorded instances of such occurrences had virtually disappeared. He calls this "clear proof that this was only the dream of a wounded imagination or of some gullible minds, with its basis rooted in paganism or papism which has no other foundation than vague noise or prejudice and is contrary to the best philosophy."[44] Turretin, therefore, rejects Buddeus's idea that the devil could have performed real "lesser" miracles.

Ostervald proposed an interesting alternative in a letter to Turretin. He suggested that God himself might have worked through the witch in order to proclaim a warning to Saul. After all, the prophecy of the death of Saul and of his sons did come true so there would seem to be some measure of divine wisdom in the message of the spirit of Samuel. Ostervald cited the biblical precedent in the story of Balak and the talking donkey (Numbers 22). This was an instance where God took advantage of the individual's superstition to convey a divine message. Ostervald carefully noted that he did not endorse any sort of superstition, but he did agree with Turretin that only God himself can work miracles.[45]

In refuting Buddeus, Turretin revealed his tendency toward rationalism. Through his denial of all miracles except those which pass his proof for historical reliability, he excluded the intervention of the supernatural in contemporary life. On a practical level, his position was not far from deism.

Having established the impossibility of Satanic miracles, Turretin turned his attention to the Mosaic miracles as a confirmation of the divine origin of the Pentateuch. Turretin pointed out that God had sent Moses to Pharaoh and the Israelites to prove the supremacy of the Hebrew God through the demonstration of the miraculous.[46]

Turretin explained that false prophets, such as Pharaoh's magicians, used human trickery and sleight of hand to deceive the people into believing that they possessed some kind of supernatural power.[47] One important test that he encouraged believers to use in examining the spirits is to ask if their teaching encourages people to follow the true God. If the teaching fails this test, then it cannot be from a true prophet of God.[48]

This principle of testing the spirits is quite in keeping with Turretin's methodology of investigation. One needs rational evidence in physical experiments and in metaphysical investigation. Religious truth, therefore, except for the few areas that he reserves as mysteries, should be accepted only if it can be verified. Any form of biblical interpretation should be particularly scrutinized because of the potential for dividing Christians.

At this point, Turretin refuted at length the possibility that the Egyptian magicians had some aspect of real supernatural power.

He cited three of their "tricks": the changing of the rods into snakes, the turning of water into blood, and the appearance of the frogs on the land. He called the first of these acts a simple substitution of rods with snakes, a clever sleight of hand. The fact that Aaron's serpent devoured those of the magicians indicates the superiority of the true divine miracle over the trickery of the magicians. The second miracle of the Egyptian magicians, where they turn water into blood, was simply the mixture of a red coloring into the water to make it appear to be blood. By contrast, Moses turned the Nile into real blood and then it back into pure water.[49] In the case of the frogs, the Egyptians could copy the work of Moses by releasing frogs secretly. However, when it came to reproducing gnats, they could not imitate the miracle of Moses at all because it was not possible through trickery.[50]

Turretin devoted so much space to the discussion of Mosaic miracles because he saw it as an essential aspect of revelation that he desired to establish it thoroughly enough to convince the deist. Since miracles prove that a revelation has a divine origin, the essential aspects of Scripture must have the attestation of the miraculous.

After establishing the authenticity of the Mosaic miracles, Turretin defended the ability of believers to test false prophets. He claimed that God would not allow the miraculous to serve as a way of leading believers into sin. Since divine miracles were always publicly demonstrated in the presence of eyewitnesses, God's message would enjoy the visible, divine confirmation of God's intervention into the realm of natural law.[51]

Other External Marks of the Old Testament

Although the miracles and prophetic nature of the Old Testament are the primary marks for the divine authority of the Old Testament, Turretin pointed to some other, including the wisdom and majesty of its writings, its antiquity, and its preservation. The human authors of the Old Testament, with the exception of Solomon, were relatively uneducated and possessed few of the worldly advantages of the leaders of the surrounding kingdoms. Such individuals would need divine assistance to produce a work so lofty and beautiful as the oracles of the Old Testament.[52]

In the area of the divine preservation of the original text of the Old Testament, Turretin denied the necessity for God to preserve the original as long as it is humanly possible to preserve all the major doctrines through the process of textual criticism. The divine preservation of the Masoretic pointing would, therefore, be unnecessary. He claimed, furthermore, that the copies of the Old Testament were accurate, using the sheer number of manuscripts of the Old Testament as evidence. He did not, however, discuss textual criticism at length. He was content to show that many manuscripts are extant and since these texts agree, for the most part, they must be very close to the original. He also observed that the originals of most works do not survive for a long period after they were written. However, for such a public work as the Bible, it would be quoted and cited in so many places that it would be very difficult to change the content of the text in very significant ways. He allowed for minor scribal errors, but denied any substantial alteration that would affect any major doctrine.[53]

The Divine Authority of the New Testament: Its Historical Reliability

Having established the divine authority of the Old Testament, Turretin turned his attention to the New Testament, which he considered to be a fuller revelation because of its clear presentation of the gospel. While applying the same rules of criticism that he would use for any other book, Turretin saw no reason to doubt the authenticity of the New Testament. His method was to apply the same external marks to the New Testament as he did to the Old Testament. He began by discussing the historical accuracy of the New Testament.

In arguing for the reliability of the testimony of the New Testament, Turretin claimed that the student of Scripture should accept the apostolic authorship of the New Testament because the books identify the authors. He accepted such identification at face value and saw no reason to employ critical methods to come up with alternate authors. The style of the New Testament books supported this idea as well. The Greek is often very simple, especially in the Johannine corpus, and it reflects the lack of education of most of the New Testament authors. Forged books certainly would have employed a better grammatical style of Greek. The New Testament books, rather, reflected the divine mission of announcing the gospel to the people and was written in a popular style, simple in its use of history, but sublime in its reflections and exhortations. He quoted 1 Corinthians 1:20–21 where Paul contrasted the philosophical wisdom of the Gentiles with the simple truth of the New

Testament. Quoting Samuel Werenfels at length, Turretin concurred that the wisdom of the apostolic doctrine is "the work of God Himself."[54] The quality of life and the testimony of Christ and the Apostles indicated that they had no selfish ambition or reason to fabricate their writings.[55] Their emphasis upon love and religious piety provided a godly character that would support a sincere report. Turretin saw no reason to doubt their findings.[56]

Turretin, therefore, established an almost airtight proof for the historical accuracy of the New Testament. Since one cannot impugn the sincerity of such men, one must trust their accounts. Turretin assumed the apostolic authorship of the New Testament books and did not attempt to discuss questions of authorship or criticism. In addition, he did not venture to harmonize the differences among the synoptic accounts. Proving the inerrancy of such books was not his concern. He chose, instead, to uphold their historical accuracy in order to defend the essential aspects of the faith.

Turretin continued at length to defend the integrity of the person of Christ also. Contrasting the Lord's humility with the arrogance of King Herod who desired worship for himself, Turretin noted that, although Christ did not refuse worship, he was the paramount example of servanthood. Christ possessed such personal qualities as wisdom, sobriety, and moderation.[57] Christ's confidence in the Father in the period immediately before the crucifixion served as a sharp contrast for Turretin with the attitude of the famous pagan philosophers such as Socrates as they approached death.[58]

Turretin admitted that the character of Christ is revealed to us through the eyes of the Apostles. He viewed this as a strength for the case for Christianity because of the trustworthiness of their testimony. He claimed that as one read the New Testament with an unbiased eye, one would discover a simple, clear narrative with no evidence of exaggeration. Supporting this is the fact that the narrative does not always portray the Apostles in a positive light. In fact, it usually makes them look like ignorant followers who misunderstood Christ's teachings. It follows that the Apostles had nothing to gain from fabricating such an account. Besides, all but one of them died as martyrs.[59]

He posited further that the Apostles could not have been sincerely deluded in their teachings. First, their behavior contained no evidence of irrationality. In addition, it is very unlikely that all of them would have been insane at the same time and would have given the same story about Christ.[60]

The sufferings of Christ and of the Apostles serve as the ultimate test of their sincerity. The practice of martyrdom continued until the era of Constantine. Turretin noted that the intensity of a faith that would lead so many believers over so long a period to die for their beliefs indicated a true experience with God himself.[61]

Accommodation in the New Testament

Turretin did not limit the concept of accommodation to the Old Testament, but argued that it takes on a new significance in the New Testament where accommodation refers to the ability of every individual to understand the more perfect light of God's revelation clearly. For example, Turretin argued that the precepts of the gospel are "accommodated to every understanding." He wrote: "[Special Revelation] should be accommodated to the circumstances of those placed in the lowest stations of life, as well as to the circumstances of men instructed in the principles of wisdom and philosophy."[62]

Christ himself used accommodated revelation when he taught in parables. This type of communication was specifically designed so the simplest peasant could understand. The gospel was not designed for the doctors of theology alone, but for everyone.[63]

Christ also expanded the command to love even our enemies to different circumstances that provided for a wide applicability. He thus "accommodates them to the various circumstances and to the various relations of men, whence arise the duties of husband and wife, of parent and child, of ruler and subject, of master and servant; all duties which are explained in the New Testament, with singular wisdom and accuracy."[64]

Turretin went to great lengths to preserve the integrity of the New Testament, which reflected his high opinion of its value. He provided, for example, a thorough explanation for the differences between the synoptic gospels and disagreements among the Apostles such as those of the Jerusalem Council. In all of his arguments, Turretin carefully upheld the divine inspiration of the text.[65]

Messianic Prophecy

Not only does the historical validity of the New Testament support its divine origin, the fulfillment of messianic prophecy served as an incontestable stamp of God upon the text. Having already examined prophecy fulfilled in the Old Testament to support the divine nature of the older revelation, Turretin analyzed at length the authenticity of Old Testament prophecy, which was fulfilled in the Messiah, Jesus of Nazareth.

Turretin placed a great deal of emphasis upon the validity of prophecy in Scripture as sure evidence of the divine nature of Scripture. Through prophecy, the true God was able to distinguish himself from false gods. Such prophecy could not be produced without divine assistance. In addition, these predictions were fulfilled publicly, so their validity would be beyond dispute.[66]

Some of the more prominent Old Testament prophecies included the promise to Abraham that through his seed all the nations of the earth would be blessed.[67] In addition, Genesis 49:10 referred to the messianic line going through the house of Judah.[68] Deuteronomy 32:21 predicted the rejections of the people of Israel and the inclusion of the Gentiles into the people of God. Several Psalms also referred to this including Psalms 7 and Psalms 87. According to Turretin, these are just a few of the many prophetic passages of Scripture fulfilled in Christ.

He stated further that the power of the prophetic oracles possessed a fourfold demonstration of strength. First, they preceded the gospel in time. Second, they predicted events with accuracy. Third, the prophets did not understand all the circumstances surrounding the life and ministry of Christ, but only the aspects that the Holy Spirit revealed to them. Fourth, human wisdom could not have predicted such writings or events.[69]

Although the name of Christ was unknown to many peoples of the world, Turretin maintained the validity of the scriptural promise that Christ would reign over the entire world as king.[70]

New Testament Miracles

In addition to supporting the witness of messianic prophecy, Turretin carefully defended the validity of the miracles of Christ and the Apostles. He defined the term *miracle* as a surprising work that breaks the ordinary course of natural law. A miracle is performed totally from the will of God in such a way that the eyewitnesses can tell that the work was truly supernatural and extraordinary.[71]

In defense of the miraculous in the New Testament, Turretin criticized Spinoza's opposition to the idea that God cannot contravene the laws of nature and that God's nature cannot be known through miracles. Citing the sixth chapter of Spinoza's *Tractatus,*

Turretin called the Jewish philosopher an atheist. He rejected Spinoza's assertion that miraculous events always have natural explanations. Turretin did agree that the laws of nature virtually always run in a fixed pattern, but he asserted that God, on rare occasions, does intervene in order to display his power.[72] Turretin likened Spinoza's reasoning to a labyrinth that is difficult to untangle. He agreed that if one eliminates the divine factor from natural law, the supernatural is, by definition, excluded. However, when one took the existence of a personal God into account, intervention into the laws of nature must, at times, occur.[73]

A key problem with the presence of miraculous events is that alleged miracles might be considered to change the very essence of nature. Christ walking on water or the three Hebrews surviving in the fiery furnace of the Babylonian King Nebuchadnezzar are examples when God's intervention involved a suspension of natural law. Turretin denied, however, that such events change the normal working of natural laws. He saw nothing to prevent God from intervening and extending the boundaries of death.[74]

Spinoza had argued that since God created the natural order, for him to change such order would be a contradiction of his very nature. Turretin took issue with Spinoza's contention by stating that God's power extends beyond the natural order that he created. While God's will determines the order, he is not limited.[75] In addition, God sent messages to the human race to document and confirm the miraculous signs of his presence. Without such demonstration of divine power, there was no undeniable evidence for God's existence at all. This is why Turretin accused Spinoza of atheism.[76]

Christ himself told the Jews that if they did not believe his message, they should believe in his works. Turretin interpreted this statement as supporting the concept that the purpose of miracles was to confirm the divine revelation.[77] If this were not the case, wrote Turretin, then Moses, the Apostles, and Christ himself would all have been blasphemers.[78] Repeating his assertion that Satan cannot perform true miracles, Turretin believed with Locke that the miraculous is reserved only for God and his servants. The devil, by contrast, possesses no power to perform such works and the so-called magicians or mediums could only produce forgeries of the real miracle.[79]

In addition to stating that only God can perform miracles, Turretin provided the reader with some methods for discerning the difference between true and false miracles. His desire here was to establish clear guidelines that showed that divine miracles are very easy to confirm.[80]

One difference between false miracles and the real ones is that true miracles occur very rarely. It is the very nature of miracles to be the exception to the normal working of natural law. If miracles were commonplace, Turretin wrote, then they would be included in the normal working of natural law and would no longer be extraordinary at all.[81] In any case, one must examine all miracles with care.[82]

In addition, Turretin pointed out that the enemies of Judeo-Christian religion witnessed miracles as well. In Matthew 13 and in Mark 6, Christ performed only a few miracles in his hometown because of unbelief. Turretin was quick to note that Christ did, indeed, perform some miracles there and did not cease his miraculous activity totally out of a response to the unbelief of the people of Nazareth.[83]

Although Turretin noted that one cannot prove the validity of the miraculous by mathematical means, Christ did desire that his followers explore the reasons for their belief in him.[84] Christ customarily provided additional revelation to those who responded initially to his teachings. The disciples are the best example of individuals who responded positively to the Lord's work until they became the eyewitnesses of the Resurrection and the Ascension. If Christ had appeared only before those who did not respond to his revelation, there would have been no response to his message. Such people did not even respond to the gospel message by the time of Pentecost.[85]

Turretin felt there was no need for additional miraculous acts in contemporary times. The main purpose of miracles was to confirm the divine nature of revelation. Since the biblical canon was closed, there would be no need for further miracles.[86]

The Propagation of the Gospel

The propagation of the gospel served as the fifth main external proof for Turretin's defense of the truth of the Christian faith. He argued that the evidence of the spread of Christianity throughout history serves as evidence of the validity of the religion.[87] He postulated that Christianity, in comparison with the other religions of the world, has experienced more success in spreading throughout different cultures, social and intellectual classes. The Christian faith, therefore, must possess practical value.[88]

In support of this claim, he described the basic facts surrounding the origins and dissemination of Christianity. Turretin claimed that the unique teachings of the Christian faith could never have been developed without divine aid. They are unique among the world's religions and do not agree with the type of religion that mere men would invent. The fact that Christianity has lasted so long and possesses so many adherents gives it further credence.[89]

In describing the spread of the early faith, Turretin stressed the idea that the disciples spread the word to the entire Roman Empire within a few short years after the resurrection of Christ. Even the secular historians of Rome, Suetonius and Tacitus, referred to the spread of the Christian faith as early as during the reign of the Emperor Nero. In addition, the fact that the faith spread in the face of repeated state persecutions was evidence that it must have possessed some type of divine sanction.[90]

An additional external proof for the truth of Christianity was the diversity of types of people who came to faith during the early Christian era. Its adherents did not come merely from the lower classes, as one might expect. Both learned and unlearned, rich and poor, people from all walks of life came to faith and swore allegiance to Christ. Turretin argued on this score that the Christian faith must have been a reasonable one for the people of Rome since an individual's level of intelligence or social standing did not prevent him from professing faith in Christ.[91]

Contrasting the spread of Christianity with its main contender for religious hegemony in the Holy Land, Islam, Turretin declared that no prince such as Muhammad could have achieved the spread of Christianity. Although Islam itself spread quite rapidly, it did so through military might. The early Apostles, by contrast, had no access to military support. In addition, they could not have spread the religion through deception because they were too uneducated to succeed in such a sophisticated endeavor. After all, the Roman world already had its own pantheon of gods and there were many other successful religions in the empire. The Apostles were obviously not capable of starting and disseminating a new religion.[92]

A further obstacle against the spread of the Christian faith was the fact that both Jews and Gentiles were historically reluctant to change their beliefs. The Roman polytheistic religion tended to absorb local deities. In addition, most of the Jews were suspicious of the teachings of the Apostles. Turretin observed that the Pharisees were not really open to God's message to them because they were so concerned about petty religious details.[93]

Turretin concluded that the early faith faced incredible obstacles and should have been wiped out without any trouble. False religions commonly died out in quick succession during this era and many of them had much more societal assistance than did Christianity. He quoted the Jewish scholar of the Sanhedrin, Gamaliel, who commanded his colleagues to leave the early followers of Christ alone saying that if their teaching was truly from God then no human power could stop them. Such a faith beginning from such humble origins could not have grown so rapidly, he argued, without divine power. The spread of Christianity serves as an essential external proof for the truth of Christianity for Turretin.[94]

The Efficacy of the Christian Faith

The efficacy of the Christian faith provided the last major external mark for its divine origin. By the term *efficacia,* he meant that the Christian faith produces demonstrable fruits that demonstrate its practical value.[95] First, it was effective in combatting idolatry throughout the Roman Empire. A key problem with the introduction of Christianity was its interaction with pagan religions. Christians often added certain pagan rites to their Christian practice resulting in a mixture of the two religions. The Apostles had to command their followers, who were mostly Gentiles, to turn from idolatry. Even the Jews had never asked the Gentiles to do such a thing.[96]

The fact that the early church effectively rooted out paganism in a society that was so rife with it demonstrates its practical utility. Turretin admitted that there was some mixing of paganism and Christianity that even the Apostles could not stop, but noted that the early persecutions of the Christians separated the true Christians from those who were really still pagans.[97] He quoted the early Apologists, such as Justin Martyr, Tertullian, and Origen, as evidence of the sincerity of the early believers in their faith, along with the secular Roman historian Pliny as well.[98]

Christian morality, according to Turretin, was very different from pagan morality. The emphasis of Christianity upon moderation and virtue was not unique. Secular philosophy taught it as well. Christianity, however, had the power to enable its followers to live morally through the enabling power of the Holy Spirit. Secular philosophical systems could only tell them what was moral.[99]

In addition, the changes in the lifestyles of Christians provide evidence of its efficacy as a religion. Such change occurred over a long period of time and throughout the empire. In enduring persecutions, the early believers suffered but maintained tremendous personal confidence and peace. These early martyrs desired to live holy lives. They practiced discipline in order to insure personal piety. In the assemblies, the parishioners held each other accountable for virtuous living. Turretin asserted that the Gentiles possessed no such system of moral accountability.[100]

Turretin concluded this section by stating that the most important arguments in favor of the Christian religion are either moral or historical in character. Old Testament prophecies fulfilled in Christ, the propagation of the gospel in the face of incredible obstacles, and the historical evidence for the resurrection of Christ could all be cited as evidence to persuade the skeptic of the validity of Christian belief.[101]

Not only was the authority of biblical revelation important for understanding his form of enlightened orthodoxy, Turretin concept of *sola Scriptura* indicates how he used Scripture in theological debate. Like his Reformed colleagues, Turretin was very sensitive to the Roman Catholic use of Pyrrhonism as an attack against the Protestant notion of the perspicuity of Scripture. He would not countenance union with the Roman church and composed an entire treatise designed to condemn their position on religious authority.

Arguments Against the Roman Catholic Position of Religious Authority

Turretin's polemics against the Roman Catholic church provide important insights into his own understanding of special revelation. The debates between the Protestants and Catholics centered upon the issue of the authority of Scripture versus the authority of the Roman church. Turretin defended the perspicuity of Scripture, stating that any layman can, indeed, understand enough of the Bible for salvation and the "doctors" can, in turn, come to satisfactory conclusions concerning difficult passages.

Turretin discussed his objections to Roman Catholic theology in several places. First, while he was studying under Spanheim in 1692, he published the treatise *Pyrrhonismus pontificus, sive dissertatio historico-theologica de variationibus pontificorum, circa ecclesiae infallibilitatem* (Leyden, 1692). This work was directed against Bossuet and was praised by Bayle. It reflected primarily Turretin's objections to the Roman Catholic use of Pyrrhonism.

Accusing the Romanists of resorting to blind faith in their use of Pyrrhonism in their polemics against the Protestants, Turretin claimed that the Catholic apologists, in their use of such a line of argumentation, were vulnerable to the attacks of both atheists and deists.

Since the Catholic apologists were advocating fideism as the key defense of the faith, they possessed no common ground upon which to form the basis for rational discussion with unbelievers who advocated the use of reason in all matters of investigation including the religious area. Turretin pointed out, by contrast, that his own emphasis upon the authority of Scripture supported through the use of reason serves as far better basis for leading such skeptics and unbelievers to faith. Without the common ground of reason, Turretin saw no dialogue and no opportunity for conversion for such people.[102]

Turretin argued that the Roman church cannot serve adequately as the supreme judge in religious controversies. He took great pains to emphasize the lack of Catholic unanimity on the subject of infallibility and pointed to the entire saga of the squabbles within the church over the supremacy of the pope versus the supremacy of the councils. Turretin asserted that the papists have no right to call the Scripture obscure while they themselves have difficulty resolving basic issues of authority within their own hierarchy.[103]

Turretin contrasted the Roman Catholic view of religious authority with the superior *sola Scriptura* doctrine of the Protestant confession. He emphasized that each individual Christian has the prerogative to read Scripture and to obtain spiritual benefit from it. Everything that is necessary for salvation can be easily understood from an unbiased reading of the biblical text. The Protestants, being blessed with the assistance of pastors and doctors, have no need for special judges in the area of controversies. Scripture, instead, should be the guiding norm in all areas of religious controversy. Further, Turretin observed that when a controversy brews over scriptural interpretation, one is not able to say that God himself is the judge. A judge should be able to respond to questions, but one cannot interview God. God has left his judgment in the Bible and it is up to his people to interpret it. One must note here that Turretin did not depart from Calvin's emphasis on the need for scholars to do the careful work of biblical exegesis. Turretin shared Calvin's fear of the Enthusiasts' misinterpretation of Scripture.[104]

Defending the power of Protestant pastors to interpret Scripture correctly for the benefit of their congregations, Turretin admitted that they are not infallible in their interpretation nor does any human being have such ability. If God had intended to give the church an infallible judge of spiritual matters there would be no need for Scripture at all. The papal claim to judge matters of religious dispute is remarkably similar, he argued, to that of the false prophets in the Old Testament. The Old Testament contains frequent admonitions to the nation of Israel not to listen to such people. The New Testament also contains admonitions to "test the spirits" and not to accept the views of those who claimed to have special religious knowledge. The New Testament commands the believer to listen to Christ instead.[105]

At this point, Turretin pointed out the errors of the Roman Catholic church in interpreting its own traditions. Quite often, Roman Catholic traditions contradicted each other. The problem with the Roman system of religious authority lay in its dependence upon fallible human judgment. Turretin thought it impossible to formulate an infallible doctrine of religious truth upon any other basis than inspired Scripture. Roman Catholic scholars did not have the power of infallibility in their works and had difficulty in interpreting the literature of antiquity. Men are naturally subject to their own imagination and anger and many Roman Catholic bishops have erred in such a manner by their own admission. He cited several examples of bishops who have erred throughout the history of the church from the time of the Council of Nicaea to Turretin's own day. In addition, the pronouncements of various popes and councils often contradicted each other. By using such arguments, Turretin ridiculed the Roman Catholic idea of the superiority of the church in judging matters of religious controversy.[106]

Responding to a papal objection to his argument, Turretin distinguished between the Old Testament method of arbitrating religious disputes and that of the New Testament. The Roman church had taken great pains to point to biblical examples of tribunals, which served as judges in areas of religious controversy, in hopes of building a case that the Roman Catholic church was serving a similar and therefore legitimate function for the church age. The Hebrews had a tribunal that was supreme in such matters since even the Levites were fallible in their judgments. After all they had to make provision for their own sins before atoning for the sins of the people. However, Turretin said that this is irrelevant for New Testament times. There were, after all, many aspects of Old Testament Judaism that had no bearing whatsoever on the Christian religion.[107] The Roman Catholic apologists pointed to the great wisdom of the Magi in predicting the exact time and place of Christ's birth. They further pointed to the seat of Moses upon which the members of the Sanhedrin sat in judging religious disputes. They implied that the special seat of Moses was so revered as to provide its occupants with special authority and, perhaps, with infallibility. Turretin scoffed at such arguments, countering that priests and supposed wise men often erred or fell into idolatry. Besides, the seat of Moses was the customary place for the rabbis to teach the Law to the Jewish people rather than a seat of infallible pronouncements independent from Scripture.[108] In addition, Christ had taught his disciples to beware of the teachings of the Pharisees and repeatedly emphasized that a mere outward adherence to the Law would not be sufficient to lead the individual to salvation.[109]

An important argument in both Roman Catholic and Protestant systems of religious authority was the role of the Holy Spirit in leading the believer to true knowledge about God. The key question was whether or not the Holy Spirit promised infallibility of interpretation. Turretin asserted that the Holy Spirit is a guide to open the individual's heart to consider the reality of divine truth as well as a guide in leading Christ's followers to live godly lifestyles. In Matthew 28, Christ promised his followers that he would provide them with a helper to guide them through the times of adversity that were certain to come. He did not promise each believer the power of infallibility.[110]

One of Turretin's main themes in his doctrine of religious truth was the concept that the public miracles of Christ and the Apostles proved that the doctrines that they taught were of a divine origin. However, he was quick to point out that the successors to the Apostles did not perform such miracles. The role of the early church, therefore, was not to create infallible doctrine, but to practice the teachings that had been passed on to them by Christ and the Apostles. The early ecumenical councils did not serve as infallible sources of religious authority, but rather as witnesses to the authoritative teachings of the New Testament. According to the Roman Catholic view, not only was the whole church infallible but each individual bishop had to be infallible as well. He saw no reason how they could be collectively infallible when they were not infallible individually.[111]

Not only did Turretin deny the infallibility of ecumenical councils, he denied the validity of the Petrine doctrine of apostolic succession. This doctrine was based on the passage in Matthew 16:18 where Christ says to Peter: "You are Peter and upon this rock I will build my Church." Turretin posited his own interpretation of this passage, writing that Christ was revealing to Peter that he would be the first one to convey the message of the gospel to the Gentiles. It was never meant to imply that Peter was to be the first of a succession of popes, each of whom would have the power of the keys to bind and to loose the very gates of entrance into heaven.[112]

Turretin admitted that the traditional Protestant argument in favor of the sole authority of Scripture did have its own host of difficulties. Quite in keeping with his own abhorrence of Protestant schism, he viewed such discord as the main weakness in the Protestant argument for religious authority. Turretin did attempt to shore up Protestant discord through his attempts to unify the Anglicans, Lutheran, and Reformed confessions around a core of essential religious truths. However, he did not deem such schism as fatal to the Protestant position since all the major Protestant groups agreed on a wide range of basic "fundamentals." He countered the Roman argument by pointing out that the Catholics were by no means harmonious within their own ranks. In support, he cited the Jesuit-Jansenist controversy and the history of the disagreements among the monastic orders.[113] Furthermore, the Protestant clergy had a history of helping to restore religious order through their use of reason and proper biblical exegesis.[114]

Taking the offensive against the Roman Catholics for using Pyrrhonism to attack the Protestants for their adoption of fideistic arguments in defense of their own faith, Turretin criticized the Roman Catholics for advocating the use of blind faith. He pointed out that it is far easier to believe a doctrine through passive, lazy acceptance rather than through the hard work called for by sound reason. The Protestant clergy, by contrast, characteristically warned their congregations against accepting truth blindly while the papists warned against the use of examination. The Protestant system, according to Turretin, held that no religious truth should be believed unless it conformed to Scripture. Furthermore, although Protestant clergy were by no means infallible, they could decide, with authority, on issues such as church discipline and on disagreements and questions concerning faith and doctrine.[115] The Apostles who desired order in the church would have approved of the functions of the synods, which held authority in that the churches under their care would abide by their decisions. However, the synods never claimed infallibility and merely served as witnesses to Scripture. Turretin concluded that believers should submit to the decisions of the synods out of a desire to preserve order and concord. In cases where an individual comes up with a questionable teaching, the synod can make a ruling on it and amend any presence of error. The key difference between the Protestant synod and the Roman Catholic Ecumenical Council is that the former never claimed to be infallible but served as a regulatory agency, while the councils claimed to be a source of religious tradition, which was put on a par with the Bible itself. Turretin, in his discussion of church order, attempted to show that the Protestant system led to order and harmony rather than discord and religious anarchy.[116]

Not only did Turretin criticize the Roman Catholics for their use of fideism in defending their religious faith, he also faulted them for their use of nonfideistic arguments. He accused Catholic apologists of being inconsistent in their use of reason especially in their biblical interpretation concerning the doctrine of the Eucharist. He said that their exegesis of Scripture was not only biased to support their own traditions, but it simply stretched the meaning of the text in ways that the biblical authors would never have dreamed. The key passage that served as the basis for the doctrine of transubstantiation, where Christ told the Apostles, "this is my body," had historically been interpreted by Roman Catholic scholars to mean that Christ was referring to his literal body. Turretin ridiculed this interpretation as a denial of the obvious sense of the passage. The context of the passage clearly indicated, he argued, that the bread was a representation of Christ's body. To take it otherwise would be to misrepresent the biblical context. He pointed out that, in other instances, Catholic scholars were very careful to preserve the context and the plain sense of biblical pericopes. Turretin chided them for their inconsistency in exegesis, especially when such inconsistency supported their own views on controversial doctrines.[117]

The issue of the perspicuity of Scripture was an important aspect of Turretin's defense of the Protestant faith. Countering the Romanist charge that the Protestants could never come to a certain knowledge of religious truth because of the obscure nature of Scripture, Turretin argued that the Protestant theological system was based on the testimony of the Apostles in the New Testament who taught clearly and distinctly. One cannot help but notice the Cartesian expression here. Emphasizing, above all, the clarity of the teachings of Christ, Turretin noted the simplicity of the Sermon on the Mount in which even the uneducated masses could understand his teachings. Further, the Apostles themselves were uneducated and yet they could understand the teachings of the Lord.[118] In the more difficult areas of theological controversy, Turretin held that all believers, even though they do not have formal theological training should study the Scriptures and employ basic hermeneutical techniques as much as they are able.[119]

In the last section of his treatise, Turretin discussed the canon of Scripture. He criticized the Roman Catholic acceptance of the Apocrypha, observing that the Jews never accepted it as part of the Holy Scriptures. He went to great lengths to describe the gathering of the Old Testament books from the time of Ezra to the completion of the book of Malachi. Furthermore, he pointed out that Christ accepted the Hebrew Old Testament as canonical in Luke 24.[120]

In defending the New Testament canon, Turretin recognized that there were many initial contenders for canonicity. The early church carefully placed the New Testament canon alongside the sacred books of the Old Testament after carefully examining the merits of each book for canonicity. By the time the Apostle Peter wrote his second letter, the church had already accepted the writings of the Apostle Paul as canonical (2 Peter 3:16). Marcion's false canon was rejected in 126 A.D. and the four gospels were accepted by Irenaeus, Origen, and Eusebius. He charged that the Apocrypha was not officially accepted as canonical until the Council of Trent. These books served no necessary function for the church, since they contain no doctrines that are essential for salvation. Furthermore, he wrote that the Roman Catholic church based some of its important doctrines on the Apocrypha such as the doctrine of purgatory.[121] The New Testament contains no quotations of the Apocrypha, although it does allude to it on several occasions. However, such allusions carry no more weight in support of apocryphal canonicity than do the New Testament allusions to secular poetry.[122] Further, Turretin asserted that various obvious errors in the Apocrypha make it unworthy of the Holy Spirit. This is an important point because Turretin did admit the possibility of minor errors to be present in the biblical canon, but he must not consider them to be "evident" errors as one would find in the Apocrypha. He wrote, however, that the apocryphal books possessed great utility and provided moral teachings, but such utility would not be sufficient to make these writings canonical.[123]

Turretin's attacks against Roman Catholic theology revealed much about his own views on the subject of religious authority. He clearly attacked the Catholic use of Pyrrhonism and argued for the perspicuity of the biblical text. His intention here was to defend the foundational doctrine of *sola Scriptura*. Turretin did admit, however, that some parts of Scripture are especially difficult to interpret even for the scholar. For the laymen, they would be virtually impossible to figure out. This posed no problem for Turretin because all the important doctrines of Scripture are quite clear, even for the layman. The central aspect of Turretin's core of essential theological truth centers on the teachings of Christ himself. He elevated the words of Christ over other aspects of Scripture and considered it to be the fullest expression of scriptural revelation.

Christological Theology

In his brief treatise entitled *Dissertatio theologica de Christo Audiendo,* Turretin sought to establish the foundation for his theological system squarely upon the New Testament discourses of Christ. Turretin emphasized the simplicity of the Christian faith in contrast to both the scholastics and the Roman Catholics.[124]

He discussed as well the problem within Protestantism of choosing among the various sects and admitted that each group has its own experts who are thoroughly grounded in the biblical languages and in the proper methods of exegesis.[125] He posited that one can find true theology primarily in the discourses of Christ. It is far better, he claimed, to side with Christ, the embodiment of truth, than with the so-called experts who are prone to error. It was impossible to argue with one who adheres strictly to the imitation of the life of Christ.[126] In Matthew 17:5, the Father commanded the Apostles to listen to Christ. The implication is that this is a primary command and is far more important than fighting over theological minutiae.[127] Furthermore, this command was not meant to be limited to the Apostles alone, but to all believers of all times. In support of this point, he cited Cyprian, who argued that the commands of Christ are foremost in Scripture.[128]

God's providence supported the centrality of Christ's teachings. Since God cares for all of man's needs, redemption is foremost of all. God, therefore, sent his Son as a model of perfection who acts as the righteous judge. Christ's commands are just and holy and his example served as an important motive for the believer to be obedient.[129]

Turretin asserted that Christian doctrine must be very simple and easy to understand.[130] He contrasted the simplicity of Christian doctrine with the complexity of ancient philosophy. The pagan philosophers said many true and useful things, but their teaching was quite imperfect compared with the teachings of Christ. Turretin listed many of the errors of pagan philosophers, such as the Stoics, who confused God with the created world, and the Pyrrhonists, who were against religion in general and pretended that nothing at all can be known for certain. Socrates, Cicero, and Seneca spoke with hesitation concerning the afterlife.[131] In addition, he

called the works of Plato and Aristotle profitable reading, but difficult to grasp fully. He cited Romans 1:22 and 1 Corinthians 1:21,
which condemn the "wisdom of the wise" and point to the simplicity of the gospel.

Turretin contrasted the writings of the Old Testament prophets
with the teachings of Christ, arguing that the latter are far superior
in their simplicity and clarity. The writings of the prophets were
designed to lead the believer to listen to Christ. Their teachings
were far too rudimentary and the light of the prophets too weak
to provide a full picture of proper Christology. However, they did
point to Christ and, in doing so, fulfilled their calling.[132] Turretin
writes: "The law was given by Moses, but grace and truth came
through Jesus Christ (John 1:17). It is, then, not in the rudimentary
teachings of Moses, or in the weakness of the Prophets, but in the
fullness of Christ, that we ought to find grace and truth."[133]

Next, he contrasted the clear teachings of the Lord with those
of the Roman Catholic church. The Romanists had several seats
of authority, including popes, councils, church fathers, traditions,
and the decisions of theologians. Turretin commented:

> It would suffice to observe that those who propose such rules, look
> far and wide and through a thousand difficult detours, but the true
> teaching is close to them and to their doors. In effect, the discourses
> of the Savior are so simple, so clear, so popular (more so when it
> relates to the essentials of things) that even a peasant can understand
> them. But the Fathers, Councils, and popes, and all traditions are so
> complicated that one can study them at length without lessening their
> work and research which are without end, and one can never be sure
> to have arrived at the correct answer![134]

As to the relationship between Christ and the authority of the
church, Turretin wrote:

> The name of the Church is without doubt universal and holy, and it is
> with respect and submission that we ought to listen to this bride of
> Christ. . . . But like many societies, there are diametrically opposed
> principles that are attributed to this name and this dignity, and it is
> certain, however, that the sole Church which ought to be listened to is
> that which teaches the true doctrine of Christ. The result is that we
> should judge the Church by the doctrine of Christ rather than by the
> doctrine of the Church. It would serve nothing to say that it is not all
> churches indifferently, but only the Church *catholic* than can judge the
> true faith because if one understands this universal name of churches
> that exist or have exited in the world, what does one gain by invoking
> their authority? The Church, understood in this sense, can it ever as-

semble in order to judge articles of faith? And is there in some part of the world one particular church that could usurp this title? Do you understand by this that a majority of particular churches can impart true principles and that the majority is always right? But aren't there a thousand examples to the contrary in Scripture and in the annals of the Church? Do you say that the orthodox Church and the orthodox theologians are the ones we must listen to? You are right, but who does not see that each one must attribute these beautiful titles and thus they prove nothing?[135]

As to the church fathers, Turretin pointed out that they are prone to err as well. Some lacked certain aspects of instruction or were not precise in their writings. Others were given to drunkenness, anger, envy, or lies. It is easy, he wrote, to find them contradicting each other. This is also the difficulty in understanding the meaning of many of their writings, some having been lost, and others containing the insertions of scribes. He went on to indicate examples where traditions were not valid, such as the blasphemies of Nestorius and the councils of Constantinople of 528 and 533 A.D.[136] He concluded that: "In general, only the Apostles among those who have received the Spirit of Christ, are guaranteed against all error. There is in the world no doctor, no assembly, no book or canon, even those which have the authority of antiquity, that we can permit to serve as a superior judge in religious matters." He cautioned the student of Scripture: "Guard yourselves against false teachers. Take care that no one seduces you. . . . Examine all things; retain what is good. If even an angel from heaven pronounces another gospel than that which you have heard let him be condemned."[137]

He distinguished, as well, between the teachings of the master and those of his followers, claiming that those of the masters are more certain. The followers of Socrates, Aristotle, and Plato certainly did not totally agree with their masters and divided themselves into various schools of thought.[138]

Turretin finally cautioned his readers against the foibles of human writers: "Finally, while all human authors who write about holy truth are full of deficiencies, mixing truth with falsehood, the useless with the important, and by this refute oftentimes the discourses of Christ, Christ's teachings furnish those who read them with joy and peace and the divine spirit of faithfulness with respect and piety." In addition, he contrasted Scripture from the words of Christ: "Whatever are the excellencies of the entire writing, one cannot prevent anyone from recognizing the greater perfection in the discourses of the Savior and in the story of His life; so much that one who meditates deeply and carefully upon it (without neglecting at the same time the lights which furnish the rest of Holy Scripture) will certainly receive the true theology, a truly Christian theology."[139]

The Influence of J. A. Turretin's Position on Special Revelation

Turretin was by no means alone among Reformed theologians of his era in his use of accommodation as a major principle in special revelation. His close friend and confidant, Jean-Frédéric Ostervald, agreed substantially with Turretin on the subject. In his comments on Matthew 11:11, Ostervald speculated that God tolerated the vices of the ancient Hebrews, such as polygamy and divorce, because of their limited ability to understand more advanced religious truth. In addition, New Testament believers possessed more complete knowledge of God than did John the Baptist.[140] François LaPlanche speculated that on this point Turretin may have had a direct influence on not only Ostervald, but on other prominent theologians as well including Jacques Abbadie, David Martin, and Jacques Basnage.[141]

Even with his major opponent in the Genevan Academy over the abrogation of the Formula Consensus Helvetica in 1706, Benedict Pictet (1655–1724), there was a measure of agreement on the issue of accommodation. Although Pictet is usually characterized as an archconservative who was opposed to the secularlizing trend at the academy in the early eighteenth century, LaPlanche called him a "theologian of transition."[142] Pictet was not afraid to employ the methods of biblical criticism popularized by the French Academy of Saumur while attempting to defend the essential nature of biblical inspiration and infallibility.[143]

Without question, Turretin influenced the next generation of Genevan theologians on the topic of accommodation, especially his protege, Jacob Vernet, who followed his arguments with precision. Vernet's denigration of the Old Testament stemmed primarily from his view of accommodation taken from Turretin and he took great pains to acknowledge his debt to his mentor.[144]

Turretin's use of the concept of accommodation and biblical error in both the Old and New Testaments is in accord with his position on the essentials of religious belief. He was attempting to protect the fundamental beliefs necessary for salvation in order to provide a basis of union between Protestants and also to provide a rational defense of the Christian faith against the deist and atheist. His reliance on the marks of fulfilled prophecy and biblical miracles made it difficult for him to defend the literal accuracy of the early portions of Genesis. Instead, he accepted their religious validity and refused to comment on their scientific accuracy. The revelation to the patriarchs was accommodated to the limited level of the people and would be more fully revealed through Christ.

In Turretin's use of the concept of biblical accommodation he abandoned many aspects of Calvin's thought. Granted, he never cited Calvin's arguments as incorrect and did not explicitly deny the interior witness of the Holy Spirit in establishing the divine authority of Scripture. His use of the external biblical marks, however, represented a divergent emphasis upon the need to establish a rational defense of the faith against deism and atheism. For Turretin, the knowledge of God was discovered in the same way that one found any other form of information—through the use of reason. This is a marked departure from Calvin and from his Reformed successors, including Jean-Alphonse's father, Francis, who recognized the difference between rational knowledge and the knowledge of God. With Jean-Alphonse, who gained his categories of religious knowledge from the tradition of Saumur, Reformed theology moved toward rationalism and ultimately into the Socinian camp.

This is not to say that Jean-Alphonse was influenced directly by the Socinians. He was a student of the rationalizing tendency of the Academy of Saumur and was strongly influenced by the Remonstrant tradition in Amsterdam in the person of his close friend and confidant, Jean LeClerc. The Remonstrant tradition, in turn, had followed the lead of the theologian and authority on international law, Hugo Grotius, on such issues as biblical evidentialism and biblical accommodation. Given his close affinity toward LeClerc and the critical methodology of Saumur, it was not surprising that Turretin's positions would resemble that of Socinus on the issue of accommodation.

Furthermore, Jean-Alphonse's extensive use of natural theology went beyond even Socinus. He was critical of Socinus for rejecting natural revelation as a proof for the existence and nature of God, but praises the seventeenth-century disciples of Socinus for correcting this error. Turretin attempted to establish as many of the basics of orthodoxy as possible without having to resort to special revelation to present a cogent apologetic to the growing tide of deism. Biblical revelation, when accommodated, was by its very nature limited and in its more primitive form (i.e., the early portions of the Pentateuch) cannot stand on its own. The problem was not that God is limited, but that man is. Revelation must be accommodated to man's limited ability to understand it. The message that God conveyed through Scripture contains correct knowledge about God and becomes progressively clearer. There was no necessity, however, for Scripture to be accurate, in terms of history and science, especially in its more primitive form. Scripture was inspired and authoritative to lead one to a knowledge of essential truths, but its accommodated nature removed the necessity that it be without error.

Clearly, Turretin's approach to biblical accommodation approached the Socinian camp. It is interesting to note that Turretin barely mentioned Calvin in any of his writings, except to say that Calvin was one of many early reformers responsible for splitting the Reformation movement over the rigid insistence on doctrines that Turretin deemed to be of secondary importance at best. It is not surprising that Turretin attempted to achieve a pan-Protestant union based on the fundamental articles of the faith.

In summary, for Turretin, a truly Christian theology is a rational system, based upon external marks and designed to eliminate scholastic speculation. His system emphasized the progressive nature of revelation and exalted the words of Christ as of higher value than the rest of Scripture. Christ himself possessed the greatest amount of light and his sermons contained the basic gospel message while virtually ignoring such difficult doctrines as predestination. Turretin's system of Reformed theology, adhering closely to the Sermon on the Mount, emphasized the practical aspects of the Christian life. In its use of external marks and in its pragmatism, it resembled Remonstrant theology as much as it does Reformed. Turretin attempted to eliminate the divisive aspects of scholastic creeds while building a system based upon the fundamentals of the faith. The next chapters will outline this system of fundamental articles as well as his attempts to break the back of Reformed scholasticism while constructing a basis for a pan-Protestant union.

5

The Demise of Reformed Scholasticism and the Abrogation of the Helvetic Formula Consensus of 1675

In addition to his desire to defend the Reformed faith, Turretin constructed a theological system based upon the fundamentals articles of the faith. Significantly, he never used a systematic approach to the issue of predestination, since he deemed it nonessential for salvation and the main stumbling block to Protestant union. Although his father was one of the principal architects of the Helvetic Formula Consensus, Jean-Alphonse led the movement away from such credal religion through the abrogation of the Formula in 1706 and the secularization of the curriculum of instruction at the academy. For Turretin, the Consensus formed the very heart of the type of theology that caused divisions among believers and especially between the leading Protestant confessions of faith in Switzerland, Germany, and England. Protestant union or even unity would not be possible as long as the objectionable pronouncements of the Consensus were enforced. Not only did Turretin succeed in having the Formula Consensus abrogated in Geneva, but he continued to negotiate for its abrogation within the cantons of Switzerland, especially in Lausanne.

Albert Montandon, in his analysis of the theological evolution that took place in Geneva after the death of Francis Turretin, labels this period of the growing dominance of the anti-scholastic party as a "period of tolerance."[1] He chose 1694 as the starting point for this new era because it was the year of Jean-Alphonse Turretin's ordination where he expressed his determination to promote the method of theological examination that Tronchin had taught him. Montandon, writing in the late nineteenth century, agreed with Jean-Alphonse's assessment that the scholastic approach to theological education was no longer viable. He wrote:

It was not a matter of responding [to heterodoxy] by persecution, exile or death. . . . It was no longer possible to use the same means that his [Turretin's] successors used during the Reformation. It was, rather, that God helped men to realize that to fight this battle successfully, they had to abandon the old tactics of revising, modifying and controlling [through the composition of traditional] Calvinistic works. The past with its confessions of faith and dogmatic requirements had served as the basis for the enemy.[2]

Turretin publicly expressed the same sentiment as well as his vision for the academy in his oration of 1 January 1700: "The century of the Reformation caused division and schism; the century that we have just finished consecrated these division by the formulas of discord; now that we have woken up to a new century, we ought to start it by covering the errors of our fathers with a coat of love, and in seeking to unite all churches in the same spirit by the bonds of peace."[3] Turretin took his own proclamations seriously and refused to discuss controversial dogmas.

The first step toward the abolishment of the scholastic theological method was to change the curriculum of instruction at the academy. With the help of his colleagues Jean-Robert Chouet, Antoine Léger, and Pierre Gautier, Turretin pushed for the establishment of a chair of mathematics at the academy. Mathematics was important, they reasoned, for the proper understanding of physics and for the student to acquire the mental discipline usually gained from the study of logic. In addition, mathematics had practical uses in architecture and it was already a very popular field of study throughout Europe. Michael Heyd points out that the popularity of mathematics helped explain the problem that the academy was having in attracting foreign students. If it was to compete against other prominent institutions for students, the academy would have to keep pace with "changing intellectual fashions."[4]

The chair of mathematics was approved by the Company in 1703. They nominated the French minister, Etienne Jalabert, for the post because he had already been teaching mathematics in Geneva for several years and was quite popular among the students.[5]

In his oration before the Council entitled "De studiis emendandis et promovendis," Turretin supported the nomination of Jalabert. In this speech, Turretin argued that the process of learning and improving man's mental condition could only result in an increase in piety and virtue. His philosophy of education advocated the gaining of knowledge for its own sake, which would lead inevitably toward godly devotion. Heyd notes that Turretin's philosophy of education was essentially secular and elevated "the polished man of letters who was dedicated to the pursuit of truth and the advancement of the sciences; and who was able to judge correctly and distinguish the true from the false; who was moderate and temperate, searching only after things which were accessible to human knowledge and avoiding vain controversies."[6]

This secular philosophy of education was quite different from the scholastic form. It did not focus on the intricacies of interpretation of theological problems, but advocated the discovery of new knowledge. Turretin recommended the inductive and experimental method of learning of Bacon.[7]

Turretin, however, criticized the scholastic method of investigation precisely because it did not lead to new knowledge. He saw little value in the questions of logic concerning "universals predicates and categories" or in syllogistic reasoning. Instead, he praised the method of Descartes and the study of mathematics and of geometry as better uses for the human mind.[8] He continued:

A last area of progress would be the abandoning or at least the reduction of the strict requirements of the scholastic heritage. One should occupy oneself more voluntarily to natural history. One should conduct more experiments. One should learn more about the vault of heaven, the kingdom of the animals, the properties of minerals and plants. The entire laboratory of nature would be opened to our investigations. In this area, the works of Aristotle, Theophrastus and Pliny would be relevant. And because all these things are beginning to be better and more exactly known today, I think, without better advice, that they should be taught more fully in our schools.[9]

Turretin's oration encouraged the Council to accept Jalabert and the chair of mathematics. Heyd cautions, however, that this reform did not initiate changes in the curriculum, but merely formalized those changes which had already been taking place.[10]

Changes in the curriculum continued after 1704, both in the teaching of the humanities and of law. A compulsory year of Greek as an intermediate step between study at the college and at the academy was approved and, by 1722, a special two-year humanities course was also initiated. In addition, the law faculty was reorganized in 1722–23 with the foundation of two chairs of jurisprudence and the integration of natural law into the curriculum. The latter development was significant for theology because the foremost authority in the field was none other than the famed expert on international law, Hugo Grotius. These changes reflect the modernization of the course of studies at the academy to meet changes in academic curriculums that were taking place at institutions throughout Europe. Significantly, these developments hastened the demise of the traditional scholastic approach to education at the academy.[11]

In the midst of the modifications of the course of studies offered at the academy, Turretin's mentor and colleague, Louis Tronchin, passed away in 1705. Deprived of the support and encouragement of his former teacher, Turretin pressed on to fulfill Tronchin's vision for the academy. He succeeded him to the theology chair and replaced him as the most vocal spokesman within the Company in favor of the abrogation of the creed.[12]

The abrogation of the Formula the following year marked the high point in Turretin's ascendancy within the Company of Pastors. The move against the Formula was precipitated by the request of an ordinand, Vial de Beaumont, who agreed to subscribe to it but without the traditional *sic sentio* (thus I believe). He preferred the statement *contrarium non docebo, pacem ecclesiae non turbabo* (I will not teach contrarily, nor will I disturb the peace of the church).[13]

Vial's request came before the Company of Pastors for discussion. By this time, Turretin, as rector of the academy, had gained a great deal of power within the body and had persuaded the majority of members that the Formula was outdated. He argued in favor of Vial's request, pointing out that even this subscription was too strong since one might swear to something that one did not believe.[14] In addition, these issues were not at all central to the Christian faith but were only "indifferent" matters. It would be far preferable, he argued, to disregard the Formula when one could adhere to the Word of God and to the Helvetic Confession. Further, the Reformers themselves would not have been admitted to the Company of Pastors if they were presented with the prerequisite of signing the Formula. Lastly, many of the Swiss churches were beginning to move away from the Consensus while the English prelates and Saxon princes were virulent in their opposition to it.[15]

Surprisingly, the majority of the Company of Pastors agreed to the change, but a significant minority led by Benedict Pictet and Benedict Calandrini, appealed to the Small Council. On 7 May the Council urged them to reconsider the matter and the Company of Pastors complied. Then the Council, led by Pierre Fatio, the famous lawyer and a supporter of Turretin, advocated maintaining the Formula but adding a milder form of the oath, *Sic docebo et Contrarium non docebo, scilicet quoties hanc materiam tracandam suscipiam, sive ore, sive calamo, sive privatum, sive publice* (thus I will teach and contrarily I will not teach, certainly as long as this subject is suspect, either by mouth, by pen, either privately or publicly).[16] Twelve out of thirty-four members of the Company abstained from voting, but contested the decision before the Council. Pictet and Calandrini argued before the Council that the abolition of the signature would threaten the orthodoxy of the Helvetic Confession and the Synod of Dort and would renew the threat of Arminianism to Reformed orthodoxy. The Small Council agreed to require a subscription that the ordinand would not teach anything against the canons of Dort. The Council of 200, however, would not ratify this agreement, but it did approve the original decision on 10 September that the ordinands were not required to sign the Formula, but only to swear adherence to the teachings of the New and Old Testaments and the contents of Calvin's catechism. It is significant that not only did the candidates for the ministry not have to sign the Formula, but they also did not have to pronounce formally their belief in the canons of Dort and in the Second Helvetic Confession.[17]

The Company recognized several factors that swayed their opinion toward the abolition of the Formula. They realized how many divisions such statements of faith caused among the various Protestant sects. The Company also considered the importance of the issues discussed in the Formula to be "very obscure and very difficult and not essential for salvation."[18] The Company finally admitted that the Formula dealt primarily with "indifferent" matters and that the articles of the Formula no longer rendered any service to personal piety, the worship service, or the manner of preaching. The questions raised in the Consensus were relevant in a time of reaction against the Academy of Saumur. The French Academy, however, had been closed prior to the Revocation of the Edict of Nantes in 1685, over twenty years before. The primary target of most of the provisions of the Formula no longer existed. The fact that the requirement of signature could prevent many well-qualified ordinands from the ministry was another important consideration. The Company concluded:

> All the arguments have been well weighed and examined by the Company and it has formulated an opinion which does not touch on the doctrine contained in the Regulations of 1649 and in the Consensus. In the future those who are candidates for the ministry will not be obliged to sign anything, but will be exhorted verbally by the Moderator to teach nothing in the Church or in the Academy against the Regulations, in order to preserve peace and union and to protect the uniformity of instruction.[19]

Important to note, Turretin was the moderator for this session of the Company, while Pictet did not even attend. This was an indication that the conservative party realized that they had lost control. After the decision of the Company was finalized, Turretin and Jean-Jacques Sartoris, who had moderated the previous session of the Company, presented its recommendation to the Council. Although the minority group sent its opinion to the Council as well, the final decision favored abrogation. The new ordination service consisted of a series of charges to the ordinands without any requirement of signature. The text reads:

> You promise and swear before God to believe and to make profession to believe all that is contained in the Holy Scriptures of the Old and New Testaments, which are the true and unique rule of our faith.
>
> You promise further not to teach anything which does not conform to the confession of faith or to the catechism of this Church, as contained in the summary of that which is taught to us in Holy Scripture.
>
> Finally, you are exhorted to teach nothing in the Church or in the Academy against the canons of Dort, against the Regulations of the Venerable Company or of those of the churches of Switzerland; and this is for the benefit of peace and for uniformity in the manner of instruction.[20]

Between 1706 and 1725, the minority group that desired to maintain the old Formula began to die off, including Pictet in 1724. They were replaced by individuals more predisposed toward the liberal position of Turretin. By June of 1725, Turretin had succeeded in convincing the majority of pastors that the primary basis for maintaining the strength of Protestant orthodoxy was to emphasize the fundamental points of biblical revelation. Without the strength of its main defender, the advocates of the Formula found themselves in a distinct minority. The Company then voted in 1725 to abrogate the Formula altogether. Further, they decided to charge new ordinands with the following statement: "You promise to keep the doctrines of the holy prophets and Apostles as they are contained in the books of the Old and New Testaments, whose doctrine we have summarized in our catechism."[21] James Good comments that the Genevan church thus became "confessionless."[22] The Company did add Jean-Frédéric Ostervald's catechism in 1731, but it did not contain any statements regarding the characteristic Reformed doctrines of original sin and predestination.

Liturgical Revision

Besides the elimination of the creed, new additions to the Reformed liturgy further diminished the influence of Reformed scholasticism over the theological climate of Geneva. Interestingly enough, these changes led to a more structured liturgy.[23] The movement toward rationalism thereby increased the emphasis upon the forms of worship while diminishing the rigors of dogma.[24]

Ironically, one of Jean-Alphonse Turretin's major allies in these changes was his cousin, Benedict Pictet, who had opposed the abrogation of the Formula. Pictet had enjoyed an extremely close relationship with his uncle, Francis Turretin, and was the first one called to the elder Turretin's bedside as he was nearing death. It is not surprising that Pictet wrote an inspiring eulogy praising the virtues of his departed uncle. Their relationship explains, in part, why Pictet defended the Formula, while also supporting many of the changes that contributed to the development of enlightened orthodoxy.

The two colleagues worked together to form a more structured service in which they instituted a brief explanation after the reading of Scripture and to add prescribed prayer at the end of the service. To facilitate the latter, they composed a series of general prayers for each week of the year. They were also commissioned in 1705 to compose a series of prayers for the youth as well as a prayer of preparation for the Lord's Supper.[25]

In addition, the Genevan Company of Pastors desired to have a revision of the Psalter in contemporary French. Since 1543 the Genevan church had been using a series of forty-nine Psalms put into verse by the French poet Clement Marot and by Theodore Beza. The problem with the Genevan Psalter was that the music was too simple, so that there was virtually no method in the singing. Many of the lyrics also contained graphic descriptions of the imprecatory Psalms that were a source of mockery among the opponents of the French Reformed movement. As a result, the French Reformed service was severely lacking in lay participation, and very few parishioners bothered to sing the Psalms with any vigor.[26]

In the light of the obvious need for change, the Company commissioned Pictet to lead the efforts for revision and asked that all the imprecatory Psalms be eliminated. Pictet completed the work in 1694, but it was not used in the Genevan churches until 1698.[27]

Pictet's revisions were generally well received, with the exception of theologian Pierre Jurieu, who led the synod of Rotterdam to condemn the revision as "patriarchal and papal tyranny." Part of his criticism came as a result of his extreme conservatism and disdain for any major alterations in the worship service from the "purity" of the early reformers. Jurieu was very suspicious of the theological developments at Geneva because of the rise of the liberal element, which was opposed to the Formula Consensus within the Genevan Academy. He felt that any imposition on the part of Geneva would be similar to papal pronouncements. Furthermore, the neighboring city of Bern, the strongest advocate of the Formula within the Swiss confederation, would not allow the use of the Psalter in the territories under its control. This was a reactionary move that reflected Bern's suspicions that the theological developments in Geneva might lead to heterodoxy elsewhere.[28]

Pictet was also responsible for compiling a book of hymns taken from the New Testament. Commissioned by the Company of Pastors, Pictet presented a book of fifty-three songs that were especially applicable to the communion service. Pictet included a preface in which he outlined the history of hymns from the first century. He also cited the opinion of Erasmus on the importance of such music for proper worship.[29]

Another badly needed change in the worship service was the benediction, which had previously been tediously long. In 1705, Pictet's colleague on the theological faculty, Benedict Calandrini, composed a shorter version, but members of the Company of Pastors refused to use it. This resulted in a fourteen-year period of confusion in which Reformed pastors used the old longer benediction and some the new shorter version. Finally, in 1719, Calandrini's version was enforced and by 1725, Turretin wrote yet another new benediction that was even shorter and was immediately enforced in the Reformed Churches in the Genevan environs.[30]

A third major area of revision of the French Reformed service was the liturgy itself. In their desire to remain faithful to Calvin, the French Reformed liturgy was quite simple and centered on the preaching of the word while resisting the temptation to copy the more ordered and poetic aspects of the Anglican or Lutheran liturgies. As a result, the Reformed services were quite unstructured and, with the poor quality of the Psalter, by 1700 lay participation had sunk to an all-time low. Ostervald complained to Turretin on 23 July 1701: "It is also very important to pay attention to the reformation of worship because it is currently in a deplorable state. More than half the pastors in this state are convinced that these changes must be made prudently."[31] Ostervald was quick to blame Calvin for the problems with the French liturgy and by no means revered Calvin's theology. He believed it contained some ideas that were "as absurd" as some aspects of Roman Catholicism. Referring to Calvin's liturgical style as cold and dry, Ostervald expressed his dismay to Turretin on 10 May 1702: "Our reformers have terribly disfigured (the worship service) under the guise of reform. Our adversaries are correct when they say that Calvin introduced a form of worship unknown in the entire era of the early church."[32]

The reform of the liturgy was extremely important to Ostervald and he remarked to Turretin that it was the most valued accomplishment of his academic career. Turretin and Ostervald believed that the changes in the liturgy would do more to change the Reformed church than any official change in doctrine. Furthermore, both argued that the purpose of the liturgy was not to preserve orthodoxy, but to inspire the believer toward proper worship of God.[33]

In his revision, Ostervald felt that it was perfectly reasonable to take from what he considered to be the best aspects of the Lutheran and Anglican services. This sentiment not only reflected his disposition in favor of Turretin's plans for a pan-Protestant union, but also indicated that Ostervald was not afraid of changes that would make the Reformed service seem more "high church" in its liturgical style. His desire was to form a meaningful worship in a structured fashion modeled after the purity of the early church. Interestingly, he felt that the Anglican church was closer to the apostolic model than was the Reformed. According to biographer Jean-Jacques Von Allmen, Ostervald "saw in the Church of England a structure that all believers could adhere to. It reflects the true image of the universal church because it does not have a pope and since the time of the Reformation, the Church of England has maintained all that could be preserved, not believing itself to be more wise than the universal church." One way of approaching the devotional style of Anglicanism was to have a special service once a week, a half-hour in length, devoted solely to worship without the sermon. This service included a structured time for adoration, confession, Scripture reading, and short prayers of devotion.[34]

Ostervald's suggestion was well received in Geneva, with Pictet and Turretin leading the way within the Company for its implementation. Part of the reason for the success of this new service was the elimination of some of the mid-week sermons that left many of the pastors so overworked that they had little time remaining for the other tasks of the ministry.[35]

Ostervald competed his first revision of the liturgy in 1713, which he had started as early as 1701. The major reason for the delay was the inevitable fear of the conservative reaction against any changes in the worship service. Prior to the official publication of the revision, the new service was tried at Neuchâtel during the summer of 1702 and in Geneva the following summer with Turretin, Tronchin, and Jean-Robert Chouet as its major proponents.[36]

Lastly, Pictet and Turretin were major advocates in favor of the adoption of a new Reformed catechism authored by Ostervald. Typically, depending on whether one was in German- or French-speaking areas of the Alpine region, catechumens would memorize either Calvin's catechism or the Heidelberg catechism. Because of the catechism's length and detail, which often soured one of their first religious experiences, neither was very popular among the youth. Support for a revision was uniform among the pietists, as well as among both liberal and conservative elements within the Reformed church. Ostervald completed his revision entitled *Le Catéchisme ou instruction dans la religion chrétienne,* which was modeled after both the Anglican Book of Common Prayer and the creeds of the early church. In a letter to Turretin dated 19 March 1701, Ostervald expressed his desire to "provide a very simple catechism, containing a summary of the work of God in history and in which the foundations of religion would be established, and where, in following the Symbol, the Decalogue, the Lord's prayer, and the material of the sacraments, one explains their principal points, either in doctrine or in practice."[37]

Ostervald's revision was not well received by the Bernese, who, not surprisingly, complained that it was not faithful to the theology of Calvin and was either silent or unclear on most of the controversial doctrines of the Remonstrants. In addition, some members of the Bernese clergy felt that the catechism did not express the doctrine of justification by faith clearly enough. It is interesting to note that Ostervald's description of the doctrine of justification focused on the idea of intellectual assent to a number of fundamental articles of the faith. Ostervald wrote in the catechism that true faith "is a belief, a persuasion of the truths that God has revealed in his word. One recognizes such faith by good works and by the study of holiness."[38]

A further comparison of Ostervald's catechism with Calvin's shows other marked deviations. For example, Ostervald refused to use the language of Nicaea to describe the Trinity, preferring to employ biblical expressions only. Furthermore, his descriptions of predestination were not very substantive and stated only that "God does not deprive men of salvation, but they render themselves unworthy by their unbelief and by their sins." Louis Gonin comments on this point that Ostervald did not want to lead the catechumens toward an area of theology that he considered "horribly obscure."[39]

In the long run, Ostervald's catechism became the dominant version used within the Reformed churches of the region. In 1734, Ostervald published a shorter version, at the insistence of Turretin, entitled *L'abrégé de l'histoire sainte et du catéchisme,* which became extremely popular partly because of its succinctness and partly because it was affordable for purchase. This version became dominant within the French Church of the Desert in southern France and, in 1758, Roman Catholic authorities in the Bordeaux region ordered 5,928 copies burned. In all, over 300,000 copies were published.[40]

The Controversy Over the Formula Consensus at Lausanne

Turretin desired not only to rid Geneva of the domination of the hated formulary, but also to eliminate its influence throughout all of Switzerland, especially in the Pays de Vaud. He was not alone in this regard. Turretin, Samuel Werenfels, and Jean-Frédéric Ostervald were often referred to as the "Swiss Triumvirate" for their joint efforts to rid all Switzerland of the Formula.

The conflict over the abrogation of the Formula Consensus in Lausanne provided an important forum for Turretin to press his views concerning the necessity to insist upon the maintenance of only the fundamental articles of the faith. The series of confrontations at Lausanne were part of a wider movement toward a pan-Protestant union of Anglican, Lutheran, and Reformed churches that included such international figures as Gottfried Wilhelm Freiherr von Leibniz of Hanover, Balthazar Winkler of Magdeburg, the Antistes of Zurich, Peter Winkler, Daniel Ernest Jablonksi of Berlin, Jean LeClerc, and the archbishop of Canterbury, William Wake. The specific nature of the Formula Consensus served as a major roadblock for such attempts at accord, so the advocates of union deemed it necessary to have it abrogated throughout the Swiss confederation.

Importantly, the French-speaking cantons were more influenced by developments in the French Reformed church than by their German counterparts, especially Bern, which was the dominant force in ecclesiastical affairs in Vaud. In addition, the Pays de Vaud, being primarily French-speaking, had a natural resentment against the domination of a German-speaking city such as Bern. Good writes: "Vaud had sympathized with Calvin's view of the Church as autonomous in its government, but Bern on the other hand sympathized with Zwingli in making the Church and State closely united."[41] Furthermore, Bern was extremely conservative in its defense of the Formula and kept a watchful eye over developments in Geneva after the abolishment of the requirement of subscription in 1706. They were extremely suspicious of Ostervald's new catechism of 1702, and preferred to retain the Heidelberg Catechism and the Little Catechism of Bern. The theological leaders of Bern detested Ostervald's new liturgy of 1713 because of its similarities with the English Book of Common Prayer.[42]

Lausanne, even prior to the Revocation, had not adhered closely to the Formula. Only 51 out of 160 ministry candidates had subscribed to the Consensus from 1675–1700. The major reason was that the authorities of Lausanne had not required them to sign. The controversy began in earnest in 1698 when several members of the Academy of Lausanne were accused of holding erroneous opinions that verged on Arminianism. In February 1698, a German pastor in Lausanne, a certain M. Ulrich, accused five students, Jurassien Faigaux, Pierre-François Bergier, Pierre Porta, Jeremie Arthaud, and Joste Terraz, of failing to adhere to the Formula Consensus. An inquiry was opened by the academy, in which a number of witnesses were questioned, with the result that an official report was sent to Bern, with additional comments by the professor of philosophy, Jeremie Sterky, who had been the secretary during the proceedings. Bern, in turn, asked for a fuller inquiry, so the Council sent a commission to Lausanne to look into the matter further.[43]

Most of the faculty at the Lausanne Academy had assented to the Formula Consensus as long as the qualified signature, "as far as it agrees with Scripture" was allowed. Only Sterky and the professor of Hebrew, Gabriel Bergier, objected to the necessity to sign any form of the Consensus. The liberal party was attempting to be diplomatic and spoke out against the Formula with extreme prudence and reservation.[44]

The Bernese commission came up with several conclusions after their investigation. First, the source of the strife was Geneva, where the liberal party was gaining dominance. Second, the commission suspected the renegade-Calvinist, turned-Arminian, Jean LeClerc, of having some influence. He also happened to be engaged in correspondence with several important theological figures in Geneva, primarily Turretin. Third, these errors reflected a failure to understand that Arminian theology might result in a leaning toward Socinianism.[45]

The commission ordered the Lausanne Academy to be more careful in insuring orthodoxy by requiring the students involved to sign the Formula and to renounce all heterodox opinions on threat of banishment and loss of their ministerial credentials. The Bernese required unqualified adherence to a new oath, *Le Serment d'Association,* which specifically condemned Pietism, Arminianism, and Socinianism. However, by 1706 the qualified signature *non contrarium docebo* (I will not teach contrarily) was allowed by the rector, Jean Pierre de Crousaz, also a professor of philosophy.[46]

The debates over the Consensus in Lausanne reflected a division between the conservative pastors of the Pays de Vaud and the more liberal professors at the academy. The issue developed into a crisis when, in 1715, sixteen ordinands signed the Consensus with the qualified signature, "as far as it agrees with Scripture." This led to the Classis at Morges to send a complaint to Bern along with the recommendation that full subscription to the Formula be required. The liberal party had gained much strength at the academy with the support of Abraham Ruchat, professor of church history, Jean Barbeyrac, Gabriel Bergier, professor of Hebrew, and Georges Pierre Polier, also a professor of Hebrew. The faculty sent a formal defense of their position to Bern, which referred the case to its Academic Senate. This was made up of ten laymen, who were members of the Great and Small Councils, and ten clergymen, who would make a recommendation to the Small Council. Barbeyrac was visibly upset by the complaints and sent a letter to Turretin outlining a defense of his actions as rector of the academy. He wrote:[47]

> It is certain that the Classis of Morges gathered a considerable amount of information in order to represent to the Council that the new opinions had made considerable progress among the young ministers and in order to cast suspicion on several members of the Academy, and to ask that in the future the new ordinands who entered into their Classis would have to sign the Consensus again in the manner that they demanded. Monsieur de Crousaz understood that they suspected him most particularly, after speaking to Monsieur le Thiesmor Steiger. . . . It was said to us that this man received them poorly enough and since that time we have not heard anything else about it. The authors of this affair are some of the most ignorant men of the Classis.[48]

Barbeyrac continued to explain that there was little support for his position in the Bernese Council, where he estimated that only three or four members were predisposed toward the abolition of the Consensus. In addition, he claimed that he had never prevented anyone from signing the Formula. In fact, he argued that he had required signature to the Formula but had allowed a qualified signature "as far as it agrees with Scripture." He defended this allowance with the explanation that this signature was a common practice in other cantons.[49]

In February 1716, Barbeyrac explained further to Turretin that he had written to the Bernese Council denying that there was any trace of Arminian thought at the Academy of Lausanne. He also pointed out that the qualified subscription was contained in the end of the preface to the Helvetic Confession and, therefore, possessed some measure of justification. He defended the qualified signature on the grounds that the section of the Formula dealing with the vowel points of the Masoretic text was more of an article of grammar than an article of faith.[50]

By December of 1717, after having received a copy of the register of the Lausanne Academy listing all the signatures to the Formula, the Council pressed the matter further by sending a series of questions to the Lausanne Academy. They hoped that the academy would respond with the assurance that they were taking the proper measures to enforce the dictates of the Formula Consensus. These questions are as follows:

1. Do the ordinands subscribe to the Serment d'association when they are ordained?
2. Where did the idea come from that the Academy permits the ordinands to sign the Consensus in a modified manner?
3. Under whose rectorate did the Academy begin to permit the qualified signature?
4. Why did the Academy not inform the Council of this?
5. What is the opinion of the Academy on this subject?[51]

The response by the Academy of Lausanne, written by Barbeyrac, honestly portrayed the faculty's criticism of the strictness of the Formula. It gave an accounting of their allowance of the qualified subscription. Their critique of the Consensus was quite in keeping with the arguments that Tronchin had set forth when the Consensus was under debate in Geneva over thirty years before. In addition, the report denied any adherence to Arminianism at the academy and advocated adherence to the old Helvetic Confession. Lastly, the report stated that the doctrine of hypothetical universalism did not affect any fundamental article of the faith and that adherence to it should not be prohibited.[52]

The Senate of Bern was, to say the least, displeased with the reply. Their response to the report was not immediately sent to Lausanne, but an unofficial, French translation was circulated there. This private version expressed extreme dismay that the Lausanne Academy would not enforce full subscription to the Formula during a time when Socinianism and Arminianism threatened the dominance of "orthodox" Reformed theology. In addition, the translation indicated the sentiment that the provisions of the Formula were essential to defend fundamentals of the faith and were not mere *adiaphora* or secondary matters. The letter did distinguish between a *formula fidei* and a *formula doctrinae*. The former would regulate belief and the latter would merely apply to the academic curriculum. The Bernese commission would, therefore, allow some measure of latitude in personal belief but not in instruction at the academy. They wanted to protect the next generation of pastors and professors from any hint of heterodox thought. From their perspective, the very future of the Reformed movement in the Pays de Vaud was at stake. This was a minor compromise and the letter indicated the desire to enforce the stricter signature of the Formula.[53]

After the Lausanne Academy sent a formal reply in March 1718, the Small Council of Bern responded on 13 June by forbidding any further public discussion of the issue and requiring a full subscription to the Formula without any qualified signatures. The penalty for refusing to comply with this provision would be the revocation of ministerial credentials. The candidates for the ministry at Lausanne complied with this requirement, but received some solace from insiders at Bern who related that the Bernese did recognize this distinction between *formula doctrinae* and *formula fidei*. This would allow the candidates personally to disagree with some of the harsher measures of the Formula while agreeing not to denounce it publicly.[54]

Barbeyrac, however, was so incensed over the intransigence of the Bernese that he resigned his post as rector of the academy and took a new position at Groningen, Holland. After the commission sent its recommendations to the Lausanne Academy, Barbeyrac complained to Turretin that it was a poor decision.[55]

On 6 January 1718, in the midst of the controversy over the Formula at Lausanne, Turretin wrote to his close friend, the archbishop of Canterbury, William Wake, asking him for his advice on the matter. Wake's response, dated 24 February 1678, provides interesting insights into the Latitudinarian position on the Swiss Formula. Wake wrote:

I am very sorry for the controversie you mention, which is risen up in the Evangelical Cantons. I heartily wish it may come to a peaceable end; which in my opinion such affairs can never do, unless more libertie be allowed in point of subscription of some sort of formularies than most churches seem willing to consent unto. The moderation of the Church of England has been very exemplary in this respect; and we have felt the good effect of it in that peace we enjoy among our ministers, notwithstanding their own difference of opinion in many considerable articles of Christian doctrine. The 39 Articles, published about the beginning of the reign of Queen Elizabeth and collected from those which had been set forth in the last year of King Edward VI, with several prudent amendments with respect to the synods, indifferently, by bishops and clergy of different persuasions, we have left every one to interpret them in his own sense; and they are indeed so generally framed, that they may, without an equivocation, have more senses than one fairly put upon them. . . .

I do not mention these things, as if I equally approved myself of them. But this I own, that the main articles of Christianity being equally secured by the creeds of the church; the public worship by a sound and orthodox liturgy; and the clergy by a larger formulary obliged not to preach or write anything contrary to what has, in the judgment of the body of ministers and pastors of every church, been approved of, as most agreeable to the holy scriptures; I think it sufficient for men to be obliged to declare their own faith and assent only to what is most clear, and certain, and necessary for every one who is to be admitted to any office in the opposition, nor by preaching, writing or otherwise, to contradict the received doctrine or usages of churches with which he communicates, without being forced to an explicit declaration of his own judgement in such matters; in which he may innocently differ from others of his brethren and yet be a useful man in the church of Christ.[56]

Turretin was so moved by this letter that he urged Wake to compose a formal draft that could be used to influence the authorities in Bern that the subscription to the Formula was not necessary. Wake complied with a formal six-page letter written in Latin. The letter detailed the British involvement in the Synod of Dort and specified that King James I did not desire any religious controversy over the finer points of the doctrine of predestination for fear that such subtleties would cause division within the Church of England. Wake quoted the Anglican delegate to the Synod, Bishop John Davenant, who was content to say that the main points of predestination were to ascribe to God the work of saving sinners and to man the fault of reprobation. Wake was convinced that the fundamental articles of religion were sufficient and believed that restraint in such technical matters was important to prevent further schism among the Protestant confessions that would provide Rome with an undue advantage in the quest for religious dominance in Europe.[57] Wake explained:

> If therefore these articles concerning which a dispute is already being waged between the citizens of Berne and Lausanne may to all appearances not only cause factions, hatreds and enmities in the Swiss churches, but also prove an obstacle to the union of all the reformed churches which is so greatly desired by every one; if all the Lutherans in Germany, Denmark and Sweden, and by far the greatest part of the Churches of England and Ireland will most certainly demand a greater freedom of opinion in these matters; and if even in the Evangelical churches themselves of Belgium, Switzerland and Germany, very many will find an occasion of offence, if not actually of schism, it may be left to the consideration of any discerning judge of these things whether it would not be much wiser to forestall those evils betimes, than, as the saying is, to be wise too late, and when the disease has grown too grave, to apply remedies in vain.[58]

Wake concluded the letter by encouraging the leaders of the Swiss church to bring peace to Bern and Lausanne and to reject the Formula, being content with a subscription to the Helvetic Confession of 1566.[59]

Wake's letter was not used to mediate in the dispute because the controversy was seemingly settled in June of 1718, by the decision of the Bernese Council. Although the case appeared closed, Turretin was not at all convinced because in September 1718, De Crousaz had written to him suggesting that Wake might be able to help the liberal party at the Lausanne Academy. He again invoked the opinion of Wake, who was very respected in Bern, in order to encourage the Bernese to withdraw their demands to enforce the Formula in Lausanne. Turretin requested that Wake compose a statement for the December 1718 celebration of the bicentenary of the Reformation in Zurich. Wake's statement was lengthy, covering nine folio pages, and described the theological history of England beginning with the Lambeth Articles of 1595. Wake emphasized the moderation of the English theologians in the face of religious discord, pointing out that the prudence of the English theologians had prevented much possible strife and schism. He then turned to the history of the Continental Reformation and noted the differences of opinion among the delegates to the Synod of Dort. Both sides of the debate over the Formula Consensus were also in agreement on the fundamentals of the faith. He pointed out that there were sufficient areas of agreement in order to make compromise and agreement possible. He wrote concerning the difficulty of proving the aspects of the Formula that dealt with the origin of the vowel points of the Hebrew text:

Who is of greater authority in Hebrew studies than Buxtorf and Cappellus? and who can determine the issue joined between them about the authority of Hebrew points? Who can know exactly how far the holy scriptures as we possess them at this day, both as to content and as to their very words, are divinely inspired? Who will dare to pronounce what is the authority of the Septuagintal version, so much extolled by Isaac Vossius and others? Or what is the pre-eminence of the Samaritan codex?[60]

This document stressed the importance of the fundamental articles of religion and reflected Turretin's sentiment that the fundamental articles of the faith could serve as the primary source of unity among Protestants. Norman Sykes points out, however, that in England, only a strong civil magistrate had been able to force the theologians to remain silent on disputed doctrines. Wake's comments seem somewhat hypocritical in such a context, but he did desire to preserve harmony among believers and disdained theological disputes over minor matters, whether it be in England or in Switzerland.[61]

By May of 1719, the Bernese renewed the controversy by deciding to make sure that the members of the Academy of Lausanne were keeping their word in enforcing the Formula. They conducted a formal visitation that precipitated much opposition in Lausanne. The Bernese wanted to test the professors of the Lausanne Academy orally, but they refused, preferring to respond in a written fashion, so that they could carefully craft their responses. The Bernese commission completed its report at the beginning of the next year and the Small Council delayed for two more years before they presented their recommendations to the Council of Two Hundred. The recommendation was to enforce subscription to the Formula and to the *Serment d'Association*. The main result, however, was that the delay provided the opportunity for public debate over the issue not only in Switzerland, but in Holland and Germany as well. It was this public forum that provided Turretin and his confidant, the archbishop of Canterbury, William Wake, the opportunity to make their case throughout Switzerland and the Republic of Letters.[62]

Meanwhile, Zurich strongly supported Bern and was more conservative in its wish for unconditional adherence to the Formula. Both Bern and Zurich argued that the Formula served the same purpose in Switzerland that the 39 Articles had served in England.

Through his correspondence with Peter Zeller, the Antistes of Zurich, Wake became convinced that compromise was possible because the conservative faction held that adherence to the Formula was not a matter of faith but rather a matter of maintaining theological peace. Turretin disagreed and claimed that the churchmen of Zurich really desired full acceptance of the Formula.[63]

It was in the midst of this crisis, at the end of 1719, that Turretin composed the *Nubes testium*,[64] which he wrote as an apologetic piece to defend the liberal party in Lausanne as well as in Geneva. This work, which will be discussed later in detail, emphasized the necessity to insist only upon a small core of fundamental doctrines and formed the heart of Turretin's theology of Christian union.

Between 1719 and 1722, there was a lull in the crisis between Bern and Lausanne because of several deaths within the Bernese Council. During the interim, on 23 March 1721, Wake commented to Turretin on the progress of the Kings of England and Prussia in pressuring Bern to compromise on the issue of subscription to the Formula. Wake wrote:

> Lord Townsend did not only promise to propose what you desired to the king, but he persuaded the other ministers to join with him. His majesty has consented to send a letter to the cantons, and I was charged with writing a draft. I copied the plan you sent to me exactly. . . . The king has signed the letter and it is now on its way to Bern. I hope that the two kings (of England and of Prussia) will unite in the same request which will not be refused.[65]

When the Bernese Council finally did come out with a formal decision on the matter, they refused to compromise and ordered the Academy of Lausanne to subscribe to the Consensus in 1722. Vuilleumier listed the orders that the Council sent to the Lausanne Academy:

1. Avoid personal questions;
2. Establish as much uniformity as possible between the Academies of Bern and of Lausanne and, in this goal, to oblige all the ministers of the Pays de Vaud, as well as of German speaking areas, to sign the Consensus "according to the approved explication" and to prepare anew the Oath of Fellowship . . . ;
3. To proceed with the execution of this order, two members of the Little Council will be sent to Lausanne with the order to dismiss immediately those who refuse to sign as they had said and to take the oath;

4. Before being executed, the decisions above will all be submitted to the Council of 200 for ratification.[66]

The vote in favor of ordering subscription was ninety-eight to twenty-eight and many at Lausanne were hopeful that the minority party at Bern, who favored abolition of the subscription, would gain more votes in the Council. The presence of such a significant minority in Bern strengthened the opposition to the Formula in Lausanne. They felt it was just a matter of time until the Bernese would realize the futility of attempting to force the Academy of Lausanne to submit to their demands.[67]

Seizing this opportunity, Turretin invoked the authority of the King of Prussia, Frederick William I, and urged him to draft a letter to the cantons of Bern and Zurich pressing for moderation. He did so on 21 February in a very strong letter addressed to the cantons of Switzerland in general. In addition, in May 1722, the body of Protestant sovereigns of Germany wrote a similar letter to the Swiss cantons and Frederick William I composed an additional appeal in April 1723. These letters had relatively little effect, however, but they contributed to good relations between the liberal party in the Swiss Reformed church and the secular leaders of the German Lutheran states.[68]

Turretin then urged Wake to draft a new letter containing the signature of the king himself in order to encourage further the Bernese to adopt a conciliatory stance. The letter, dated 10 April 1722, was sent to all the cantons and expressed the desire for Protestant union. Wake stated that the Formula was causing an unnecessary division between the Swiss and the German Lutherans thereby blocking all possibility of union. The letter stated:

> That you may consent to make this concession to the peace of the Reformed Church; namely, that no one shall be required to sign the above-mentioned Formula Consensus contrary to your customary indulgence in matters of this kind. Further that it should on the contrary be forbidden by you that any one, under the pretext of setting forth a true profession of faith, should disturb the peace of the church, and by untimely controversies concerning a question too difficult and obscure and (as some consider) in no wise affecting the true end of eternal salvation, should inflict much hurt on religion and the state. How useful, salutary and at this time especially how necessary thus advice is, your eminent piety and prudence will readily indicate to you; since in carrying it out, it is a matter equally affecting your own affairs and the common cause of Protestantism. Nor have we any reason to doubt that you will gladly embrace it, since you will thereby both gratify us

and in the best manner consult the quiet and safety of the Reformed Churches.[69]

Bern was willing to compromise only to the extent that signature would not be a matter of faith and by 23 May 1722, seven out of twenty-five ordinands refused to sign and were excluded from the ministry. One of the professors, Polier, also refused to sign, but he submitted a formal statement that satisfied the Council and he was allowed to maintain his professorship.[70]

After the submission of the Lausanne Academy, a second letter from George I expressed regret over the requirement for subscription to the Formula. This letter included Wake's opinion that "the most learned men whom we have consulted on this mater are unanimously of opinion that the articles treated of in this Formula are both very obscure in themselves and also not necessary to be believed for salvation."[71]

In February 1723, Bern allowed a milder form of adherence to the *Serment d'Association* and the ordinands who had previously refused to sign adhered to the compromise. It was a political uprising, however, that led to the solution of the debates over the formulary. On 31 March 1723, Major Duval led a revolt of the French-speaking citizens of the Vaud region against their German-speaking masters of Bern. Duval's revolt was put down and he was hanged for treason. The result of this, however, was the growing realization in Bern of the great discontent in Lausanne at Bernese domination on the matter of the Formula. By April 1723, Bern issued a decree that imposed silence on all issues relating the Formula and sent a conciliatory letter on behalf of all the cantons to the king of England. Although, they still required signature to the Formula and the *Serment d'Association,* Bern allowed the compromise signatures, which seemed to satisfy all parties. The ordinands who had refused to sign accepted the compromise and were ordained to the ministry.[72]

The use of the oath died a slow death in Lausanne. In 1746 it was replaced with a more simple "Serment de Religion," advocating adherence to the Helvetic Confession. There was no mention of a refutation of Socinianism, Pietism, or Arminianism. By 1758, the Ecclesiastical Ordinances made no mention of the Formula, which had ceased to have much significance.[73]

As one can see from the series of incidents in Lausanne over the Formula Consensus, the period following the Revocation of the Edict of Nantes was a time of insecurity for the Reformed scholastic movement throughout Switzerland. In order to insure their

brand of orthodoxy, the conservative party resorted to the intervention of civil power. The liberals, however, were able to gain
power in the civil government and soon this movement was de-
feated. Beardslee comments that "Reformed scholasticism was an
artificial growth. It seemed necessary at a time when Protestantism
needed all its weapons; it proved to have little in common with the
lives of the people for whom it spoke."[74]

6

The Fundamental Articles and Attempts at Protestant Reunification

Jean-Alphonse Turretin's attempts to rid Switzerland of the Consensus was only part of his overall plan to form a union among the main members of the Protestant Reformation movement, the Reformed, Anglican, and Lutheran churches. He hoped that the abrogation of strict confessions of faith would remove barriers to a union of orthodox Protestant belief that could withstand any attacks, whether it be from Roman Catholic polemicists or atheistic philosophers. He was untiring in his attempts to formalize a statement of unification and spent countless hours composing letters to the kings of England and of Prussia, as well as to their ministers. When the count of Metternich visited Neuchâtel in 1707, he told Turretin that the king of Prussia was positively predisposed toward union. In addition, the king of Prussia wanted to know the views of both the Academy of Geneva and the Company of Pastors on the issue of union.[1]

Turretin responded with a carefully crafted letter in which he stated the position of the Company. In this letter, Turretin expressed the idea that the Genevan church had always believed that the Calvinists and the Lutherans could come to an agreement on the essential aspects of religious faith because neither confession contained any aspect of idolatry or fundamental error. The issues that separated the two were, he argued, quite unnecessary for salvation. The Company hoped to establish congregations in German territories and allow the Lutherans to form a congregation in Geneva, thus paving the way for an eventual single ecclesiastical union.[2]

Turretin turned his attention next to the methodology of forming such a union. He did not recommend holding public disputations since such meetings would only highlight the differences between the two groups. He cautioned that divisive issues ought to be discussed only with moderation and caution. He would prefer to allow worship of both confessions in both Geneva and Prussia, commenting that whenever adherents to the Augsburg Confession communicated with the Genevan divines, they were received with open arms. He speculated further that if the Lutherans would extend the same courtesy, communication would be quite open and free between the two churches.[3]

Having informed the Prussians of the conciliatory stance of the Genevan Company of Pastors, Turretin made the subject of union with the Lutherans in Prussia his theme in his address as rector of the academy. To further indicate his desire for union, he dedicated his address to the king of Prussia. As a result of these attempts at conciliation, Geneva and the king of Prussia mutually agreed to allow a Lutheran minister to form a Lutheran congregation in Geneva. The king desired to break down the wall of separation and invited a dialogue with the Lutheran theologians concerning the matter. The duke of Saxony concurred and desired to have some Reformed ministers in his court in order to "involve all the ministers and professors in good-natured fellowship and in the work of mutual charity." He pointed out that he had done everything possible, according to the constitutions of the empire, to oppose the plans and practices of Roman Catholicism.

Turretin continued to correspond with the count of Metternich and the count of Wartenburg on the subject of union. On 29 April 1707, Turretin wrote to Metternich: "If there is something else, sir, that can give us hope for success, it is to see a powerful and pious Prince who applies himself with so much zeal and who employs a minister as able and as well-intentioned as you."[4]

On 18 June 1707, the count of Wartenburg replied to Turretin and informed him that the additional Lutheran services available in Geneva had greatly added to the possibilities of a religious union. As a further conciliatory gesture, the king of Prussia rewarded Turretin with a special gold medal and membership in the Royal Academy of Berlin.[5]

Turretin corresponded with several of his close friends, including Ostervald, LeClerc, and Leemans, concerning his negotiations with the Anglicans and the Lutherans. Ostervald agreed with Turretin that the debates over the Formula in Lausanne were hindering their attempts at union. Ostervald described, in a letter to Turretin dated 5 July 1719, that one could form union on two levels. The first level would be an agreement on the essentials of the faith and the second would be an agreement on more secondary matters. The second category would obviously be much more difficult to achieve since the requirements for agreement would be much greater. It would most likely serve as a source of division rather than as a source of accord. The Formula Consensus was a clear example of the second category. Ostervald did not see such a specific creed as practically beneficial because it excluded so many believers. Interestingly enough, he would not countenance an alternate creed that supported the Salmurian teachings because it also would be too narrowly defined.[6]

In a later letter, Ostervald predicted, however, that the attempts at union with the Lutherans would ultimately fail because the Lutheran theologians themselves were very conservative and were not naturally predisposed toward agreement with the Reformed churches of Switzerland. He cited their difficulty in forming accords with the Lutherans in Sweden as an example of this potential difficulty. Nevertheless, Ostervald encouraged Turretin to continue his efforts at union and push for the abrogation of the Formula throughout Switzerland. Without such abrogation, he wrote, any attempts at union would not succeed.[7] In addition, Ostervald pointed out that union would be difficult because the theologians did not possess authority to speak for the state. One would have to negotiate, not with the theology professors or the pastors, but with the head of the state.[8]

This actually worked out to Turretin's advantage because the kings of England and Prussia were more desirous for union than were the majority of theologians. The problem in these two countries was the differences of opinion among the clergy. In England, the debates between the Conformists and the Nonconformists made the project so difficult that Ostervald predicted to Turretin that the English government would not attempt it.[9] However, Ostervald noted that the English prelates had read several of Turretin's speeches and were favorably impressed with his rationalistic approach to Christian faith, especially in his opposition to the specific creeds of the scholastic Calvinists. Of course, Turretin's good relations with the English churchmen dated back to his studies in England. LeClerc, for his part, predicted, in a letter to Turretin, that the attempts at union with the Lutherans would be extremely difficult. He claimed that the Lutheran theologians were neither sufficiently prudent, enlightened, nor well read to agree to reunification. The princes, for their part, were neither enlightened nor firm enough to gain the support of the theologians. However, LeClerc recommended to Turretin that he should press on with his attempts at union in any case because by sowing the seed of moderation he could gain important ground toward similar attempts at some future time.[10]

Leemans expressed similar sentiments as early as 1700. He told Turretin that the Lutherans had not forgotten their lack of representation at the Synod of Dort. However, he noted that the Lutherans were also worried about the relationship between Arminianism and Socinianism and, because of this fear, they might well agree to some kind of accord.[11]

Turretin's main ally in the attempt at Protestant reunification was William Wake, who had been tireless in his own attempts for ecclesiastical accord with the Gallican church. Wake was well connected among the Gallican theologians in Paris, the foremost of whom was Ellies Dupin, who was representative of the moderate element within the French church. According to Leonard Adams, Wake did not want a formal union with the French Catholics, but rather an "intercommunion" defined as a "working relationship of understanding and probable progress toward ecumenism on the essential elements of catholicism in its broadest sense." The basis for such an accord would be the fundamental articles of the faith necessary for salvation. Sacramental theology would form a secondary layer of fundamentals on which the two sides could disagree without risking separation. Wake was willing to compromise on a key element of the Book of Common Prayer by offering to eliminate the famous Black Rubric, added by John Knox in order to eliminate any vestiges of papism from the liturgy.[12] Dupin also was willing to compromise by stating that the pope should be merely the first bishop among equals and should not have authority to interfere in the affairs of the French church.[13]

Wake's efforts suffered a severe blow when Dupin died in 1719, but Wake carried on a similar correspondence from 1719–31 with one of Dupin's colleagues at the Sorbonne, Piers de Girardin. Such efforts had little chance for any real success in the era following the revocation of both the Edict of Nantes and the Gallican Articles. However, Wake was interested in a much wider union than with the Gallicans alone and worked with Turretin in favor of a pan-Protestant accord based on the fundamental articles. Part of his interest in this project came as a result of his sympathies for the exiled Huguenot community and he became intricately involved in a host of theological controversies not only in Switzerland and Geneva, but in Holland and Prussia as well.[14]

Turretin was an important ally for Wake because of his stature within the Republic of Letters and his influence within the academy, the Company of Pastors, and the Genevan City Council. Both Turretin and Wake realized that the conflict between Bern and Lausanne over the Formula Consensus was an important chapter in the history of reunification. Both the Lutherans and Anglicans were against the strict Reformed statements on the subject of predestination. The removal of such creeds from the Reformed camp would help open the door toward negotiations with the Lutherans.

LeClerc was correct, however, that the Lutheran theologians of Saxony were against Protestant union. However, when the elector of Saxony converted to Roman Catholicism, the Lutherans were beginning to realize that it could well be in their best interest to negotiate with their Reformed and Anglican brethren.[15]

Foremost among the Lutheran theologians, who greatly assisted Turretin in his efforts at union, was Daniel Ernst Jablonski of Prussia. On 31 July 1716, Jablonski outlined to the king of Prussia the main similarities and differences between the Lutheran and Reformed churches. The areas of agreement included the Lord's Supper, Christology, predestination, and grace. The differences centered on church ceremonies such as in the Lord's Supper, auricular confession, the sign of the cross, and the use of surplices.[16]

Having outlined the major issues involved, Jablonski discussed a possible compromise. First, both sides need to admit that their differences did not affect any fundamental point of doctrine and should not be the cause of schism. Second, both sides should allow each other to maintain ceremonial differences while they could set up a joint commission to investigate what ceremonies were particularly objectionable and could be set aside. Lastly, both churches should adopt the name "evangelical" and thus form a united front against Rome.[17]

The efforts at reunification would not move along these lines, however, because it was impossible to divorce political issues from theological ones. Both Frederick I and his son, Frederick William I were in favor of union. Frederick I's second wife, Sophie Charlotte, was George I's sister, and her connections with the Hanoverian court and with Leibniz broadened the Prussian king's predisposition in favor of ecclesiastical accord. Political and theological differences, however, made the possibility of real progress extremely difficult. George I's chief advisor, Count Andreas Gottlieb Bernstorff, was lukewarm at best about the project, and personal animosities between George I and Frederick William I further complicated matters. In addition, it was difficult to get the theologians to agree. In 1703, Frederick I called a meeting in Berlin, between Lutheran and Reformed theologians to discuss accord. Included among the Lutheran delegation was Gerhard Walter Molanus, the most ecumenically minded of the group, who was well known for his lengthy correspondence with the French Bishop

Jacques Bénigne Bossuet. Samuel Strimesius was chief among the Reformed advocates for union and he later composed a number of treatises on the subject of ecclesiastical accord. The colloquy at Berlin did not achieve any long-term success, however, because opponents to union published an advance copy of a proposal for a union, which was given secretly to the king by John Joseph Winkler, the Lutheran superintendent in Magdeburg.[18]

By June of 1719, Wake informed Turretin that the differences between England and Prussia would probably preclude union. Furthermore, Count Andreas Gottlieb Bernsdorff, one of George's key diplomat in relations with Prussia, was not consistently zealous about the reunification project. He felt that it would be wiser not to discuss union for fear of destroying the negotiations between the Catholic and Protestant states of Germany regarding the oppression of Protestants in Catholic areas.[19]

In 1722, at a conference in Regensburg, two ecumenically minded, Lutheran theologians of pietist leanings, Johann Christian Klemm and Christoff Mattaeus Pfaff, were able to obtain approval from the Protestant princes for a plan of accord based on the fundamental articles. However, by this time, the vast majority of Lutheran theologians condemned the project and it never made any progress.[20]

The attempts at reunification, therefore, faced the dual difficulty of overcoming both theological and political obstacles. Wake and Turretin had attempted a political settlement while trying to remove the major theological objections to the project. By 1721, Turretin despaired that even his Reformed brethren were experiencing internal conflicts over the need to update the liturgy and could not even agree on a revised version of the Psalter.[21]

Although political realities and theological conservatism ultimately led to the failure of Wake's and Turretin's attempts at reunification, the dream of a united Protestant front was a major factor in shaping Turretin's theological views. He formed a position that focused on the "essentials" of belief, while practically ignoring the subtleties of theology that had characterized his Reformed, scholastic predecessors.

Turretin on the Fundamental Articles

Turretin's position on the issue of the "fundamental articles"[22] of the faith provides insights into his move away from the Reformed scholasticism of his father and toward a rationalistic or an enlightened form of orthodoxy. In addition, it indicates one of the most important areas in which Reformed theology was being influenced by the Remonstrant tradition. This is not surprising, considering his close affinity with the French Reformed tradition of the Academy of Saumur. This had been closed in 1681, four years prior to the Revocation of the Edict of Nantes. The Academy of Saumur had used fundamental articles in a manner similar to the Remonstrants in attempts to forge an accord with the various Protestant confessions of Europe.

The Reformed use of fundamental articles had both positive and polemical origins. In a positive sense, it grew out of the catechetical method of theological instruction and developed into an integral aspect of Reformed prolegomena by the mid-seventeenth century. Ironically, J. A. Turretin's father, Francis, was primarily responsible for integrating fundamental articles into his prolegomena to theology. It should be noted, however, that fundamental articles were used extensively in the sixteenth century, primarily within the context of ecclesiology. This was the case with Calvin. Some sixteenth-century Reformed theologians, such as Johannes Maccovius, in his *Loci communes* (1650), used fundamental articles within their prolegomena, but they did not go as far as Francis Turretin did in making fundamental articles foundational to their entire theological system.

The polemical source for the Protestant discussion of fundamental articles was the Counter-Reformation argument that Scripture was obscure and that only the church could decide the essential articles of the faith. As a result, Roman Catholic scholars argued that all of Scripture as well as church traditions should properly be classified as fundamental. It is not surprising, therefore, that the Jesuit Adam Tanner argued in 1601, at the Colloquy of Ratisbon, that even such arcane issues from the Apocrypha as whether or not Tobias's dog wagged its tail should properly be classified as fundamental.[23]

According to Otto Ritschl, the Protestant response to the Roman Catholic approach to fundamental articles took three forms. First, the response from the Remonstrant and Socinian side of the Protestant camp reduced the fundamental articles to those doctrines necessary for salvation which Scripture expressly denotes as fundamental. They took a narrow view of fundamental articles that limited the number of articles necessary for salvation. This allowed for a significant amount of latitude on what they considered to be secondary points, which one could differ on without risking separation. The second position was that of the traditionalists, such as George Calixtus, a Lutheran, who attributed the fundamental articles to the pronouncements of the ecumenical councils of the early church. Lastly, the majority of Reformed and Lutheran theologians grounded the fundamentals within the salvific doctrines of the faith that are revealed in Scripture.[24]

The importance of the views of such thinkers as Jacob Acontius (d. 1566) and Hugo Grotius (1583–1645), was that their position became dominant within the Reformed camp by the beginning of the eighteenth century. Acontius contended in his *Stratagemata Satanae* (1564), dedicated to Queen Elizabeth, that Satan had succeeded in his strategy of dividing the Reformation. Acontius formulated the idea of separating primary articles of faith necessary for salvation from secondary articles in which there can be disagreement without affecting unity. Part of Acontius's justification for this separation was his belief in the Noetic, or intellectual, effects of the Fall that make it impossible to understand for certain doctrines other than those which are explicitly taught in Scripture. He pled for mercy upon heretics on this basis, noting that they, as opposed to atheists, held to scriptural authority.[25]

Grotius, whose evidential approach to apologetics and legal expertise were so influential in the Remonstrant tradition, used fundamental articles as a basis for ecclesiastical union with even the Roman Catholic church, which he considered to be merely one church among many. Although Grotius affirmed the Virgin Birth and the Second Coming of Christ, he denied that the Trinity and the two natures of Christ were fundamental articles because they were added in the Constantinian era and were not explicitly taught in Scripture.[26]

The danger to Reformed orthodoxy of this position was that it emphasized Christian practice to the potential exclusion of many of the historic doctrines of the post-Nicene church. For example, the Socinians claimed that any article deemed to be fundamental must be clearly stated in Scripture. This removed such doctrines as the Trinity or speculation about the nature of election from the category of fundamentals. In addition, the Remonstrants advocated a cause-and-effect relationship between acceptance of fundamental articles and saving faith. The Reformed position, conversely, advocated that those who have saving faith will believe the fundamentals.[27]

The use of fundamental articles as a basis for ecclesiastical accord had particular relevance for the French Reformed church, which was at the forefront of attempts at reconciliation with the Lutherans and the Church of England.[28] The Academy of Saumur, founded by Du Plessis-Mornay, was quite active in such ecumenical endeavors. At Saumur, Isaac D'Huisseau composed the anonymous *Réunion du christianisme*[29] in which he argued for religious toleration even for the Socinians on the basis of fundamental articles. D'Huisseau asserted that, even though Scripture does not identify the fundamental articles in formal terms, they were clearly revealed in Scripture and have been historically and universally accepted by Christians of various theological persuasions. Those doctrines which the theologian deduced from Scripture through the use of reason, by contrast, festered as a kind of "gangrene poisoning" that has splintered the church for centuries.[30]

Although D'Huisseau was Reformed, his stance was virtually identical to the Arminian or narrow use of fundamental articles. Alfred Soman has pointed out remarkable similarities between the *Réunion* and Jacob Arminius's published speech entitled *A Compendium of Religious Quarrels Between Christians* (1606).[31] It is not surprising, therefore, that the position of D'Huisseau would result in a backlash by such theologians as Pierre Jurieu who not only recognized the Arminian tendencies in the work, but considered it too conciliatory toward the Roman Catholics during an era when the Huguenots were allowed only those benefits explicitly permitted under the Edict of Nantes.

Although the position of D'Huisseau remained a minority opinion within the Reformed camp for the remainder of the seventeenth century, it came to dominate the Reformed scene by the middle of the next century. The main protagonist in this shift was Jean-Alphonse Turretin. Jean-Alphonse was not alone in this development. Along with Samuel Werenfels and Jean-Frédéric Ostervald, the so-called Swiss triumvirate were seen as champions of enlightened orthodoxy. Furthermore, the Republic of Letters provided them with a forum for using fundamental articles as a basis for ecclesiastical union.

Jean-Alphonse Turretin's approach to fundamental articles was very similar to the one that dominated the Remonstrant camp. This is reflected in his close relationship with the Remonstrant theologian and literary critic, Jean LeClerc, who, ironically, had been educated in Geneva and had studied under Francis Turretin before rejecting the Reformed faith for a system that he felt squared more with Scripture and with reason.

Turretin's most famous work, in which he outlined his views of the fundamental articles, was his *Nubes testium* or *(Cloud of Witnesses)* published in 1719. It is not surprising that he dedicated the work to William Wake, the archbishop of Canterbury. Turretin and Wake carried on a lengthy correspondence on the prospects of church union. Wake also campaigned vigorously for a complete union of Anglican, Reformed, and Lutheran confessions throughout Europe.[32]

The *Cloud of Witnesses* was essentially a textbook outlining the basis for union. Such accord, however, never materialized and, in spite of Wake's and Turretin's tireless efforts on its behalf, its prospects were considered dim even during their lifetimes. LeClerc expressed this sentiment in a letter to Turretin dated 5 June 1710, saying that the divisions within the Church of England were too distracting to allow them to focus on any kind of union with the Reformed churches on the continent.[33]

In spite of the odds against ever achieving such ecclesiastical union, Turretin pressed forward in his negotiations with leaders of both church and state. He even pushed for Lutheran worship to be allowed in Geneva, which was accomplished in 1707. His *Cloud of Witnesses* served as a rallying cry for those who were predisposed toward such accord.[34]

The emphasis on practice was the hallmark of the Arminian, as well as the Pietist, critique of the Reformed and Lutheran scholastics and Turretin made it one of his primary points. Defining the essence of religious belief as reflecting itself in pious, prudent conduct, Turretin emphasized the need to act with kindness and with an open mind toward those who differed in adiaphoric or secondary matters. Although the emphasis on *praxis* was characteristic of the Remonstrant tradition on the subject, Reformed theologians such as Johann Heinrich Heidegger and Francis Turretin refused to yield ground on this issue and believed that the fundamentals are invalidated without correct practice.[35]

It should also be noted that, although Jean-Alphonse Turretin agreed with the antischolastic bias of the Enthusiasts, he was not at all an advocate of their particular form of theology. He ardently opposed them on a number of points, primarily their emphasis on extrabiblical revelation and their opposition to rationalism. By contrast, Jean-Alphonse revealed a rationalistic view of the work of the Holy Spirit when he stated that the Spirit works through reason when the individual understands the doctrines necessary for saving faith. One is saved, therefore, by an intellectual assent to the fundamental articles.[36]

Jean-Alphonse defined the fundamental articles as "those principles of religion, which so relate to the essence and foundation of it, and are of so great importance, that without them religion cannot stand, or at least will be destitute of a chief and necessary part."

In other words, fundamental articles are those doctrines which are necessary for salvation. The problem comes with determining the specific identity of these beliefs. In a manner consistent Arminianism, he prefers to insist upon the absolute minimum number of articles in order to allow for the widest possible measure of agreement.[37]

Turretin noted that one can determine the difference between fundamental and nonfundamental articles from both nature and from Scripture. From nature, one can discover basic moral precepts based on the human conscience. Scripture further illumines those doctrines which are fundamental, those which are secondary and those which are not essential at all. In either case, fundamental articles are clearly revealed. Turretin explained:

> Certainly the design of religion is not to exercise the wit and understandings of men, nor to burden and overwhelm their memories with so vast a number of all sorts of truths; but to implant in their minds the fear and love of God, and excite them to certain duties.[38]

Having established the basis for determining the fundamentals of the faith, Turretin proceeded to discuss several principles for defining them. The first was that Christians have an obligation to believe only those truths which are clearly taught in Scripture.[39] God, as the supremely wise "instructor of men," uses due caution to make sure that he reveals the fundamental truths in a clear manner. This concept has the necessary inference that people of different intellectual capacities can all recognize the fundamentals because they are so clear. He wrote: "Fundamentals are plain, adapted to common capacities, and free from all subtle and intricate distinctions of the schools."[40] Since the majority of the authors of Scripture were common men of limited education, it makes sense that the essential truths of the Bible would be easy to understand. This is obviously a response to the Counter-Reformation argument against the perspicuity of Scripture.[41]

Furthermore, God alone has the ability to determine which beliefs are absolutely essential for salvation so it would be impossible to compile a precise list of fundamental articles. Turretin reasoned that the well-intentioned seeker who truly desires to know God should have no difficulty learning what he needs to know in order to be saved.[42]

In addition, the fundamentals are few in number. This was a common notion in both the Remonstrant and the Socinian approach to the subject. Socinus had made precisely the same point as did Grotius. In fact, Turretin's close confidant, Jean LeClerc, made it as well in his first published work in 1681.[43]

Turretin criticized Reformed scholasticism by stating that the fundamentals relate to religious piety and never contradict godly living. The main design of the Christian gospel is piety, but Turretin cautioned that not every idea that results in piety is fundamental. He was careful at this point to distinguish his position from that of the Enthusiasts.[44]

He continued by arguing that many of the distinctive Nicene doctrines such as the Trinity may still be fundamental even though they are not clearly revealed.[45] He explained:

> If therefore, the mode and circumstances, the causes and adjuncts of a thing are to be accounted fundamental, it will follow that an abundance of things, of which we can have no clear perceptions, and which do far exceed our capacities, are nevertheless fundamental.[46]

On this point, at least, he distinguished his position from that of the Socinians. Turretin did emphasize that reason plays a major role in determining the fundamental articles, but he was prepared to allow for some element of biblical mystery in the areas of the Trinity and the Incarnation.

However, it is impossible to determine the exact number of fundamental articles. Some doctrines are fundamental to those who have received a great deal of revelation, while those who have not been exposed to the gospel are responsible for a far lesser number of necessary truths. He then listed several doctrines that are essential for salvation such as Christ's crucifixion, that he was the true Son of God, that one is saved by faith alone, and that the Christian becomes a new creature at the point of regeneration.[47] Turretin asked:

> How many truths precisely ought he to know, that he may be truly saved? I will answer in a word. Let a man but sincerely love truth, and seek it heartily, begging help from God and making use of those who are capable of giving him light; and let him not omit, or neglect any proper means that he may make continual progress in the ways of truth and holiness; and such a one may certainly conclude that God will not be wanting to him, not suffer him to remain ignorant of anything necessary for him to know, or if he is unknowledgeable of any necessary truth, or does err and make mistakes in some areas, God will graciously pardon him, even as a father does his own children.[48]

This argument carries with it the inference that the content of the fundamental articles developed gradually throughout biblical history. Because God progressively revealed himself to man throughout Scripture, the patriarchs of the Old Testament possessed less of a knowledge of revelation than did Moses who, in turn, possessed still less than did the Apostles. The guiding principle in such an observation was that God holds a man responsible only for the revelation that God has provided. When God reveals a lesser degree of light, the number of fundamental articles correspondingly decreases. Turretin wrote:

> Fundamental articles are not the same to all men, but differ according to the different degrees of revelation, and according to the different capacities and circumstances of men. The reason is plain; for since God has made very different revelations of himself, and has given very different capacities to men and has placed them in stations and circumstances that most widely differ; it is therefore impossible that all men should be obliged to the same measure of knowledge, or the same standard of faith.[49]

This idea of progressive revelation was not new. Calvin held to a form of it, but did not include the rationalistic tone that Turretin gave to the subject.[50] In addition, such Reformed scholars as Pierre Jurieu and Francis Turretin held that the Old Testament saints possessed as many of the fundamentals as did the members of the Apostolic church.[51]

The principle of degrees of revelation applies not merely to biblical history, but also to the various circumstances of mankind. The native in Africa who never heard of Christ or the retarded child who possessed a limited ability of understanding would have to believe a far lesser number of fundamental doctrines for salvation. Turretin emphasized that all of the fundamental articles that concern the existence of God are biblical presuppositions that can be demonstrated through natural theology. This was important because it answers the problem of the unbelieving pagan who has never heard the gospel. This individual does receive the fundamental elements of the faith and is responsible for acting upon them and can conceivably be saved without special revelation.[52]

Having provided several principles for understanding the fundamentals, Turretin turned to the question of separation, which was central for his plans for a pan-Protestant union. In a manner consistent with the Reformed position, he argued that one must separate only in areas of difference in primary articles (Galatians 1:8–9; Corinthians 6:14–15). One must treat those who differ on secondary points as Christian brothers and practice forbearance in such areas of disagreement. The Apostle Paul made this same point himself in reference to his conflict with the Apostle Peter in the Jerusalem Council of Acts 15. Furthermore, if Christians were to practice separation over all minor doctrinal matters, the resultant proliferation of sects would render the Protestant cause powerless.[53]

Turretin's stance on separation has particular relevance for his position on religious toleration in cases of theological error. Individuals may err in two different ways with regard to the fundamentals. They can either deny the fundamentals or add to them. He cautioned the believer to be extremely careful not to err in either manner. In addition, one possessed the perfect right to be dogmatic concerning the truth of the fundamentals. However, in non-fundamental matters, one should refrain from expressing an opinion carelessly because of the possibility of causing division.[54]

Turretin emphasized that the exegete of Scripture must admit his limitations and admit that toleration is the best means of winning over the heterodox. In addition, denominational squabbles have provided unbelievers with powerful reasons to oppose the practical efficacy of Christianity. When Christians practice tolerance, this argument is ineffective.[55]

Turretin's position on tolerance bears striking resemblance to that of Isaac D'Huisseau and Sebastian Castellio. Ironically, Turretin's stance gained dominance within the Genevan Academy that Calvin himself had founded. Castellio had, in a sense, finally triumphed over Calvin.

Turretin's concept of toleration, however, did not extend to the Roman Catholics, whose sacramental system contradicted the fundamental concept of salvation by grace through faith. Submission to the church in matters of faith left the door open for all sorts of errors because of man's fallibility, meaning that both the Roman Catholic concepts of papal supremacy and conciliarism were also open for heterodoxy. The danger he saw in allowing any group to legislate on such weighty matters as the determination of Christian doctrine lay in the possibility of them adding to or subtracting from what God has clearly taught in Scripture.[56]

Secondly, he disagreed with the Roman Catholic position that any doctrine that the Bible teaches is fundamental. He commented: "But, as had already been observed, who can imagine that all things found in Scripture, of whatever sort, as proper names of men, places, animals, plants, and all circumstances of the most minute actions, are so necessary to be known, that none can be saved without knowledge of them?"[57] Rather, only biblical doctrines specifically related to salvation can be fundamental truths. Other teachings concerning chronologies and matters that do not specifically relate to doctrinal truth can easily be discarded from the list of biblical essentials. One should not argue over such non-fundamentals since they have relatively little significance upon the spiritual lives of believers.[58] The differences with the Roman church do not center on speculative doctrines, but on practical, fundamental ones.

However, should the Roman church reform itself on the fundamental articles, Turretin sees no reason why negotiations toward union would not be possible. He wrote:

> In a word, let them shake off the popish yoke which . . . is intolerable; let no violence be ever offered to conscience; let all men judge of religion from the word of God only; let everything that savors of idolatry be banished from their worship and then we shall not be backward, but readily concert measures towards a reconciliation and union with them.[59]

In contrast to his pessimism toward union with the Roman Catholics, Turretin held that the Reformed and Lutheran confessions should unite because of their agreement on the fundamentals. Interestingly enough, the Reformed orthodox had long been attempting such a union, arguing that their differences were on secondary points such as the nature of Christ's presence in the Eucharist. Turretin's desire for negotiations on this basis was not new. However, he went to such extremes in simplifying the distinctive doctrines of the two camps that their positions were virtually indistinguishable from one another.[60]

Turretin explained that both Lutherans and Reformed churches believe in the Augsburg Confession and in the doctrine of *sola Scriptura*. The primary disagreement centered upon the nature of Christ's presence in the Eucharist. Both Lutheran and Reformed theologians agreed that Christ is truly present but differed over whether this implies a physical or spiritual presence. Turretin avoided the issue of the nature of the *communicatio idiomatum*, preferring to simplify the real differences that remained between the two positions as scholastic subtleties that obscured their true agreement. He seemed unaware that the Lutherans considered the nature of the Lord's Supper to be a primary fundamental and the major stumbling block to union.[61]

Turretin pointed out that the Reformed doctrine of the nature of predestination and the order of God's decrees were not fundamental either and should not be considered a stumbling block to accord with other Protestant confessions. He wrote:

> Why do theologians argue among themselves over the order of the decrees with so much passion and pride when God decreed everything by his own most simple act? Those who conduct themselves the best according to the designs of God are those who leave to Him the hidden things and concern themselves with understanding the things He has revealed. Those who believe will be saved and those who do not will be condemned. To know this is to know enough concerning the decrees of God.[62]

This refusal to speculate on the decrees of God was characteristic of the position of Isaac D'Huisseau. The problem with the conservative orthodox position, Turretin argued, lies in the insistence that all the minute aspects related to soteriology are essential to the faith. He condemned the resultant disharmony between believers over such issues that form, at best, secondary and speculative ideas. He preferred to emphasize divine sovereignty and simply blame man for his own sin without specifying the order of decrees. All who truly repent will be saved while God is master over all the affairs of men. He rejected supralapsarianism as contrary to natural law and emphasized the basic knowledge necessary for salvation.[63]

Turretin charged that the Reformed churches should soften the harshness of their definition of predestination. In a letter to Wake, he noted that he had only commented once on predestination in his *Compendium of Protestant Dissent* in order to minimize theological controversy.[64]

He concluded that so much agreement on even the controversial area of sacramental theology provided a basis for negotiating an accord with the other Protestant groups. He particularly favored agreement with the Lutherans, citing the example of Melanchthon's friendly relationship with Calvin. Turretin explained: "Previously, therefore, it has been plainly shown, that there is so great an agreement among Protestants, and that their disagreement is so inconsiderable, that they may well exercise mutual forbearance, and enter into a hearty union with one another." If such communion was denied, the Christian law of charity would be violated.[65]

Turretin ended the *Cloud of Witnesses* by suggesting several avenues for promoting "agreement and forbearance." First, one should maintain a deep sense of true faith toward God and examine the relative importance of each doctrine in a prudent manner. Second, one should exercise extreme caution in insisting upon many of the "more obscure" teachings of Scripture and obey the precept "that the Holy Scripture is the only rule of our faith" as opposed to the "human" decisions of Roman councils and popes. Third, the student of Scripture, in spite of his expertise in biblical exegesis, must admit the possibility that one can err and as a result, one should handle the Bible in a humble manner. Minor issues of interpretation must never be allowed to break the bond of love between believers who have the responsibility of sharing the Lord's Table when there is agreement on the essentials of the faith.[66]

In spite of the failure of his attempts to forge an ecclesiastical union between the various Protestant confessions, Jean-Alphonse Turretin reduced the scope of the fundamental articles so much that many of the distinctive reformed doctrines were relegated to nonfundamental status. This was especially the case in the area of progressive revelation in which the Old Testament saints could be saved with an understanding of a lesser number of fundamental than their apostolic counterparts. His assertion that the heathen or the mentally handicapped needed to believe fewer fundamentals than those who had access to the New Testament was a major departure from the Reformed position and reflected his rationalistic emphasis. The implication is that, in some cases, one does not need special revelation in order to be saved. Such teachings reflected his Salmurian and Arminian predisposition. Clearly, his views on the subject were closer to the Remonstrant stance than to the Reformed. Furthermore, Turretin's Arminian tendency led him toward a religious tolerance based upon the acceptance of a few basic fundamental articles, which were clearly revealed in Scripture and necessary for salvation.

Turretin's Defense of the Fundamental Articles

In the *Cloud of Witnesses,* Turretin assimilated religious faith into a kind of practical philosophy. The distinctiveness of Christianity was blurred somewhat because of Turretin's assumption that the number of fundamentals varies according to the specific circumstances of individuals. This left the possibility of salvation through mere response to natural revelation without the necessity of a knowledge of Christ. This idea elevated natural theology to a virtual autonomous position. Although Turretin would certainly have denied the independent nature of natural theology, he did allow for it under special circumstances, such as when a pagan possessed absolutely no possibility of a knowledge of special revelation. It was precisely this doctrine that aroused objections from the circles of the conservative theologians.

The *Cloud of Witnesses* became the source of considerable controversy in 1727 when a young Vaudois minister, Théodore Crinsoz de Bionens, composed an anonymous attack on it entitled, *An Investigation of the Fundamental Articles.* Turretin countered with a defense of his original thesis in which he strengthened and clarified his original arguments.

Ironically, the most famous response to the *Cloud of Witnesses* did not come from his conservative critics, but from Bionens, a former candidate for the ministry at Lausanne, who had refused to sign the *Serment d'Association* in 1722. He had remained persistent in his opposition to the dictates of Bern. Bionens stayed in Lausanne until 1723, when he accepted a pastorate in Nyon. He developed a good degree of expertise in Old Testament studies and composed several treatises on prophetic and apocalyptic literature. He also pointed an accusing finger at Turretin for denying the statement of the Apostle Paul that Christ is the sole foundation for the Christian faith.

In Turretin's defense of his treatise on the fundamental articles of religion, he outlined the reasons for Bionens's attack as well as Bionens's objections. The affair began when Bionens, still suffering emotionally from his expulsion from the Lausanne Academy for his failure to adhere to Bern's obligatory oath, composed a treatise condemning the requirement. After having been encouraged by several of his friends and colleagues in Lausanne to publish the work, Bionens in October 1723 sent it to Turretin for comment. Turretin was the most logical referee of the manuscript because of his role as an intermediary in the Lausanne affair. Much to Bionens's surprise, however, Turretin did not like the treatise because of its advocacy of a reduced role of the state in the affairs of the church. Receiving Turretin's criticisms, Bionens was quite upset and wrote to Turretin to attempt to gain his support. This accomplished nothing, however, and Turretin wrote back that further discussion would not be of any help.

Bionens attempted to have his work published without Turretin's support, but was turned down both at Bern and later at Geneva. Bionens accused Turretin of influencing the Scholarques of Geneva to stop the publication, but Turretin had no authority to have the publication halted. Bionens's suspicions were given further credence when, in 1726, he attempted to have his annotated translation of the Book of Job published in Geneva. The work was rejected because of his disagreement with the traditional interpretation of the famous passage in Job 19 concerning the resurrection. Bionens was shocked that the censor would refuse the work on this basis since Calvin himself had interpreted the passage in a similar manner. Although Bionens was able to finally publish the translation in Rotterdam in 1729, he believed that Turretin had effectively blackballed him among the intellectual community in Geneva.

There is no doubt that Bionens composed his attack on Turretin's *Cloud of Witnesses* out of a personal grudge. He expressed this sentiment by stating: "The door of the publisher, [in which such] a dictator in the Republic of Letters [assumes] the power of closing to anyone he wants, ought to be opened to all those of good intentions. The good public demands that one oppose enterprises of this nature." This statement was so shocking to the friends of Turretin that Ostervald comforted Turretin with the comment that he did not have the kind of personality that could ever be that of a tyrant. Turretin was a sickly man who did not have such an imposing stature.

Bionens disagreed with several aspects of Turretin's treatise on the fundamentals of the Christian faith. First, he disagreed with Turretin's definition of the fundamentals. Bionens explained that the fundamental articles should be such that every person endowed with common sense should believe them for membership in the church and for salvation. Second, Bionens believed that the fundamental articles should be declared formally in specific terms. One should not take as fundamental those truths which have to be deduced. In other words, if the Bible does not explicitly state that a certain doctrine is fundamental, one should not take it to be so. Third, Bionens held to a fixed number of fundamental articles for all people in all places, circumstances, and intellectual capacities.

Bionens argued that Turretin's definition of the fundamental articles was too vague and confusing especially on the issue of progressive revelation. He took issue with Turretin's stance that the Old Testament saints or the heathen could be saved with a knowledge of a lesser number of fundamental articles than the New Testament believers. Bionens stated that this left the possibility open for salvation without a knowledge of Christ. He argued further that Turretin had confused fundamental articles with the truths of "edification," which are intended for those who are already saved. God holds believers responsible according to their ability to understand, but a minimum knowledge of Christ is necessary for salvation. Bionens also preferred a more specific listing of the fundamentals that could still serve as a basis for negotiations for ecclesiastical accord. He cautioned against a list so short that it could eliminate many of the distinctive doctrines of the Christian faith. Bionens based his own definition of fundamental articles on 1 Corinthians 3:11: "For no one can lay a foundation than the one already laid, which is Jesus Christ." The possibility of salvation apart from a specific knowledge of Christ would destroy the very foundation of the faith.

Turretin's response was three times longer than Bionens's original treatise.[67] Turretin first noted the bad humor of Bionens and asserted that one should never enter into disputes over religious controversies when the passions dominate an individual's reason.[68] Turretin clarified his definition of the fundamentals by stating that these articles are those which every person endowed with a common measure of reasoning ability, with adequate time and means for instruction, needs to believe in order to become a member of the church and be saved.[69]

Bionens argued that it is often very difficult for scholars to determine what is clear. For the nonscholar, it was much more difficult to determine what doctrines are clear. Turretin countered that such an argument carries an air of Pyrrhonism. Turretin defined a clear truth as one that both scholar and layman can comprehend. The more educated, however, would have a fuller understanding of such fundamentals.[70]

Bionens had accused Turretin of holding to a contradictory position when Turretin stated that there were not only few fundamental articles but their number was also indeterminable. Bionens related the issue of the justice of God to the number of fundamental truths. He wrote that it is a contradiction to say that a man can be saved even though he ignored one of the fundamental truths. Either the truth is fundamental and necessary for salvation or it is not. If the truth is not necessary for salvation, it is not fundamental.[71]

Turretin responded that the number of fundamentals is generally small but not fixed. The idea of a fixed number of fundamentals for all people was especially objectionable for Turretin because it would provide an unfair advantage to the Christian scholar and would destroy his concept of progressive revelation that was basic to his entire theological system. He argued that God holds individuals accountable only for the amount of light that they have received. He argued that Scripture itself does not list a specific number of fundamentals. The individual who truly seeks after God will know a sufficient number of the fundamentals in order to be saved. There is, therefore, no need for a specific listing of the fundamental articles.[72]

Bionens argued that Turretin confused the fundamental truths for Christians with those intended for Jews. Obviously, these fundamentals are different because the Hebrews would have to believe in the future coming of a Messiah and could not be expected to have a specific knowledge of Christ. In addition, God places few demands upon infants, or upon those who are retarded or do not have the ability to understand the gospel. Turretin countered that he agreed with Bionens that the number of fundamentals varies according to the biblical dispensation or the individual level of intelligence. Bionens's objection really, therefore, was in agreement with Turretin's own views.[73] On this point, Turretin defended his stance on progressive revelation and progressive capacities to understand that revelation. God, as the fair and honest judge, cannot evaluate every person on the same grounds. This would be unfair. God must judge each individual according to the level of revelation received.[74]

Turretin explained that just as God has provided man with the ability to discover how to nourish his own body, he has also provided the ability to know how to nourish the soul.[75] God provided both natural and supernatural sources of such knowledge. However, one cannot say that all men throughout history have received the same amount of such information. God demands more of those to whom he has given more revelation. The number of fundamental articles, therefore, must vary according to the situation of the individual and only God himself knows for certain the amount that is necessary for each person.[76]

Turretin's response to Bionens by no means ended the debate. In fact, it fanned the flames even further. Part of the reason for this was that Turretin had resorted to attacking Bionens personally by stating that he "was stuck on himself."[77] It is not surprising that Bionens responded with yet another treatise entitled *Apologie de Mr. de Bionens, Contre un ecrit intitulé Défense de la dissertation de Mr. Turretin, sur les articles fondamentaux de la religion* (1727). This response was published in Yverdon by the same Pietist-minded publisher of the first volume, Jean-Jacques Genath. Unlike in the first work, however, Bionens now decided that it was time to remove the mask of anonymity and attack Turretin more openly. Bionens repeated the entire episode of the rejection of his treatise on the *Serment d'Association* and included several passages from this work that the Genevan censors had rejected.[78]

The majority of those who followed the debate favored Turretin primarily because of his international reputation and stature, but also because of the weaknesses of Bionens's arguments. Most of the respondents regretted the brashness of Bionens and viewed the entire episode as more of an embarrassment than anything else.

One respondent, Turretin's confidant Elie Saurin, assured him of the absurdity of Bionens's charges. Bionens had asked Saurin to have the work published, but Saurin refused on the grounds of his friendship with Turretin. Saurin agreed that the number of fundamental articles varies according to the individual, but pointed out that in certain aspects the fundamentals of religion are always the same. He explained that there are a number of core fundamentals that do not change, such as the existence of a personal God, but others do change, such as the specific knowledge of God's redemptive work in Christ. Saurin allowed for the possibility of salvation outside of Christ if one lacked the natural faculties to reject a knowledge of Christ or if one lived in circumstances in which it would be impossible to know about him.[79] Samuel Werenfels commented that it was Bionens's "practice that determines his theory," meaning that Bionens had allowed his personal feelings to play a major role in his theological critique of the *Cloud of Witnesses*.[80]

The entire affair was much more damaging to Bionens than to Turretin. The Lausanne scholar had already lost his ministerial status and therefore, was suspect from the point of view of the advocates of the Formula Consensus. By attacking Turretin, he lost any support from the more liberal-minded theologians who opposed the Formula. In fact, according to Henri Vuilleumier, the conservative faction was quite happy to see their theological opponents fighting among themselves.[81]

This episode, in spite of its personal nature, highlighted Turretin's position on the fundamental articles as well as his form of enlightened orthodoxy. Turretin had constructed a theological system that emphasized the practical aspects of theology, especially personal piety and the amount of information that one needs to know in order to gain salvation. In addition, he answered the question concerning the "heathen in Africa who never hear of Christ." Every individual is responsible for the light that God has given him. God will judge no individual unfairly.

Turretin designed his system of fundamental truths to remove the objectionable aspects of scholastic theology that had divided the Reformed church from their Protestant brethren. It was also designed to eliminate many of the objections of deists and atheists against the Catholic faith. It was virulently anti-Roman Catholic, however, since Turretin dreamed of forming a united Protestant front against the unorthodox and Pyrrhonical teachings of Rome. By building a theological system that was essentially practical and simple, Turretin changed many of the distinctive aspects of Reformed theology and eliminated both theological creeds and speculations.

Conclusion

Jean-Alphonse Turretin's enlightened orthodoxy represented a complete break with Reformed scholasticism. This new form of orthodoxy elevated reason as the main arbiter in religious affairs and advocated the reduction of the fundamentals of the faith to those doctrines strictly necessary for salvation. By reducing the scope of theological discourse, enlightened orthodoxy served as a basis for a pan-Protestant union in which all objectionable doctrines could be virtually ignored. Any discussion of the decrees of God concerning election or reprobation were no longer relevant. Arguments over the nature of Christ's presence in the Eucharist were also beside the point. Furthermore, the doctrine of biblical accommodation provided a basis for squaring the more objectionable parts of the Old Testament with reason and the ethics of the Sermon on the Mount. Scripture could, therefore, be authoritative without being inerrant.

In analyzing the context and development of enlightened orthodoxy, the writer has endeavored to answer four questions: What was the nature of the Reformed scholastic system of theology in Geneva that Jean-Alphonse Turretin found so objectionable? Second, how did the liberal party at the Academy of Geneva, led by Jean-Robert Chouet and Louis Tronchin, set the stage for Jean-Alphonse Turretin's work in breaking the back of the old scholastic system of education? Third, what was the nature of Jean-Alphonse Turretin's system of enlightened orthodoxy? Lastly, how did Jean-Alphonse Turretin apply his theological position to change the theological climate in Geneva as well as in other parts of the Swiss confederation?

This work has sought to show that Jean-Alphonse Turretin's views on the subject of religious authority were not all that revolutionary. They were the natural outgrowth of the direction that the liberal party at the academy had set well before the younger Turretin enrolled at the academy. The new scientific culture of Cartesianism penetrated only gradually into the academy and did not immediately replace the Aristotelian framework of the scholastics. Only by the early eighteenth century were the methodologies of scientific experiments and mathematics accepted as integral parts of the academic curriculum. The scholastic framework was rejected through the introduction of this new curriculum and through the abrogation of the Formula Consensus in 1706.

By the next generation, Newtonianism would replace Cartesianism as the model for study in physics and scientific study would gain increased importance at the expense of theology at the academy. Philosophy was an entirely separate field of study from theology at the academy, due, in part, to the suspicion of the Reformed tradition of the use of philosophy in theological matters.

Chouet set the stage for the secularization of education through his acceptance of such a separation between philosophy and theology holding that science should be studied for its own sake in order to increase the reservoir of human knowledge. Turretin's own philosophy of education reflected this bias. A more thorough knowledge of God's creation, he reasoned, could only lead to increased reverence toward the Creator.

Jean-Alphonse Turretin contributed greatly to the study of theology devoid of dogmatic demands through his emphasis upon the autonomy of human reason in all fields of study, including theology. His system of natural theology was far more extensive than his scholastic predecessors would have permitted. Natural theology became the very basis for his entire theological system thus establishing the common ground of reason with atheists and deists in order to convince them of the reasonableness of the Christian faith.

As a result of this enlarged role of natural theology, special revelation was less important than for any of his scholastic predecessors in Geneva. Although he viewed the Bible as coming from God, he limited the extent to which it could regulate Christian doctrine. One could not insist upon explicit definitions of predestination, for example, because the Bible does not clearly teach its technical aspects. One should only maintain those doctrines which are clear and necessary for salvation. The result was that Turretin failed to insist upon most of the doctrines that made Reformed theology distinct from other forms of Protestant thought. This did not alarm Turretin, however, because he believed that the scholastic insistence upon minute definitions of dogma only served to cause schism and discord among the various Protestant sects. He saw this as being counterproductive, furthermore, in an era when Protestantism needed to form a united front to combat the growing sophistication of Roman-Catholic polemics. The Catholic use of a partial form of Pyrrhonism criticized Protestantism precisely for its doc-

trine of *sola Scriptura,* which led inevitably toward disagreements
among believers as to the true interpretation of difficult passages.

One should not view Jean-Alphonse Turretin's form of enlightened orthodoxy as a rejection of scholasticism in favor of a return
to the purity of Calvin. Turretin did not make use of Calvin's primary defense of the divine authority of Scripture, the interior witness of the Holy Spirit; he limited the role of the Spirit in
regeneration to the point where salvation was virtually equivalent
to intellectual assent to a few fundamental doctrines. To prove
these truths, Turretin did not rely upon the self-authenticating nature of Scripture but used the external marks of its authority to
construct a rational defense of biblical historicity.

He relied primarily upon the marks of fulfilled prophecy and the
historical evidence of the miraculous as the marks that confirmed
the divine nature of Scripture. Importantly, such proofs resembled
the apologetic systems of Grotius and the Remonstrants LeClerc
and Limborch as well as that of Socinus and reflected little of
Calvin's approach to defending the faith.

In addition, Turretin held that Scripture did not have to be inerrant. His use of the concept of accommodation assumed that the
doctrines that Scripture taught were true, but many of the details
of chronology or of ancient history could well have been errant.
After all, he reasoned, God was accommodating himself to the
limited, ignorant minds of ancient people.

Turretin believed strongly in the concept of progressive revelation, arguing that those individuals living before the patriarchal era
would need a lesser degree of revelation in order to gain salvation
than would those living after the time of Christ. The older parts
of Scripture, therefore, were less accurate and less specific concerning "fundamental" truths than would be the revelation of
Christ in the New Testament. Turretin saw the entire scriptural
revelation as coming from God himself, but he emphasized the
Christological aspects of the New Testament as containing a fuller
degree of light.

Furthermore, Turretin's exegetical method, as exhibited in his
De Sacrae Scripturae interpretandae methodo tractatus (1728),
reflected a marked move away from Calvin. Hans Joachim Kraus
comments that Turretin's procedure was "far ahead of his time."
Kraus cites Turretin's method as consisting of five major points:

> 1) scripture is to be interpreted in the same way as any other book;
> 2) the exegete must be attentive to the interpretation of words and
> expressions; 3) he is to determine the purpose of the author in the

context and explain it as clearly as possible; 4) he is to use the natural light of reason and to bear in mind that nothing contradictory to general concepts can be transmitted and accepted; 5) the "opinions of the sacred writers" must not be judged by present-day standards and systems but must always be understood in terms of their own time.[1]

Turretin's system of theology, therefore, focused on the fundamental articles of the faith that were primarily the direct teachings of Christ himself. The major thrust of these articles were not overly complex and mainly concerned personal piety and devotion to God. The result was a theological system that emphasized moral behavior and love among Christians. Turretin still believed in the doctrines of the Trinity and the Incarnation, but the dominance of reason in his theological system made such doctrines seem almost secondary to pragmatic and ethical concerns. In this respect, Turretin's enlightened orthodoxy resembled the antischolastic reaction of the Enthusiasts, but beyond this ethical concern enlightened orthodoxy had little in common with the Pietists. Turretin believed in a closed canon and denied the reality of contemporary miracles because there were no rational means to confirm such alleged divine activity.

In the next generation, his successors, such as Jacob Vernet, who succeeded Turretin as a professor of theology at the academy, would adopt Turretin's use of reason in theology. They would also apply it to the traditional areas of theology that had been preserved from the scrutiny of reason because they were deemed "mysterious." The result was that the theologians of mid-eighteenth-century Geneva could reject or call into question doctrines such as the Trinity and the Incarnation because they did not square with reason, while the ethical and pragmatic aspects of religious thought could be maintained.

It is interesting to note that Vernet was an ancient opponent of Voltaire during the latter's tenure in Geneva in the mid-eighteenth century. Vernet objected to the fact that Voltaire was calling the theological faculty at the academy a Socinian group. Even though the term, *Socinian,* was typically a pejorative expression, Voltaire's accusation was literally correct. The theological faculty at the academy had subjected the cardinal doctrines of the Incarnation and the Trinity to the scrutiny of reason and had found them wanting. Vernet himself, in his discussion of the Apostles Creed, called Jesus of Nazareth the unique Son of God based upon his virgin birth, his godly character, and his intimate union with God. However, Vernet did describe Jesus as the unique third Person of the Trinity. Furthermore, by 1814, the revised catechism ignored the doctrines of redemption and the divinity of Christ, preferring to label Jesus as the first-born of all creation who should be honored, but certainly not worshipped.

Turretin's successors at the academy were not, therefore, advocates of the Enlightenment philosophy of Voltaire. They had, however, accepted Turretin's methodology of open theological inquiry and his secular view of education to the point that they also accepted the same presuppositions as their atheistic and deistic opponents, that religion should be subject to reason and that ethical concerns were the most beneficial results of theological study. They were not atheistic in their religious beliefs, but they had moved in that direction by adopting much of Socinian belief.

Turretin was not a harbinger of Enlightenment thought. He was the author of an enlightened orthodoxy that attempted to square the Christian faith with the methodology of the Enlightenment. Although this enlightened orthodoxy rejected many of the distinctive elements of the Reformed faith, Turretin would never have countenanced the rejection of a core of essential Christian doctrines such as the Trinity and the Incarnation. However, his emphasis upon a faith based on reason eventually led to the destruction of many of the very fundamentals of Christian belief that he had so ardently argued to preserve.

Notes

Introduction

1. On Francis Turretin see Eugène de Budé, *Vie de François Turrettini: théologien genevois, 1623–1687* (Lausanne: G. Bridel, 1891), and Gerrit Keier, *François Turrettini: sa vie, ses oeuvres et le consensus* (Kampen, the Netherlands: J. A. Bus, 1900); Timothy Phillips, "Francis Turretin's Idea of Theology and its Bearing upon his Doctrine of Scripture" (Ph.D. diss., Vanderbilt University, 1986); Paul T. Jensen, "Calvin and Turretin: A Comparison of their Soteriologies" (Ph.D. diss., University of Virginia, 1988); and John W. Beardslee, "Theological Development at Geneva under Francis and Jean-Alphonse Turretin" (Ph.D. diss., Yale University, 1956). The only major biography of Jean-Alphonse Turretin is Eugène de Budé's *Vie de J. A. Turrettini, théologien genevois (1671–1737)* (Lausanne: Georges Bridel, 1880). Budé also edited three volumes of Turretin's correspondence, *Lettres inédites addressés de 1686–1737 à J. A. Turrettini, théologien genevois* 3 vols. (Geneva: Jules Carey, 1887). Budé wrote several other biographies that touch on Jean-Alphonse Turretin; among them is his treatment of Benedict Pictet, Turretin's cousin and colleague on the theological faculty, *Vie de Bénédict Pictet, théologien genevois (1655–1724)* (Lausanne: Georges Bridel, 1874). For a discussion of Turretin's position on natural theology see Michael Heyd, "Un role nouveau pour la science: Jean-Alphonse Turrettini et les débuts de la théologie naturelle à Genève," *Revue de théologie et philosophie* 112 (1982): 25–42. Other studies include Maria C. Pitassi, "L'Apologétique Raisonnable de Jean-Alphonse Turrettini," *Apologétique 1680–1740: Sauvetage ou naufrage de la théologie,* Olivier Fatio and Maria C. Pitassi, eds. (Geneva: Publications de la Faculté de Théologie de l'Université de Genève, 1990): 180–212; Pitassi, "Un Manuscrit Genevois du XVIIIe Siècle: La Refutation du Système de Spinosa par Mr. Turrettini," *Nederlands Archief voor Kerkegeschiedenis* 68 (1988): 180–212; Martin I. Klauber, "The Context and Development of the Views of Jean-Alphonse Turrettini (1671–1737) on Religious Authority" (Ph.D. diss., University of Wisconsin-Madison, 1987); Martin I. Klauber and Glenn Sunshine, "Jean-Alphonse Turrettini on Biblical Accommodation: Calvinist or Socinian?" *Calvin Theological Journal* (April 1990): 7–27; Martin I. Klauber, "Jean-Alphonse Turrettini and the Abrogation of the Formula Consensus in Geneva," *Westminster Theological Journal* 53 (Fall 1991): 325–38.

2. Tronchin was the son of Theodore Tronchin, a professor of theology at the Academy of Geneva and a delegate to the Synod of Dort. The younger Tronchin studied under Moïse Amyraut at the Saumur Academy where he became acquainted with the doctrine of "hypothetical universalism," a doctrine that his father vehemently opposed. By 1656, Louis Tronchin became the pastor of the Lyon congregation in Geneva and in 1661 professor of theology at the academy. Tronchin was the leader of the liberal party at the Academy of Geneva that defended the Saumur doctrines. On Tronchin see Walter Rex, "Pierre Bayle,

Louis Tronchin et la querelle des Donatistes," *Bulletin de la Société de l'histoire du protestantisme français* 105 (1959): 97–121; Rex, *Essays on Pierre Bayle and Religious Controversy* (The Hague: Martinus Nijhoff, 1965); Martin I. Klauber, "Reason, Revelation and Cartesianism: Louis Tronchin and Enlightened Orthodoxy in Late Seventeenth-Century Geneva" *Church History* 59 (September 1990): 326–39.

3. The faculty at the Saumur Academy had rejected the harshness of the pronouncements of the Synod of Dort concerning the nature of predestination and had also proposed that the medieval Jewish copyists, the Masocretes, had altered the text of the Old Testament when they added vowel pointing to make the text more understandable. The traditional view had been that the vowels were part of the original text. The theological positions espoused at Saumur will be covered more thoroughly in the first chapter of this work.

4. Chouet, a nephew of Louis Tronchin, became professor of philosophy at the Academy of Geneva in 1669, after serving in a similar capacity at Saumur for the previous five years. He was elected as a member of the Small Council in 1686 and secretary of the Council from 1689–98. Finally, he was elected as a syndic in 1699. On Chouet see Eugène de Budé, *Vie de Jean-Robert Chouet: professeur et magistrat genevois (1647–1731)* (Geneva: Reymond et Cie, 1899); Michael Heyd, *Between Orthodoxy and the Enlightenment: Jean-Robert Chouet and the Introduction of Cartesian Science in the Academy of Geneva* (The Hague: Martinus Nijhoff, 1982); Heyd, "Jean-Robert Chouet et l'introduction du Cartesianisme à l'Académie de Genève," *Bulletin de la Société d'histoire et d'archéologie de Genève* 15 (1973): 125–53; Heyd, "Cartesianism, Secularization and Academic Reform: Jean-Robert Chouet and the Academy of Geneva, 1669–1704" (Ph.D. diss., Princeton University, 1974).

5. Jean-Alphonse Turretin, *Opera omnia theologica, philosophica et philologica*, 3 vols. (Franeker, the Netherlands: H. A. de Chalmot et D. Romar, 1774–76).

6. Jean-Alphonse Turretin, *Dilucidationes philosophico-theologico-dog-matico-morales, quibus praecipua capita tam theologiae naturalis, quam revelatae demonstrantur et ad praxin christianam commendantur accedunt, I. Orationes panegyricae et varii argumenti item henoticae de pace ecclesiae II. Commercium epistolicum inter regem borussiae Frederic I. et Pastores Genevenses de syncretismo protestantium*, 3 vols. (Basel: J. R. Imhoff, 1748).

7. Jean-Alphonse Turretin, *Cogitationes et dissertationes theologicae. Quibus principia religionis, cum naturalis, tum revelatae, adstruuntur & defenduntur; animique ad veritatis, pietatis, & pacis studium excitantur* (Geneva: Typis Barrillot & Filii, 1737).

8. Jean-Alphonse Turretin, *Nubes testium pro moderato et pacifico de rebus theologicis judicio, et instituenda inter protestantes concordia. Praemissa est brevis & pacifica de articulis fundamentalibus disquisitio* (Geneva: Fabri & Burrillo, 1719).

9. Jean-Alphonse Turretin, *Pyrrhonismus pontificus sive theses theologico-historicae de variationibus pontificorum circa ecclesiae infallibatem* (Leiden, 1692).

10. Both LeClerc and his mentor Philippe van Limborch at the Remonstrant Seminary in Amsterdam followed Hugo Grotius and Faustus Socinus in their use of the evidential, historical proof for the veracity of the Christian faith. See LeClerc, *Sentimens de quelques théologiens de Hollande sur l'Histoire critique du Vieux Testament* (Amsterdam: Henri Desbordes, 1685), and Limborch, *Theo-*

logia Christiana ad praxin pietatis ac promotionem pacis Christianae unice direc-tea (Amsterdam: George Arnold, 1735). The standard biography of LeClerc is Annie Barnes, *Jean LeClerc et la République des Lettres* (Geneva: Droz, 1938). For a discussion of the relationship between LeClerc and Turretin see M. Christina Pitassi, *Entre croire et savoir: le problème de la méthode critique chez Jean LeClerc* (Leiden: E. J. Brill, 1987). LeClerc ironically studied under Francis Turretin and rejected his strict orthodoxy for Arminianism. He found a career at the Remonstrant Seminary where he published voluminously on a number of topics and became one of the leading publishers of learned journals in the era. His lengthy correspondence with Jean-Alphonse Turretin expresses an accord on many theological points as well as a close personal friendship.

11. The external marks of Scripture dealt with proofs for biblical authority outside from the text itself. They included the antiquity of Scripture, the unity of Scripture, the testimony of martyrs and pagans, Jews and Muslims, the effectiveness of the propagation of the gospel, fulfilled prophecy, and the evidence for biblical miracles. Calvin and his Reformed followers used external proofs to support the faith of those who already believe. Jean-Alphonse Turretin used them as a basis for belief.

12. Jacob Vernet (1698–1789) was Turretin's prize student who succeeded him as professor of theology. In his *Thesium theologicarum,* Vernet denied both the Trinity and Original Sin, arguing that the Trinity was not a biblical doctrine but was added in the third and fourth centuries. Claims that he was a Socinian were exaggerated and Vernet denied them. The fact remains, however, that he had moved beyond his mentor, J. A. Turretin and away from orthodoxy. It should be noted that Turretin exerted a tremendous amount of influence on Vernet. Besides being his primary theological instructor, he sent his son Marc to travel abroad with him on the traditional postgraduate sojourn among the leading Reformed theological academies of Europe. In addition, Turretin later performed Vernet's wedding and their correspondence reflects a warm affection. Vernet edited Turretin's *De Veritate religionis Judiacae et Christianae* and thoroughly studied all of his writings. It was no surprise that upon Turretin's death in 1737, Vernet delivered a stirring eulogy in which he praised his former teacher with reverence. On Vernet's move away from orthodoxy see Eugène de Budé, *Vie de Jacob Vernet, théologien genevois (1698–1789)* (Lausanne: Georges Bridel, 1893), pp. 183–87; and James I. Good, *History of the Swiss Reformed Church since the Reformation* (Philadelphia: Publication and Sunday School Board, 1913), pp. 282–301.

13. George H. Tavard, *Holy Writ or Holy Church: The Crisis of the Protestant Reformation* (London: Burns & Oates, 1959), p. 118.

14. Martin Luther, "On the Bondage of the Will," in *Luther and Erasmus: Free Will and Salvation,* ed. E. G. Rupp (Philadelphia: Westminster Press, 1969), p. 23.

15. Richard H. Popkin, *The History of Scepticism from Erasmus to Spinoza* (Berkeley and Los Angeles: University of California Press, 1979). Pyrrhonism was a philosophical movement that followed the ideas of the Greek philosopher Sextus Empiricus. It was a system that emphasized the idea of skepticism. It held that one could not gain certain knowledge through the use of reason. See Popkin, *The History of Scepticism from Erasmus to Spinoza* for more details.

16. John D. Woodbridge, "Biblical Authority: Towards an Evaluation of the Rogers & McKim Proposal," *Trinity Journal* (Fall 1980): 189.

17. On Isaac de la Peyrère see Richard H. Popkin, "The Marrano Theology

of Isaac de la Peyrère," *Studi internazional di Filosofia* (1973): 202–22, and Popkin, "The Development of Religious Skepticism and the Influence of Isaac de la Peyrère's Pre-Adamism and Bible Criticism," in *Classical Influences on European Culture A. D. 1500–1700*, ed. R. R. Bolgar (Cambridge: Cambridge University Press, 1976), pp. 271–80.

18. John T. McNeill, *The History and Character of Calvinism* (New York: Oxford University Press, 1957).

19. On Wake see Norman Sykes, *William Wake: Archbishop of Canterbury, 1657–1737*, 2 vols. (Cambridge: Cambridge University Press, 1957).

20. The definition of the term *Reformed scholasticism* has been the subject of considerable debate in recent years. The debate centers on the alleged deviation of the "scholastics" from the central aspects of Calvin's theology. One school argues that the Reformed scholastics were primarily rationalists who exchanged Calvin's Christological focus for one based on divine decrees. A second interpretation, espoused principally by Richard A. Muller, defines it primarily in its organizational pattern that made Reformed theology more precise in response to the Counter-Reformation polemic. The use of the term *Reformed scholasticism* is discussed at length in the first chapter of this work.

21. W. Robert Godfrey, "Tensions Within International Calvinism: The Debate on the Atonement at the Synod of Dort, 1618–1619" (Ph.D. diss., Stanford University, 1974).

22. The Academy of Geneva was founded by Calvin in 1559 and it was bolstered when several ministers from Lausanne, protesting Bern's imposition of secular authority and discipline, came to Geneva in 1559. Several joined the faculty of the academy, including Theodore Beza, who became the rector in 1559. The academy served as an internationally renowned training school for Reformed ministers, especially for French-speaking Europe.

23. Good, *Swiss Reformed Church*, pp. 282–301. One should employ the term *Socinian* with extreme caution. It was often used as a mere epithet to mean heretic. It could also be used to refer to the theological system of Socinus, namely the excessive use of reason in scriptural interpretation to the point of denying theological mystery such as the Trinity and the Incarnation of Christ. The latter is the meaning here.

Chapter 1. The Nature of Reformed Scholasticism, and the Debates over the Adoption of the Helvetic Formula Consensus in Geneva

1. See, among others, David Steinmetz, *Luther and Staupitz* (Durham, N.C.: Duke University Press, 1980); Timothy George, *Theology of the Reformers* (Nashville, Tenn.: Broadman Press, 1988), pp. 57–74; Brian A. Gerrish, *Grace and Reason: A Study in the Theology of Luther* (New York: Oxford University Press, 1962).

2. Calvin's education was primarily humanistic and he did not have as thorough an exposure to scholasticism as had Luther. Alexandre Ganoczy argues that Calvin's knowledge of scholasticism was, at best, limited to Gratian's *Decretals* and Lombard's *Sentences*. In addition, Calvin's references to scholastic theology in the *Institutes* are limited to the refutation of Roman Catholic error and only in three instances in support of his own arguments. However, in these three citations, the point that Calvin is making is so obvious that reference to scholastic argu-

ments is merely perfunctory. Among the many works on the importance of humanism to Calvin studies see Quirinius Breen, *John Calvin: A Study in French Humanism* (New York: Archon Books, 1968), and Alexandre Ganoczy, *La Bibliothèque de l'Académie de Calvin* (Geneva: Droz, 1969); Ganoczy, *Le jeune Calvin: Genèse et évolution de sa vocation réformatrice* (Weisbaden: Franz Steiner Verlag, 1966); William J. Bouwsma, *John Calvin: A Sixteenth Century Portrait* (New York: Oxford University Press, 1988).

3. Bengt Hagglund, *History of Theology,* trans. Gene J. Lund (St. Louis, Mo.: Concordia Publishing House, 1968), p. 288.

4. Ibid., p. 356. Descartes was introduced to Suarez through the Jesuits and Leibniz boasted that he read Suarez as easily as one would read a novel. The English translation is: Francisco Suarez, *On the Various Kinds of Distinctions,* trans. Cyril Vollert (Milwaukee, Wis.: Marquette University Press, 1947). John Platt argues that the influence of Suarez was particularly strong among the Dutch universities. See John Platt, *Reformed Thought and Scholasticism: The Arguments for the Existence of God in Dutch Theology, 1575–1650* (Leiden: E. J. Brill, 1982), pp. 229–31. Richard A. Muller points to the influence of Suarez on Arminius. See Muller, "Arminius and the Scholastic Tradition," *Calvin Theological Journal* 24 (November 1989): 275; Idem, *God, Creation and Providence in the Thought of Jacob Arminius: Sources and Direction of Scholastic Protestantism in the Era of Early Orthodoxy* (Grand Rapids, Mich.: Baker Book House, 1991).

5. Martin Grabmann, "Die Disputationes metaphysicae des Franz Suarez in ihrer methodischen Eigenhart und Fortwirken," in *Mittelarterliches Geistesleben,* ed. Martin Grabmann, 2 vols. (Munich: Max Heuber, 1926–36), 1:559.

6. Armand Maurer, *Medieval Philosophy* (New York: Random House, 1962), pp. 366–67.

7. Timothy J. Cronin, *Objective Being in Descartes and in Suarez* (Rome: Gregorian University Press, 1966), pp. 77–78.

8. Suarez, *On the Various Kinds of Distinctions,* pp. 58–59.

9. Brian Armstrong, *Calvinism and the Amyraut Heresy: Protestant Scholasticism and Humanism in Seventeenth-Century France* (Madison: University of Wisconsin Press, 1969).

10. Ibid., p. 32.

11. Richard A. Muller, *Dictionary of Latin and Greek Theological Terms* (Grand Rapids, Mich.: Baker Book House, 1985), p. 8.

12. Ibid., p. 18.

13. Richard A. Muller, *Post-Reformation Reformed Dogmatics. Volume 1: Prolegomena to Theology* (Grand Rapids, Mich.: Baker Book House, 1987), pp. 13–52.

14. Brian Armstrong, "The Changing face of French Protestantism: The Influence of Pierre Du Moulin," in *Calviniana: Ideas and Influence of John Calvin,* ed. Robert V. Schnucker (Kirksville, Mo.: Sixteenth Century Journal Publications, 1988), p. 148.

15. Muller, *Post-Reformation Reformed Dogmatics,* pp. 28–40.

16. Richard A. Muller, *Christ and the Decree: Christology and Predestination from Calvin to Perkins* (Grand Rapids, Mich.: Baker Book House, 1988), p. 11.

17. Ibid., p. 13.

18. Ibid.

19. Muller, *Post-Reformation Reformed Dogmatics,* p. 83.

20. Ibid., pp. 96–97.

21. Ibid., p. 93. See also Ernst Bizer, *Früorthodoxie und Rationalismus* (Zu-

rich: EVZ Verlag, 1963), p. 6. I have taken the phrase "Calvin against the Calvinists" from Basil Hall, "Calvin Against the Calvinists," in *John Calvin*, ed. Gervase E. Duffield (Appleford, Great Britain: Sutton Courtenay Press, 1966), pp. 18–37.

22. Muller, *Post-Reformation Reformed Dogmatics*, p. 93.

23. Ibid., pp. 94–96.

24. Ibid.

25. Muller cites five reasons for this as follows:

(1) from the definition of our theology as a theology in *via*, searching out its salvation between the fall and eschaton; (2) from the limits placed on natural theology; (3) from the redefinition of a natural theology of the regenerate as belonging to Christian praise rather than to "fundamental theology," as it were; (4) from the emphasis on the object of theology as God revealed and covenanted in Christ; and (5) from the stress upon the character of theology as theoretical-practical with the emphasis upon *praxis*.

Ibid., pp. 309–10.

26. Ibid.

27. Muller, *Christ and the Decree*, p. 95.

28. Ibid., p. 82.

29. Ibid., p. 96.

30. Ibid., pp. 97–173.

31. On the relationship between Francis Turretin and the Princeton theologians see Earl W. Kennedy, "An Historical Analysis of Charles Hodge's Doctrines of Sin and Particular Grace" (Ph.D. diss., Princeton Theological Seminary, 1969); Beardslee, "Theological Developments."

32. On the Saumur Academy see Pierre D. Bourchenin, *Etude sur les académies protestantes en France aux XVIe et XVIIe siècles* (Paris: Grassert, 1882); E. Merzeau, *L'Académie protestante de Saumur (1604–1685)* (Alençon: Guy, 1908); Joseph Prost, *La philosophie à l'Académie protestante de Saumur (1606–1685)* (Paris: H. Paulin, 1907); L. J. Metayer, *L'Académie protestante de Saumur* (Paris: "La Cause," 1933); Hartmut Kretzer, *Calvinismus und franzosische Monarchie in 17. Jahrhundert: die politische besonderer Berucksichtigung von Pierre Du Moulin, Moyse Amyraut und Pierre Jurieu* (Berlin: Drunker & Humblot, 1975).

33. On Moïse Amyraut see François LaPlanche, *Orthodoxie et prédication: l'oeuvre d'Amyraut et la querelle de la grâce universelle* (Paris: Presses universitaires de France, 1965); Idem, *L'Ecriture;* Idem, *L'Evidence du Dieu Chrétien: Religion, culture et société dans l'apologétique protestante de la France classique (1576–1670)* (Strasbourg: Association des Publications de la Faculté de Théologie Protestante de Strasbourg, 1983); Roger Nicole, "Moyse Amyraut (1596–1664) and the Controversy on Universal Grace: First Phase (1634–1637)" (Ph.D. diss., Harvard University, 1966); David Sabean, "The Theological Rationalism of Moïse Amyraut," *Archiv für Reformationsgeschichte* 55 (1964): 204–16; Richard Stauffer, "Un Précurseur français de l'oecumenisme: Moïse Amyraut," *Eglise et théologie* 24 (December 1961): 13–49; Armstrong, *Calvinism*.

34. Nicole comments further on the definition of hypothetical universalism:

Amyraut held that God, moved by compassion for the plight of fallen mankind, designed to save all men and sent His son Jesus-Christ as a substitutionary offering for the sins of all men and of every man—this is Amyraut's *universalism*. This sacrifice is not effectual unto salvation, however, unless God's offer of grace is accepted by man in repentance and faith, which acceptance is the fruit of God's special grace, conferred on those only whom He has chosen—this is the *hypothetical* aspect of Amyraut's view.

Nicole, "Moyse Amyraut," p. 3. Schaff comments on Amyraut's position:

> He [Amyraut] was disposed, like Zwingli, to extend the grace of God beyond the limits
> of the visible Church inasmuch as God by his general providence operates upon the
> heathen, and may produce in them a sort of unconscious Christianity, a faith without
> knowledge; while within the Church he operates more fully and clearly through the means
> of grace. Those who never heard of Christ are condemned if they reject the general grace
> of providence; but the same persons would also reject Christ if he were offered to them.
> As regards the result, Amyraut agreed with the particularists. His ideal universalism is
> unavailable, except for those in whom God previously works the condition of faith, that
> is for those who are included in the particular decree of election.

Philip Schaff, ed., *The Creeds of Christendom,* 3 vols. (Grand Rapids, Mich.:
Baker Book House, 1959), 1:181–82.

35. Philip Schaff, *The Creeds of Christendom,* 1:485.

36. On Cappel and the issue of the vowel points of the Moasoretic text see
Richard A. Muller, "The Debate over the Vowel Points and the Crisis in Orthodox
Hermeneutics," *The Journal of Medieval and Renaissance Studies* 10, no. 1
(1980): 53–72.

37. Louis Cappel, *hoc est arcanum punctationis revelatum, sive De punctorum vocalium et accentuum apud Hebraeus vera et germana antiquitate* (Amsterdam: Johannem Maire, 1624).

38. Cappel, *Critica sacra, sive De variis quae in sacris Veteris Testamenti
libris occurrunt lectionibus libri sex . . . cui subiecta est eiusdam criticae adversus iniustum censorem iusta defensi* (Paris: S & G Cramoisy, 1650).

39. John R. Robinson, "The Doctrine of Holy Scripture in Seventeenth Century Reformed Theology" (Ph.D. diss., Université de Strasbourg, 1971), pp.
109–10. See also Stephen G. Burnett, "The Christian Hebraism of Johann Buxtorf
(1564–1629)" (Ph.D. diss., University of Wisconsin, Madison, 1990).

40. Ibid. The major issue of debate centered on the authenticity of the biblical
text. Roman Catholic apologists claimed that so many errors had crept into the
text through its transmission that the church needed to declare a contemporary
text authentic for current use. The Protestants, by contrast, argued in favor of
the adequate preservation of the text in its original languages. The problem with
the Masoretic addition of the vowel points was that Roman Catholic scholars used
it to show that the unpointed text would be impossible to interpret with any
degree of certainty. Cappel's argument in favor of the late dating of the addition
of the vowel points struck at the heart of the Counter-Reformation polemic and
aroused tremendous controversy within Reformed circles. See Timothy Phillips,
"Francis Turretin," p. 689n. Richard A. Muller points out that Cappel had attempted to preserve the concept of the divine origin of the vowel points by
positing an oral tradition. However, when he argued that the vowel points in the
textus receptus were corrupted in their transmission and needed to be corrected
by ancient translations, his opponents feared that the priority of the Hebrew
version would be jeopardized. Muller explains that it was Francis Turretin and
Johann Heinrich Heidegger who framed the most sophisticated response to Cappel. Their argument contained three major assumptions:

> the *autographa* or original manuscript copies of the scriptural books as dictated by the
> spirit to the biblical authors must be distinguished from the *apographa* or later copies;
> the authority of scripture considered in terms of the content or meaning of the text . . .
> from the authority of the words of the text, that actual *scriptura;* and the vowels consid-

ered according to sound, the *valor* or *potestas* of the vowel point form the *figura* or symbol, the vowel point itself.

For these theologians, the Hebrew was superior to all translations and it alone was the authentic version of the Old Testament. Muller, "Vowel Points," pp. 61–68.

41. Robinson, "Holy Scripture," pp. 113–15.

42. Ibid.

43. Ibid., p. 120.

44. Beardslee, "Theological Developments," p. 25.

45. Schaff, *Creeds,* 1:477–89.

46. Beardslee, "Theological Developments," pp. 16–17.

47. Heyd, "Cartesianism," p. 18.

48. Johannes Piscator, professor of theology at Herborn in Nassau, had taught that only the passive righteousness of Christ is attributed to the elect. Christ's active obedience was on his own behalf in order to fulfill the Law.

49. Grohman, "Genevan Reaction," pp. 135–53.

50. Ibid., pp. 154–257.

51. Beardslee, "Theological Developments," p. 52.

52. Grohman, "Genevan Reaction," pp. 260–65. Philippe Mestrezat, a native Genevan, studied at the Genevan Academy and was ordained in 1641, the same year that he was named professor of philosophy. After serving as a pastor from 1644–49, he replaced Morus as professor of theology in 1649. He also served as rector of the academy from 1649–54 and also from 1670–72.

53. Ibid., pp. 316–33.

54. Ibid.

55. Heyd, "Cartesianism," pp. 53, 226.

56. Ibid.

57. Johannes Cocceius (1603–69) was professor of theology at Leiden from 1650 until his death. The hallmark of his theology was the central role of the covenants throughout biblical history. He viewed the primary value of the Old Testament in terms of its typology in reference to Christ. The major objection against Cocceius was based on his rejection of the value of the Old Testament Law for the New Testament believer. On Cocceius see Heiner Faulenbach, *Weg und Ziel der Christi: Eine Untersuchung zur Theologie des Johannes Coccejus* (Neukirchen: Neukirchner Verlag, 1973); Charles S. McCoy, "Johannes Cocceius: Federal Theologian," *Scottish Journal of Theology* 16 (December 1963): 252–270.

58. Heyd, *Between Orthodoxy and the Enlightenment,* p. 48.

59. Good, *Swiss Reformed Church,* p. 164.

60. Ibid., pp. 164–65.

61. Ibid., p. 167.

62. Ibid.

63. Jean Claude (1619–87) was one of the most famous of the Reformed pastors of France and enjoyed an international reputation. He taught and served as a pastor at Nîmes and Charenton.

64. Grohman, "Genevan Reaction," pp. 386–90.

65. Beardslee, "Theological Developments," p. 67.

Chapter 2. Reformed Liberalism at the Academy of Geneva: The Education of Jean-Alphonse Turretin

1. Tronchin described several reasons for his opposition to the Formula Consensus. In spite of the fact that its authors were claiming that its adoption would

not harm a possible accord with the German Lutherans, Tronchin adamantly stated that the opposite was the case. He labeled the Consensus "the foundation of schism." In addition, he explained that it was so detailed that it had the potential of causing division within the Reformed camp. He illustrated this possibility by showing that there was already considerable dissent among theologians of the various Swiss cantons concerning the contents of the Formula.

In addition to the issue of its divisiveness, Tronchin pointed out that most of the statements of the Formula do not relate to matters essential for salvation. For example, a belief that the Holy Spirit inspired the Masoretes to insert the correct vowel points into the Hebrew text would not be a fundamental doctrine. One could disagree with this concept and yet remain orthodox. Further, many of the founders of the Reformed tradition would have had difficulty with the statements of the Formula Consensus. Both Calvin and Beza, for example, did not hold to the inspiration of the pointing of the Masoretic text. Diodati, in fact, had pointed out problems of numbering in the Hebrew text. Tronchin listed several other prominent Reformed divines of history who would have had problems with aspects of the Formula. He capped off his argument by asserting that many of the Puritan theologians of England could not have signed the document in full conscience.

The Reformed community of France, furthermore, did not hold to the statements of the Formula. Tronchin wished that Geneva would continue its practice of siding with the French Reformed church rather than with the Swiss on controversial doctrinal and political matters. After all, he argued, the French had provided the Swiss with the leaders of the Reformation, Calvin, Farel, and Beza.

The logical result of the passing of such a creed, according to Tronchin, would be the exclusion of many godly and orthodox men from the ministry. Further, many who would sign it would be adhering to statements that they did not fully understand. Archives Tronchin, vol. 68, fols. 32r–32v.

Tronchin enumerated several other political reasons for rejecting the Formula Consensus. First, he reasoned that the entire concept of unifying the Reformed churches of the cantons would be useless if, in doing so, it would cause animosity among Reformed theologians of other countries. Since the primary goal of unification was the strengthening of a Protestant consensus against the power of Rome, the Formula could, indeed, prove to be counterproductive.

Second, if the goal was to unite the Swiss cantons under a common creed, it would be quite reasonable to use one of the many creeds that the cantons already possessed, creeds that were much less specific than was the Formula Consensus, but that were sufficient enough to insure orthodoxy.

In addition, the Formula aroused much opposition not only from individual theologians, but also from significant elements of some of the cantons. For example, the Academy of Lausanne, as a whole, favored its rejection. Tronchin pointed out that many of the professors at Lausanne would not be able to sign it in full conscience, and those who did agree with it were disconcerted about the potential conflicts with their colleagues over its passage. Many of the pastors and professors there, according to Tronchin, preferred to remain silent concerning the issues raised in the debate in order to maintain harmony with their peers. Tronchin lamented that it is, indeed, a sad state of affairs when Christians find themselves compelled to choose between silence and division. It would be much more beneficial to forget the whole idea of adopting the Consensus rather than to force such a series of unhappy circumstances upon such committed Christians. Archives Tronchin, vol. 68, fols. 64r–64v. "Minute d'une lettre de Louis Tronchin à un "Monseigneur," n.d. The Archives Tronchin are a valuable collection of letters, treatises and documents of the Tronchin family. They are located at the Bibliothèque publique et universitaire at the University of Geneva.

2. "Bon Dieu! N'est-ce pas se moquer de Dieu et des hommes que d'aller débiter en chaire des semblables sottises; s'ils avoyent eu le même sujet il y a trente ans; Que votre Eglise et votre académie eussent été heureuses! Dieu veuille luy avoir fait miséricorde, et luy avoir pardonné les déreglemens que sa passion et son peu de charité luy ont fait commetre." Archives Tronchin, vol. 54, fol. 22r. Daniel Chamier to Louis Tronchin, 24 November 1687.

3. Heyd, "Cartesianism," p. 230.

4. Ibid., pp. 230–31.

5.

Pour la Philosophie, elle fleurit ici extrêmement, M. Chouet, fils du libraire, et neveu de M. Tronchin, enseigné celle de Descartes, avec grande réputation et un grand concours d'étrangers; aussi faut-il avancer que c'est un esprit extrêmement délicat et également poli et solide. . . . Il fait tous les Mercerdis des expériences fort curieuses, ou il va beaucoup de monde. C'est le génie du siècle et la méthode des philosophes modernes.

Cited in Charles Borgeaud, *Histoire de l'Université de Genève: L'Académie de Calvin*, (Geneva: George & Co., 1900), p. 412.

6. Ibid., pp. 406–17.

7. Heyd, *Between Orthodoxy and Enlightenment*, p. 47.

8. Ibid.

9. Ibid., p. 50.

10. Richard Simon, *Histoire critique du Vieux Testament* (Rotterdam: Renier Leers, 1678).

11. Heyd, *Between Orthodoxy and the Enlightenment*, p. 47.

12. Borgeaud, *L'Académie de Calvin*, p. 434.

13. Ibid., p. 417.

14. Heyd, "Cartesianism," p. 204.

15. Heyd, *Between Orthodoxy and the Enlightenment*, pp. 116–24.

16. Ibid., p. 204.

17. Ibid., p. 168.

18. Ibid., p. 169.

19. Elizabeth Labrousse, *Pierre Bayle: Hétérodoxie et rigorisme*, 2 vols. (The Hague: Nijhoff, 1964), 1:102.

20. Heyd, "Cartesianism," p. 84.

21. Archives Tronchin, vol. 47, fol. 25r. Chouet to Louis Tronchin, n.d.

22. Ibid., fol. 28r. Chouet to Louis Tronchin, 19 July 1662.

23. Ibid.

24. Heyd, "Cartesianism," p. 88.

25. Ibid., p. 90.

26. Ibid.

27. Ibid., p. 93.

28.

vous me demandez comment cette Maxime que tout ce qui est en Dieu est Dieu même peut s'accorder avec les relations personnelles qui sont dans la divinité, mais vous me dispenserez s'il vous plait de répondre à cette nouvelle question. Comme Philosophe je ne raisonne jamais de la Trinité, je la considère comme un mystère entièrement incompréhensible à l'esprit humain, et comme Chrétien je m'en tiens exactement à ce que nous enseigné la parole de Dieu sans aller au delà.

Archives Tronchin, vol. 47, fol. 138v. Chouet to Sarrasin, 1 September 1680.

29.

On luy demandera de plus si dans le moment que se fait la transsubstantiation, la substance ou la matière du pain est anéantie véritablement et réelement ou si elle ne fait que changer de nom, en prenant ce luy du Corps de Jesus Christ, s'il respond qu'elle est anéantie, je ne vois point comment toute la matière de la nature ou toute l'estendue du monde, qui est la mesme chose avec elle, ne l'est donc pas en même temps, car autrement une mesme chose sera anéantie. . . . et ne le sera pas, ce qui est inconcevable, et s'il dit que la matière du pain à proprement parler n'est pas anéantie, j'appréhende fort qu'on ne luy reproche qu'il abandone les sentiments et les décisions de son Eglise! L'autre proposition que nostre auteur veut établir, est que le corps de nostre Seigneur peut estre contenu sous un point, non pas mathématiques mais sensibles. . . . 4o. que tout ce qui est essentiel au corps humain, n'est peut estre qu'un grain de sable.

Archives Tronchin, vol. 47, fol. 112r. Chouet to Jean LeClerc, 27 August 1680.

30. He writes:

Je scay bien que l'Ame estant unie à cette seule partie pourroit avoir eu les mesmes perceptions et les mesmes pensées, qu'elle auroit dans un corps entier, car elle pourroit bien les avoir, quand mesme elle ne seroit unie à aucun corps, mais je doute pourtant que ce nouveau corps, sans bras, sans jambes, sans tête, sans veines, sans artères, sans sang, etc. peut bien estre appelé un corps humain, et je doute encore qu'il peut vivre longtemps, à moins qu'on ne multiplie les miracles puisque la vie du corps humain dépend principalement des esprits animaux, que le coeur ou le sang doit incessament fournir au cerveau.

Ibid.

31. W. Von Leyden, *Seventeenth Century Metaphysics: An Examination of Some Main Concepts and Theories* (London: Gerald Duckworth, 1968), p. 16.

32. Heyd, "Cartesianism," pp. 210–13.

33. Ibid., p. 213.

34. Ibid., p. 246.

35. Grohman, "Genevan Reaction," pp. 258–333.

36. Jacques Solé, "Rationalisme chrétien et foi reformée à Genève autour de 1700: les deniers sermons de Louis Tronchin," *Bulletin de la Société d'histoire du protestantisme français* 128 (1982): 33.

37. J. E. Cellérier, *L'Académie de Genève: Equisse d'une histoire abregée de l'Académie fondée par Calvin en 1559* (Geneva: A. Cherbiez, 1872), p. 41.

38. Pierre Bayle called Tronchin "the most penetrating and the most judicious theologian of all of Europe" in a letter to his brother written in Geneva while Bayle was studying under Tronchin in 1671. Pitassi, *Entre croire et savoir,* p. 103.

39. Maria C. Pitassi cites a letter from LeClerc to Tronchin dated 2 January 1681 in which LeClerc acknowledges his intellectual and religious debts to Tronchin. See Pitassi, *Entre croire et savoir,* p. 2.

40. The application of the term *reason* is very important for this period. Ernst Bizer and Hans Emil Weber, among others, have characterized the Reformed scholastics as those who elevated reason and rationalism in their formation of a tightly knit theological system with the doctrine of predestination as the primary focus. Richard Muller takes issue with this interpretation writing: "The Protestant orthodox disavow evidentialism and identify theological certainty as something quite distinct from mathematical and rational and theological certainty. They also argue quite pointedly that reason has an instrumental function within the bounds of faith and not a magisterial function. Reason never proves faith, but only elabo-

rates faith toward understanding." Muller goes on to argue that the dominance of reason over revelation was characteristic rather of the eighteenth century with the demise of the Aristotelian-Ptolemaic worldview. Tronchin's utter confidence in applying the Cartesian test of clear and distinct ideas to Scripture is characteristic of the growing reliance upon reason that helped to dismantle the Reformed scholastic movement. Muller, *Post-Reformation Reformed Dogmatics*, p. 93.

41. Rex, *Pierre Bayle*, p. 131. Louis Tronchin, *Notae in libros duos Theologiae sacrae Wendelini exceptae in praelectionibus Domini Tronchini theologiae in Genevensi Academia professoris celeberrimi, quae habuit inter p(ri)vatos p(ar)ietes, annis 1671, 1672*, Archives Tronchin, vol. 84, fols. 44–44v. Pitassi cites this passage to show the influence of Tronchin on LeClerc in passing on the Cartesian methodology and applying it to theological studies. Pitassi, *Entre croire et savoir*, p. 4.

42. Pitassi, *Entre croire et savoir*, p. 2.

43. Solé, "Louis Tronchin," p. 34.

44. Ibid., p. 35.

45. Ibid.

46. Ibid.

47. "Comme aujourd'hui le Vieux Testament qui autrefois est suffisante, ne l'est plus, selon ces Messieurs; mais on peut dire qu'il est médiatement, parce que si un homme qui le lisoit en profitoit, Dieu promiroit à lui donner l'ample et la claire révélation de l'évangile." Archives Tronchin, vol. 57, fols. 45r–45v, 6 January 1677.

48. "Toute homme qui fait tout ce que Dieu lui révèle, sera excusé de tout; le jugement de Dieu estant reglé sur la mesure de la révélation." Ibid.

49. Ibid., fols. 45v–46r.

50. Robinson, "The Doctrine of Holy Scripture," p. 51.

51. Ibid., p. 72.

52. H. Jackson Forstman, *Word and Spirit: Calvin's Doctrine of Biblical Authority* (Stanford, Calif.: Stanford University Press, 1962), pp. 16, 66, 71–75, 125.

53. "C'est pour cela que dieu veut que nous lui demandions son esprit de lumière et de sapience, afin de voir des merveilles de sa parole." Archives Tronchin, vol. 57, fol. 111r, minutes of seven letters written to Mme de la Fredonnière between 1686–87.

54.

Elle en défend la lecture si c'étoit un livre dangereux, jusque la qu'en Espagne, et en Italie, il ne faut qu'avoir un Nouveau Testament, pour se faire mener au Supplice. Juger si cela n'est pas contraire à ce que David dit Ps. 89: Ta parole est une lampe à mon pied, est une lumière à mon sentier: et à ce que dit S. Paul au 3 ch de la 2 ep. à Timoth: Tu as appris des son enfance les saintes lettres, lesquelles te peuvent rendre sage à salut: car toute l'écriture est divinement inspirée, et propre à enseigner, à convaincre, à corriger, et à instruire selon justice, pour rendre l'homme de dieu accompli à toute bonne oeuvre.

Ibid., fol. 94r, 15 June 1686.

55. See, among others, Roland N. Stromberg, *Religious Liberalism in Eighteenth-Century England* (Oxford: University Press, 1954).

56. "Mystère est une chose sacrée, cachée, couverte qui surpasse le luxe et l'entendent qui pour être comprisé a besoin de révélation de l'esprit de dieu [A mystery is a holy thing, hidden, covered that surpasses excess and needs the revelation of the spirit of God in order to be understood]." Archives Tronchin, vol. 86, n.p., 23 December 1666.

57. Ibid.

58. Archives Tronchin, vol. 57, fol. 120r, June 1686. Tronchin attempted, however, to explain as much as possible concerning biblical mysteries. He was fully confident that even the mysteries of Scripture could withstand examination. Rex comments that Tronchin argued in his lectures on Wendelin's *Theologiae sacrae* that "we must assert nothing concerning the Deity which our understanding does not require us to affirm, for we must judge things in accordance with our understanding of them." In areas of apparent contradiction, Tronchin pointed to the fact that God cannot perform what is logically self-defeating. The Roman Catholic doctrine of transubstantiation would be an example of this. Rex, *Pierre Bayle,* p. 132.

59.

C'est pourquoi quand mesme nos Réformateurs n'auroyent pas entendu, ni explique assez clairement la manière de nostre union avec Christ, en l'Eucharistie. Je ne laisserai pas de demeurer en leur communion, parce que le fond de leur sentiment est seul véritable parce que je peux éclaircir ce qui leur à estre obscur en me prévalant des lumières que je peux avoir moi-mesme, ou tirer de ceux qui sont venus après eux, et qui ont mieux pénétré qu'eux en cela, la nature des choses, et le sens de la parole de dieu.

Ibid.

60. "Je vous dire franchement que ceux qui suivent la doctrine d'une Eglise . . . sans examiner sous prétexte qu'ils n'ont pas assez de lumière pour comprendre le vrai sens de l'écriture ne me paroissent pas raissonables." Ibid., fol. 211r, n.d.

61. "Ne faut-il pas croire que ce soit une modestie louable que de n'oser pas juger du vrai sens de l'écriture pour discerner l'erreur. . . . C'est plutôt un aveuglement et une proposition indigne et contraire au devoir d'un bon chrétien." Ibid., fol. 97v, 15 June 1686.

62.

A votre avis, Madame, ce qui peut rendre sage à salut, ne peut-il pas suffire pour estre sauvé? Et ce qui est inspiré de dieu pour convaincre, ne peut-il pas décider des controverses? Pouvez-vous croire qu'un livre fait de dieu expressement pour estre la source, et la règle de la religion, ne sert pas propre à l'enseigner? Et a faire discerner la vérité qu'il veut établir, d'avec les erreurs que les hommes ont introduites?

Ibid.

63. Roger Stauffenegger, *Eglise et société: Genève au XVIIe siècle* (Geneva: Droz, 1983), pp. 414–15.

64. Archives Tronchin, vol. 57, fols. 97v, 221r; vol. 86, Sermon on 2 Corinthians 6:17; Olivier Fatio, "L'Eglise de Genève fâce à l'offensive Catholique: 1680–1684," in Olivier Reverdan, et al., *Genève au temps de la révocation de l'edit de Nantes,* vol. 50 in *Mémoires et documents publiés par la Société d'histoire et d'archéologie de Genève* (Geneva: Droz, 1985), pp. 182–85, 198n.

65. Ibid.

66. Archives Tronchin, vol. 57, fol. 95v, 15 June 1686.

67. "Tout particulier qui avec un esprit véritablement pieux, et amateur de la vérité, lira écriture pour y trouver les choses nécessaires à son salut, est capable de l'entendre par soi même; et c'est le devoir de chaque particulier." Ibid., fol. 97r.

68. Ibid.

69. Ibid., fol. 97r.

70. "Notre foi ne se fonde que sur la parole de dieu, et non sur l'autorité des

hommes, qui sont tous sujets à l'erreur." Ibid., fol. 122v, June 1686; fol. 221v, n.d.; Fatio, "L'Eglise," p. 183.

71. "J. Christ l'auteur de notre religion et les Apôtres les plus sages ministres ne les ont pas commandées, et n'ont établi qu'un culte fut simple, accompagné de la parole pour instruire les hommes." Archives Tronchin, fol. 96v., 15 June 1686.

72. Ibid., fol. 122v, June 1686; fol. 221v, n.d.; Fatio, "L'Eglise," p. 183.

73. Archives Tronchin, fol. 96v., 15 June 1686.

74. Ibid., fol. 122v, June 1686.

75. Heyd analyzes Tronchin's arguments as follows:

In his private courses on Wendelin's *Christianae Theologiae Libri duo,* Tronchin criticized the manner in which Wendelin refuted the Lutheran notion of the ubiquity of Christ. The Lutherans defended their view by making several distinctions concerning the mode of existence of the body of Christ: he existed in a certain place visibly, naturally (according to his proper nature or essence) and locally, but at the same time, he was everywhere *illocaliter,* invisibly, personally and by virtue of the divine majesty communicated to him. Wendelin rejected these distinctions not only by reference to Scripture, where no such invisible existence of the body of Christ was mentioned, but also by denying the logical possibility that a finite corporeal unit, spatially limited, could exist simultaneously in many places even invisibly. Tronchin, by contrast, had recourse to the new philosophy of nature in order to reject those distinctions and believed that the whole scholastic apparatus behind which the Lutherans tried to conceal their muddled thinking could be dismissed. According to the new philosophy, a given body was nothing else than extension, that is, the space it occupied or its "internal" place. It was therefore absurd to assume that a body be outside its place in any manner whatsoever. Furthermore, the visibility or invisibility of a body depended on its density, whether or not it could reflect rays of light; that had nothing to do with the place a body occupied. Neither could the divine personality or majesty which were communicated to the human Christ make him ubiquitous since they added a moral or spiritual dimension to Christ not a physical one.

Heyd, *Between Orthodoxy and the Enlightenment,* pp. 73–74.

76. Ibid.

77. Rex, *Pierre Bayle,* p. 131.

78. Archives Tronchin, fol. 211v, n.d.

79. "Le stile des prophetes, et des liaisons de leurs discours sont des choses différentes des autres écrits divins, qu'on ne sçauroit asseoir un jugement sur de ce quels prophecies signifient à l'égard des plusieurs circonstances." Ibid., fol. 211r.

80. Jean-Alphonse Turretin, "Oratio secunda inauguralis de theologo veritatis et pacis studioso. Dicta est Kalend. Decembr. An. MDCCV. Quo die auctor, in locum viri venerandi, Ludovici Tronchini in Domino pie defuncti, subrogatus, publicam S. Theologiae professionem adiret," in Jean-Alphonse Turretin, *Dilucidationes,* vol. 3, pp. 175–80.

81. Borgeaud, *L'Académie de Calvin,* p. 536.

82. Emile Haag and Eugène Haag, eds., *La France protestante* 1847–59 ed., s.v., "Pierre Du Bosc;" On Basnage see René Voeltzel, *Vrai et fausse église selon les théologiens protestants français du XVII siècle* (Paris: Universitaires de France, 1956) and E. André Mailhet, *Jacques Basnage, théologien, controversiste, diplomate et historien: sa vie et ses écrits* (Geneva, 1886).

83. *New Schaff Herzog Encyclopedia,* s.v. "Roell, Hermann Alexander."

84. Emile Haag and Eugène Haag, eds., *La France protestante* 1847–59 ed., s.v., "Elie Saurin."

85. Budé, *Vie de J. A. Turrettini,* p. 17.

86. Ibid., p. 20.
87. Ibid., p. 21.
88. Ibid., p. 33.
89. Henri Vuilleumier, *Histoire de l'Eglise Réformée de Vaud sous le régime Bernois*, 4 vols. (Lausanne: Editions la Concorde, 1930), 3:565; Budé, *Vie de J. A. Turrettini*, pp. 18–19.
90. Vuilleumier, *Histoire de l'Eglise Réformée*, 3:566.

Chapter 3. Jean-Alphonse Turretin on Natural Theology

1. Beardslee, "Theological Developments," p. 164.
2. See among others John H. McLachlan, *Socinianism in Seventeenth-Century England* (Oxford: Oxford University Press, 1951); Louis A. Bredvold, *The Intellectual Milieu of John Dryden: Studies in Some Aspects of Seventeenth-Century Thought* (Ann Arbor: University of Michigan Press, 1934).
3. Heyd, "Un Role nouveau pour la science," p. 26.
4. Leonard Adams, ed., *William Wake's Gallican Correspondence and Related Documents, 1716–1731*, 2 vols. (New York: Peter Lang, 1988), 1:308–9.
5. The complete English translation of Spinoza's *Tractatus theologico-politicus* is contained in Benedict de Spinoza, *The Chief Works of Benedict de Spinoza*, ed. R. J. M. Elwes, 2 vols. (London: George Bell and Sons, 1883). As a result of the anti-Christian content of Spinoza's writings, Roman Catholic authorities in France suppressed the publication and dissemination of his works, especially the *Tractatus*. Consequently, book sellers from Holland began to smuggle Spinoza's tomes into France under false book covers. The Reformed church, was also suspicious of Spinoza's works. Vernière points out that there were only three options in responding to Spinoza's theories denying the supernatural elements of Scripture. One could burn all the copies of the *Tractatus;* one could refute Spinoza point by point; or else one could grant Spinoza some ground on which he was obviously correct while defending those areas where Spinoza could be refuted, areas in which Spinoza's theories challenged the "essentials" of the Christian faith. This last option was the one chosen by Turretin. Paul Vernière, *Spinoza et la pensée française avant la révolution*, 2 vols. (Paris: Presses Universitaires de France), 1:67.
6. Such accusations were especially widespread in England because of the translation of LeClerc's treatise on biblical inspiration, which was translated into English and widely circulated. As a result of his denial of the divine inspiration of the majority of the Bible, LeClerc found it impossible to obtain an academic or clerical post in England in spite of his later affirmations of orthodoxy. On LeClerc's views on biblical inspiration see his *Five Letters Concerning the Inspiration of the Holy Scriptures* (London, 1690); Jean Roth, "Le 'Traité de l'inspiration' de Jean LeClerc," *Revue d'histoire et de philosophie religieuse* 36 (1956): 50–60; It is possible that the *Five Letters* was translated by John Locke according to the card catalogue in the British Museum. Locke was well versed on LeClerc's writings and followed LeClerc's running dialogue that lasted from 1685–87 with the French Oratorian priest and noted biblical critic, Richard Simon. See John Woodbridge, *Biblical Authority: A Critique of the Rogers/McKim Proposal* (Grand Rapids, Mich.: Zondervan, 1982), p. 198.
7. "Il n'est pas impossible que, soit ici, soit à Paris, il [LeClerc's nephew]

ait été un peu gâté sur le sujet de la Religion; car il n'y a que trop d'esprits libertins, qui parlent cavalièrement de ces matières, souvent même sans s'être donné la moindre peine de les étudier [It is not impossible that, either here or in Paris, he (LeClerc's nephew) was a bit spoiled on the subject of religion; because there were only so many libertine spirits, who spoke openly on these matters, often even without giving the least effort to study them]." LeClerc to Turretin, manuscrits français, vol. 481, 25 March 1718, fol. 296v.

8. LeClerc himself was often called a Socinian and in several of his early treatises, he had denied the divine inspiration of much of Scripture. LeClerc to Turretin, manuscrits français, vol. 481, 29 November 1726, fol. 320v.

9. On Ostervald see Robert Grétillat, *Jean-Frédéric Osterwald: 1663–1747* (Neuchâtel: Paul Attinger, 1904); Jean-Jacques Von Allmen, *L'Eglise et ses fonctions d'après Jean-Frédérick Ostervald: Le problème de la théologie pratique au début du XVIIIe siècle* (Neuchâtel: Delachaux & Niestle, 1947).

10. Ostervald to Turretin, manuscrits français, vol. 490, 20 March 1735, fol. 243r.

11. Ostervald to Turretin, manuscrits français, vol. 490, 20 March 1720, fol. 150v.

12. Turretin's lecture notes for the course entitles "Abrégés de Leçons de Théol. de Mr. T[urrettini]" are contained in the Archives Tronchin, vol. 119. The "Réfutation du système de Spinosa par M. Turrettini" is its appendix.

13. Henri Fazy, *Procès et Condemnation d'un déiste genevois en 1707* (Geneva: L'Institut national genevois, 1877), pp. 3–4.

Le sieur André Robert Vaudenet témoignoit ouvertement qu'il n'est point dans les sentiments du christianisme, qu'étant une fois dangereusement malade et voulant faire son testament, il dit au notaire qui y avait mis au commencement les termes ordinaires, qu'il n'étoit pas nécessaire de les mettre, puisqu'il ne croyait pas tout cela, qu'il n'a pas fait difficulté de dire qu'il ne croioit pas un Jesus-Christ né d'une vierge Marie, qu'il y avoit dans le livre qu'on appelle l'Ecriture Sainte des choses tout à fait contraires à la raison et qu'il ne le falloit point recevoir.

Ibid.

14. Ibid., p. 4.

15. Ibid., p. 5.

16. Heyd, "Un Role nouveau pour la science," pp. 31–32.

17. Ibid.

18. Maria C. Pitassi, "De la censure à la réfutation: L'Académie de Genève," *Révue de Metaphysique et de Morale* 93 (1988): 157.

19. Ibid., p. 158.

20. Jean-Alphonse Turretin, "Réfutation du système de Spinosa par M. Turrettini," in Pitassi, "De la censure à la réfutation," p. 161.

21. Ibid., in Pitassi, "De la censure à la réfutation," p. 161.

22. Maria C. Pitassi, Un manuscrit genevois cu XVIIe siècle: 'La réfutation du système de Spinosa par M. Turrettini,'" *Nederlands Archief voor Kerkgeschiedenis* 68 (1988): 191.

23. Ibid., pp. 196–97.

24. "puisque toutes les propriétés que je conçois dans les corps ont une connexion nécessaire avec la matière et que les propriétés des pensées n'y ont aucun rapport, les pensées n'apartiennent pas à la matière et aux corps, mais à une substance tout à fait différente." Ibid., p. 201.

25. Ibid., p. 200, n. 35.

26. Ibid., p. 209, n. 60. Pitassi quotes Coliins's argument that people change their minds and think that they are continually choosing among different options and mistake this for freedom. Anthony Collins, *A Philosophical Inquiry Concerning Human Liberty* (London: R. Robinson, 1717), pp. 83–84. The *Dissertatio Libertate humana* is part of Turretin's general treatise on natural theology entitled *Theses de Theologia Naturali in genere,* which was first published in Geneva in 1737.

27. "Spinosa étoit un vray athée. Il n'étoit pas assez peu sensé pour croire toutes ces extravagances, mais étant athée et sçachant que l'athéisme étoit en horreur partout, il a caché son systheme impie sous des termes de Dieu, de Liberté, de vertu, etc. pour tromper les hommes, et pour insinuer avec plus de sûrété son athéisme." Pitassi, "Un manuscrit genevois," p. 200.

28. Manuscrits latins, vol. 213. Praelectionem Analyses, Caput 1: De Theologiae Natura, fol. 6r. The manuscrits latins are housed in the Bibliothèque publique et universitaire in Geneva.

29. Turretin to Robethon, n.d., manuscrits français, vol. 481, fol. 216r.

30. Ibid.

31. Manuscrits latin, vol. 213, De Theologiae Natura, fol. 19r.

32. Beardslee, "Theological Developments," p. 138.

33. Turretin, *Dilucidationes,* 1.3.3.

34. Ibid., 2.2.34.

35. Ibid., 2.2.1–2.2.3.

36. Good, *The Swiss Reformed Church,* pp. 280–90.

37. Turretin, *Dilucidationes,* 1.1.9.

38. Beardslee, "Theological Developments," p. 220.

39. Turretin, *Dilucidationes,* 1.1.9.

40. Turretin, *De Saeculo XVII. Eruditio* in *Dilucidationes,* vol. 3, pp. 223–25.

41. Beardslee, "Theological Developments," pp. 219–20.

42. Ibid.

43. Ibid., pp. 223–24.

44. Ibid.

45. Turretin, *Dilucidationes,* 1.9.5.

46. Ibid., 1.8.9–1.8.10.

47. The *De Cive* was published in Latin in 1642 and translated into English in 1651.

48. Beardslee, "Theological Developments," p. 250.

49. Turretin, *Votum pro pace Europae* (Geneva, 1710) in *Dilucidationes,* vol. 3, pp. 421–33.

50. Ibid., p. 424.

51. Turretin, *Dilucidationes,* 1.9.14.

52. Beardslee, "Theological Developments," p. 253.

53. "Sed affectus illi, nonnisi usque ad certum gradum perduci, naturales sunt: Quod ultra est, vitio, non naturae tribuendum est." Turretin, *Dilucidationes,* 1.9.12.

54. Ibid., 1.9.13.

55. Ibid., 1.9.14.

56. Ibid., 1.7.31.

57. Beardslee, "Theological Developments," p. 245.

58. Manuscrits latins, vol. 213, fols, 1–2.

59. I have used the Basel edition of 1748, which is divided into three volumes, the first being Turretin's theses on natural theology. The treatise on natural theol-

ogy was translated into English by William Crawford in 1778 under the title *Dissertations on Natural theology* (Belfast: James Magee, 1778). All English quotations follow these translations with the original Latin being footnoted only when deemed essential to the argument.

60. Ibid., 1.2.4–10; 11–20; 21–34.
61. Ibid., 1.2.27.
62. Ibid., 1.2.35–1.3.–37; J. A. Turretin, *L'Existence de Dieu démontrée par la structure de l'univers,* Manuscrits de la Compagnie des Pasteurs, vol. 36, fol. 3.
63. Ibid., fol. 4.
64. Ibid., fols. 6–7.
65. Ibid., fols. 9–10.
66. Ibid., fol. 11.
67. Ibid., fol. 12–14.
68. Turretin, *Dilucidationes,* 1.2.22.
69. Ibid., 1.2.28.
70. Ibid., 1.2.59.
71. Beardslee, "Theological Developments," pp. 229–30.
72.

Enimvero, dum in Systemate Atheorum nos constituimus, nihil cognoscimus, nihil videmus; vel minimae res insolubilia nobis sunt aegnimata. Nescimus cur sint haec vel illa Entia, cur sit Materia, cur sit motus, cur nos ipsi simus, atque unde, aut quem in finem in hanc vitae lucem venerimus. . . . Cum in Systemate Atheorum nos constituimus, non modo in tenebris versamur, sed & gravissimae absurditates admittendae sunt. Dicendum est, juxta hoc Systema, pulcherimam illam ac ordinatissimam rerum compagem, quae Mundum adpellatur, brutae necessitas, aut caeci casus, productionem esse. Dicendum est, rudem illam massam, quae Materia dicitur, e qua lapides & ligna constant, excellentissimo adtributo praeditam esse, quod per seipsam existat, semper cognoscere, seipsam depicere, praeterita recolere, de futuris pronunciare, omnen intelligentiam, omnen generare.

Turretin, *Dilucidationes,* 1.2.67–1.2.68.

73. Ibid., 1.3.4–1.3.5.
74. Ibid., 1.3.9.
75. Ibid., 1.3.11.
76. Ibid., 1.3.11.
77. Ibid., 1.3.12.
78. Ibid., 1.3.16.
79. Ibid., 1.3.17.
80. Ibid., 1.3.18.
81. Ibid., 1.3.21.
82. Ibid., 1.3.22.
83. Ibid., 1.3.23.
84. Ibid., 1.3.24.
85. Ibid., 1.3.24–1.3.25.
86. Ibid., 1.3.24.
87. Ibid., 1.3.25.
88.

Unde enim tot se res offerunt, ad hominum utilitatem ac felictatem comparatae? Unde ipse Homo felicitatis capax existit? Unde de rebus ad vitam sustendandam necessarii voluptas addita est? Unde tot eximii fructus? Unde tam amoena Orbis facies? Unde Corpus Humanum tam mire effictum, & tam mire etiam, inter tot pericula, conservatum?

Unde haec, aliaque innumera, nisi ex summa Dei Bonitate, & ad benefaciendum propensione?

Ibid., 1.3.27.
  89. Ibid., 1.3.28.
  90. Ibid., 1.3.29.
  91. Ibid., 1.3.30–31.
  92. Ibid., 1.3.31.
  93. Ibid., 1.3.32.
  94. Ibid., 1.3.36.
  95. Ibid., 1.3.37–43.
  96. Ibid., 1.3.45.
  97. Ibid., 1.3.44.
  98. Ibid., 1.3.45.
  99. Ibid., 1.3. Corollaria.
100. Ibid., 1.4.2.
101. Ibid., 1.4.5.
102. Ibid., 1.4.6.
103. Ibid., 1.4.7.
104. Ibid., 1.4.9.
105. Ibid., 1.4.10.
106.

Pari modo, cum pulcherrimam illam universi Orbis compagem oculis usurpamus, in qua tanta rerum varietas, tantus ornatus, tanta constantia deprehenditur, in qua singula, si recte adverteris, suos ad usus aptissima cernuntur, in qua denique, non exiguo tempore, sed per plura jam annorum millia, nihil de pristino ornatu ordineque decessit, dum haec, inquam, omnia lustramus, sane nemo est nisi mentis inops, qui haec sine mente, sine consilo, sine Arbito fieri, in animum sibi inducere queat.

Ibid., 1.4.15.
107. Ibid., 1.4.16.
108. Ibid., 1.4.18.
109. "Nam qui dicit, Mundum sapienter, & Legibus a Deo positis administrari, & Leges illas constanter perstare, utique non aliud vocibus illis statuit, quam quad nos una Providentiae voce designamus." Ibid., 1.4.21.
110. Ibid., 1.4.22–26.
111. Ibid., 1.4.27.
112. Ibid., 1.4.28.
113. Ibid., 1.4.28.
114. Ibid., 1.5.2.
115. Ibid., 1.5.7.
116. Ibid.
117. Ibid., 1.5.8.
118. Ibid., 1.5.8–9.
119. Ibid., 1.5.8–1.5.9.
120. "in hac mentium nostrarum caligine, & his quibus includimur terminis, eos non esse qui de Dei operibus, eorumque commidis atque incommodis, pulchritudine vel deformitate, tuto judicium terre queamus." Ibid., 1.5.9.
121. "non dari forte rationes particulares, cur hunc foliorum vel granorum numerum, potius quam alium, Deus elegerit: Sed haec tamen omnia fiunt, juxta Leges generales a Deo positas, adeoque nihil eorum est quod non Divinae Provi-

dentiae subjiciatur. Illa omnia novit Deus, illis omnibus praeest, siquidem Legum ab ipso positarum consectaria sunt." Ibid., 1.5.10.

122. Ibid., 1.5.11.
123. Ibid.
124. Ibid., 1.5.13.
125. Ibid., 1.5.15.
126. Ibid., 1.5.16.
127. Ibid., 1.5.17–1.5.18.
128. Ibid., 1.5.19.
129. Ibid., 1.5.40–1.5.41.
130. Ibid., 1.5.43–1.5.44.
131. Ibid., 1.5.46–1.5.47.
132. Ibid.
133. Ibid., 1.5.50.
134. Ibid., 1.5.51.
135. Ibid., 1.6.3.
136. Ibid., 1.6.4.
137. Ibid., 1.6.5.
138. Ibid., 1.6.8.
139. Ibid.
140. Ibid., 1.6.10–1.6.19.
141. Ibid., 1.6.19.
142. Ibid., 1.6.20.
143. Ibid., 1.8.1–2.
144. "Quamobrem, si qui Homines sint, vel integri etiam Populi, qui rationem haudquaquam excoluerint, vel ab ea audienda, sive ob aliud quodcunque impedimentum, aversi fuerint, eos vera ac genuina rerum maralium Principia ignorasse haudquaquam mirum est; neque hinc sequitur Principia illa naturalia non esse." Ibid., 1.8.5.
145. Ibid., 1.8.13.
146. Ibid., 1.7.3.
147. Ibid., 1.7.15.
148. Ibid., 1.8.15.
149. Ibid., 1.8.6.
150. Ibid., 1.8.10.
151. Ibid., 1.8.12.
152. Ibid., 1.8.18.
153. Ibid., 1.9.16.
154. Ibid., 1.9.20.
155. Ibid., 1.9.22–27.
156. Beardslee, "Theological Developments," pp. 147–48.
157. Turretin, *Dilucidationes*, 1.8.28.
158. Ibid.
159. Ibid., 1.10.2–6.
160. Ibid., 1.10.1–7.
161. Ibid., 1.10.17.
162. Ibid., 1.10.19.
163. Ibid., 1.10.20–23.
164. Ibid., 1.10.24.
165. Ibid., 1.11.2–6.
166. Ibid., 1.11.8.

167. Ibid., 1.11.8.
168. Ibid., 1.11.16.
169. Ibid., 1.11.17–18.
170. Ibid., 1.11.29.
171. Ibid., 1.12.2.
172. Ibid., 1.12.4.
173. Ibid., 1.12.6–17.
174. Ibid., 1.12.8.

Chapter 4. Jean Alphonse Turretin on Special Revelation

1. Jean-Alphonse Turretin, *Tractatus de interpretandae Sacrae Scripturae,* Manuscrits latins, vol. 210, fol. 4.

2. W. G. Kümmel, *The New Testament: The History of the Investigation of its Problems,* trans. S. McLean Gilmour and Howard Kee (Nashville, Tenn.: Abingdon, 1972), p. 58.

3. Ibid., p. 59.

4. Hans-Joachim Kraus, "Calvin's Exegetical Principles," *Interpretation* 31 (January 1977): 18.

5. Turretin, *Dilucidationes,* vol. 2, *De Veritate religionis Judaicae et Christianae,* 2.13.12.; 2.2.11. The *De Veritate religionis Judaicae et Christianae* was translated into English in 1778, *Dissertation on Revealed Religion,* William Crawford, trans. (Belfast: James Magee, 1778). Turretin chides the Socinians for attributing too much of theology to the dictates of reason arguing that such an approach destroys the integrity of the Bible as a divine book and that it does not allow for many important biblical doctrines that lie beyond the power of reason to understand in a complete manner. *Dilucidationes,* 2.2.4.

6. Ibid., 2.2.16–2.2.22.

7. Ibid., 2.2.16–2.2.17.

8. Ibid., 2.2.21–2.2.22.

9. Ibid., 2.2.22–2.2.23.

10. Ibid., 2.11.13–2.11.16.

11. The term *accommodation* may be defined as a theological principle governing God's dealing with humanity: in order for God to interact effectively with us, he must come down to our level, or, in other words, he must accommodate himself to our capacity. The term is generally used with respect to the knowledge of God mediated through Scripture; that is, in Scripture the language having to do with the infinite is written at a level that man can understand, using human language, concepts, and so on. It thus also becomes an exegetical principle, since the accommodated nature of scriptural language must be taken into account when interpreting biblical passages.

12. Turretin does not use the phrase *testimonium Spiritus Sancti,* but refers to the *Spiritus Sancti* as the third Person of the Trinity who led the Apostles into all truth and empowered them to spread the gospel. In addition, he virtually makes the Christian faith synonymous with the adherence to rationally acceptable truths and abandons his father's notion of theology as an infused *habitus* in which God grants to the individual the possibility of both understanding the faith and accepting it. Timothy Phillips asserts this point forcefully and overturns the hypothesis that Francis Turretin was a scholastic rationalist. Rather, it was through

the tradition of the Socinians, Arminians, and Amyraldians, whose extensive use of reason won favor in Reformed circles by way of Jean-Alphonse Turretin and his mentor, Louis Tronchin, that Reformed Christianity became rationalized. Phillips quotes J. A. Turretin as saying that the Holy Spirit works through reason when the individual intellectually apprehends the doctrines necessary for saving faith. This is necessary to avoid the pitfalls of subjectivism and fanaticism. Timothy Phillips, "Francis Turretin," p. 404.

13. See Pitassi, "De la censure à la réfutation."

14. Although Turretin was a philosophical eclectic, he praised Descartes for his acumen and solid judgment and used a Cartesian methodology in his own theological discourse. Turretin, *Dilucidationes*, 3.223; Beardslee, "Theological Developments," p. 138.

15. Turretin, *Dilucidationes*, 2.11.27, 28, 48; 2.14.18, 25; 2.16.30, 33.

16. Ibid., 2.11.14.

17. On Calvin's position on progressive revelation see *Institutes*, II.ix.1; II.xi.1–5.

18. Turretin, *Dilucidationes*, 2.3.2–2.3.7; 2.7.17.

19. Ibid., 2.11.18.

20. Ibid., 2.11.17–2.11.18.

21. Ibid., 2.6.1.

22. Ibid., 2.3.12–2.3.17.

23. Ibid., 2.4.16.

24. Ibid., 2.4.3.

25. Ibid., 2.4.1–2.4.3.

26. Ibid., 2.11.48.

27. Heyd cites several other theologians of the era who employed similar arguments in this regard: Th. Barin, *Le Monde Naissant, ou la création du monde démontrée par des principes très simples et très conformés à l'histoire de Moïse* (Utrecht, 1685); S. Rembert, *Nouveau essais d'explication physique du ler chapitre de la Genèse* (Utrecht, 1713); and J. F. Vallade, *Discours philosophique sur la création et l'arrangement du monde* (Amsterdam, 1700). This last work attempts to prove that the biblical accounts of creation incorporated the concept of gravity. See Heyd, "Un Role Nouveau pour la Science," p. 41.

28. Turretin, *Dilucidationes*, 2.11.27, 28, 48; 2.14.18, 25; 2.16.30, 33. One should note that lectures on science properly belonged to the domain of the philosophy curriculum. See Heyd, *Between Orthodoxy and the Enlightenment*.

29. Turretin, *Dilucidationes*, 2.4.41.

30. Ibid., 2.11.48.

31. Ibid., 2.11.30–31.

32. Turretin, *Nubes testium*, in *Dilucidationes*, vol. 3, p. 42.

33. Turretin, *Dilucidationes*, 2.5.20.

34. Ibid., 2.11.42–43.

35. Ibid., 2.4.58.

36. Ibid., 2.4.62–2.4.67.

37. Ibid., 2.4.72–2.4.74.

38. Ibid., 2.4.43; 2.4.44; 2.4.67; 2.4.70.

39. Ibid., 2.8.1.

40. Ibid., 2.7.1–2.7.3.

41. Ibid., 2.15.11.

42. Ibid., 2.15.13.

43. Budé, *Vie de J. A. Turrettini*, pp. 173–75.

44. Ibid.
45. Ostervald to Turretin, 1 January 1727, manuscrits français, vol. 491, fols. 48r–48v.
46. Turretin, *Dilucidationes,* 2.14.13.
47. Ibid., 2.14.23.
48. Ibid., 2.14.25.
49. Ibid., 2.14.30.
50. Ibid., 2.14.32–33.
51. Ibid., 2.4.45.
52. Ibid., 2.11.22–24.
53. Ibid., 2.11.47.
54. Ibid., 2.6.7.
55. Ibid., 2.6.8.
56. Ibid., 2.6.11–12.
57. Ibid., 2.6.13–14.
58. Ibid., 2.6.13.
59. Ibid., 2.6.17–22.
60. Ibid., 2.6.24.
61. Ibid., 2.6.29.
62. Ibid., 2.5.25.
63. Ibid., 2.2.6.
64. Ibid., 2.12.8.
65. Ibid., 2.5.23.
66. Ibid., 2.8.4.
67. Ibid., 2.8.10.
68. Ibid., 2.8.11–12.
69. Ibid., 2.8.14.
70. Ibid., 2.8.20.
71. Ibid., 2.7.3.
72. Ibid., 2.4.3.
73. Ibid., 2.14.4.
74. Ibid., 2.14.7.
75. Ibid., 2.14.8.
76. Ibid., 2.14.7.
77. Ibid., 2.14.22.
78. Ibid., 2.14.22.
79. Ibid., 2.14.34–35.
80. Ibid., 2.14.2–3.
81. Ibid., 2.16.4.
82. Ibid., 2.16.5–6.
83. Ibid., 2.16.8.
84. Ibid., 2.16.10.
85. Ibid., 2.16.11.
86. Ibid., 2.16.15.
87. Ibid., 2.9.1.
88. Ibid., 2.9.2.
89. Ibid., 2.9.3.
90. Ibid., 2.9.4.
91. Ibid., 2.9.8.
92. Ibid., 2.9.9.
93. Ibid., 2.9.12.

94. Ibid., 2.9.19.
95. Richard A. Muller, *Dictionary of Latin and Greek Theological Terms*, p. 100.
96. Turretin, *Dilucidationes*, 2.10.9.
97. Ibid., 2.10.12.
98. Ibid., 2.10.16.
99. Ibid., 2.10.17–18.
100. Ibid., 2.10.23.
101. Ibid., 2.10.29.
102. Ibid., 2.3.11; Turretin, "Tractatus de interpretatione Sacrae Scripturae," fol. 106r.
103. Turretin, *Pyrrhonismus pontificus*, 3.4–3.14; "Tractatus de interpretatione Sacrae Scripturae," fols. 84r–85r.
104. Ibid., fol. 86r.
105. Ibid., fol. 87r.
106. Ibid., fol. 88r; Turretin, *Pyrrhonismus pontificus*, 3.1; 3.18.
107. Turretin, "Tractatus de interpretatione Sacrae Scripturae," fol. 89r.
108. Ibid., fol. 90r.
109. Ibid., fol. 91r.
110. Ibid., fol. 92r.
111. Ibid., fol. 93r.; Turretin, *Pyrrhonismus pontificus*, 3.8; 3.13.
112. Turretin, "Tractatus de interpretatione Sacrae Scripturae," fol. 94r.
113. Turretin, *Pyrrhonismus pontificus*, 3.18.
114. Turretin, "Tractatus de interpretatione Sacrae Scripturae," fol. 101r.
115. Ibid., fols. 102r–103r; Turretin, *Pyrrhonismus pontificus*, 3.34.
116. Turretin, "Tractatus de interpretatione Sacrae Scripturae," fol. 104r.
117. Ibid., fol. 107r.
118. Ibid., fol. 109r.
119. Ibid., fol. 114r.
120. Ibid., fol. 125r.
121. Ibid., fol. 129r.
122. Ibid., fol. 130r.
123. Ibid., fol. 131r.
124. Jean-Alphonse Turretin, *Dissertatio theologica de Christo Audiendo*, in *Dilucidationes*, 3.2.
125. Ibid.
126. Ibid., 3.3.
127. Ibid., 3.6.
128. Ibid., 3.12.
129. Ibid., 3.19.
130. Ibid., 3.20.
131. Ibid., 3.21.
132. Ibid., 3.22.
133. Ibid., 3.23.
134. Ibid., 3.30.
135. Ibid., 3.32.
136. Ibid., 3.31–32.
137. Ibid., 3.34.
138. Ibid., 3.35.
139. Ibid., 3.40–41.
140. LaPlanche, *L'Ecriture*, p. 708.

141. Ibid., p. 995, n. 354.

142. Ibid., p. 621.

143. Pictet noted in his *La théologie chrétienne:* "Et d'ailleurs qui ne sçait que Dieu pour s'accommoder à notre faiblesse parle quelquefois le langage des hommes [Who does not know that God, in order to accommodate himself to our weakness, sometimes speaks the language of men]?" Benedict Pictet, *La théologie chrétienne et la science du salut ou l'exposition des véritez que Dieu a révélées aux hommes dans la Sainte Ecriture avec la réfutation des erreurs contraires à ces véritez, l'Histoire de la plupart de ces erreurs et les sentimens des Anciens Pères* (Amsterdam, 1702), 1. I, c.XVI; p. 60, note d. Cited in LaPlanche, *L'Ecriture,* p. 621. Pictet was related to the Turretin family by marriage. His father, André Pictet, was the son-in-law of Francis Turretin's grandfather.

144. LaPlanche cites Vernet on this issue:

La multitude des cérémonies qui selon la loi de Moyse composoient le Service divin, ne peut-elle pas être regardée comme une sorte d'imperfection? . . . Mais cette remarque (il s'agit de l'imperfection du culte juif) ne va-t-elle point à blâmer la conduite de Dieu qui avoit institué un tel culte? . . . N'est-ce pas aussi un joug incommode et une génie inutile que tant d'ordonnances rituelles

[Cannot the multitude of ceremonies which, according to the Mosaic law, compose the divine service be regarded as a kind of imperfection? . . . But can this remark (concerning the imperfection of the Jewish service) be blamed on the conduct of God who instituted such a form of worship]? Vernet, *Instruction chrétienne,* 4th ed., 5 vols. (Geneva, 1807), 1:266–68; cited by Laplanche, *L'Ecriture,* p. 709.

Chapter 5. The Demise of Reformed Scholasticism, and the Abrogation of the Helvetic Formula Consensus of 1675

1. Albert Montandon, *L'Evolution théologique à Genève au XVIIe siècle* (Le Cateau: J. Roland, 1894), p. 109.

2. Ibid., pp. 112–13.

3. Ibid., p. 114.

4. Heyd, "Cartesianism," p. 306.

5. Ibid., pp. 307–8. Jalabert was the son-in-law of Louis Tronchin. Heyd speculates that the opposition to Jalabert's candidacy came from opponents of the liberal camp because Jalabert, as an ordained minister, would become a member of the Company of Pastors if named a professor at the academy.

6. Heyd, "Cartesianism," p. 310; Jean-Alphonse Turretin, "De studiis emendandis et promovendis," in *Dilucidationes,* vol. 3, pp. 251–72.

7. Ibid., p. 312.

8. Borgeaud, *L'Académie de Calvin,* pp. 487–88; Heyd, "Cartesianism," pp. 311–12.

9. Turretin, "De studiis," in Borgeaud, *L'Académie de Calvin,* p. 488.

10. Heyd, "Cartesianism," p. 312.

11. Borgeaud, *L'Académie de Calvin,* pp. 493–94.

12. Budé, *Vie de J. A. Turrettini,* pp. 69–71.

13. Borgeaud, *L'Académie de Calvin,* p. 164.

14. Ibid.

15. Ibid., pp. 164–65.

16. Registres de la Compagnie des Pasteurs, vol. 19, fol. 100. The Registres are located in the Archives d'Etat in Geneva.

17. The Registers of the Company of Pastors record the proceedings:

Avisé que cette nouvelle signature ne doit point être conservée. 1. Parce qu'ayant ôté le *sic sentio*, c'est-à-dire la nécessité de croire, on ne saurait conserver le *sic docebo* de quelque manière qu'on le tourne, et quelque limitation qu'on puisse y ajouter. Cela est contre la franchise, car c'est s'engager à enseigner ce qu'on ne croit pas lorsqu'on est dans d'autres pensées. 2. Que ces paroles *quoties suspiciam hanc materiam tractare*, sont entièrement équivoques, car elles imposent la nécéssité de mentir . . . ou elles n'imposent pas cette nécéssité et alors ces paroles ne signifient rien et sont absolument inutiles. 3. Que ces autres paroles *neque ore, neque calami, neque publice neque privatim*, établissent une espece d'inquisition très odieuse même sur la conversation et le commerce de lettres, on ne convient point a des matières que tout le monde reconnait être indifférentes, dans un temps surtout ou l'on tache de s'adoucir à cet egard, et ou l'on a oté le *sic sentio*. c'est-à-dire la nécessité de croire ces choses-la. 4. Que ces sortes d'engagements sont absolument impractables que tant de petites questions scholastiques et indifférentes et qu'ainsi ce serait un piège qu'on trait aux consciences. Mais outre ces revisions qui ont determiné la Compagnie à ôter cette nouvelle signature, ce corps a trouvé en général qu'il y avait de très grands inconvénients a laisser quelque signature que ce soit sur des matières comme celles-ci, que les uns et les autres avouent etre indifférentes et nullement essentielles au salut. 1. Parce que les signatures choquent extrêmement les autres Eglises qui n'ont pas les mêmes pensées, comme celles d'Allemagne et d'Angleterre. 3. Que si ces autres Eglises voulaient imposer à leur tour des signatures opposées comme elles le feraient si elles suivaient notre exemple, cela formerait un schisme entre elles et nous. 4. Qu'il y a de l'incongruité à se contenter d'une promesse verbale de se conformer à la Parole de Dieu et à nos confessions de foi et à exiger en même temps une signature sur des matières indifférentes. 5. Que dans plusieurs Eglises considérables de la Suisse, comme à Zurich, à Bâle, à Schaffhouse, on n'exige pas de signature. 6. Que tant qu'on laissera quelque signature sur ces matières, les mêmes inconvénients reviendront sans cesse. Ce sera toujours un piège qu'on tiendra aux consciences. Il y a l'impossibilité absolue à les conserver, et ce sera une semence de division dans notre Compagnie qui se renouvellera en mille occasions.

Ibid., fol. 114.

18. Ibid.
19. Ibid.
20. Ibid., fol. 125.
21. Ibid., fol. 123.
22. Good, *Swiss Reformed Church*, p. 279.
23. Ibid., p. 281.
24. Ibid., pp. 282–83.
25. Ibid., p. 14.
26. Ibid., p. 25.
27. Ibid.
28. Ibid., pp. 25–26.
29. Ibid.
30. Ibid., p. 27.
31. Budé, *Lettres à Turrettini*, 2:392.
32. Ibid., 2:197.
33. Von Allmen, *Ostervald*, pp. 84–85.
34. Ibid., p. 49.
35. Gaberel, *Histoire de l'Eglise de Genève*, 3:32.
36. Vuilleumier, *Histoire de l'église*, 3:594.

37. Budé, *Lettres à Turrettini*, 2:392.

38. Louis Gonin, *Les Catéchismes de Calvin et d'Ostervald: Etude historique et comparative* (Montauban, France: J. Granie, 1893), p. 87.

39. Ibid., p. 79.

40. Von Allmen, *Ostervald*, p. 112.

41. Good, *Swiss Reformed Church*, p. 191.

42. Sykes, *William Wake*, 2:27–28.

43. Vuilleumier, *Histoire de l'Eglise*, 3:572.

44. Ibid., p. 574.

45. Ibid., p. 577.

46. Ibid., p. 578.

47. Ibid., p. 636.

48.

Il est certain que la classe de Morges a fait une grande levée de fondiers, pour réprésenter à LL. EE. que les nouvelles opinions font beaucoup de progrès parmi les jeunes Ministres pour jetter des soupçons sur plusieurs membres de l'Académie, & pour demander qu'à l'avenir les Impositionnaires, qui entreront dans leur Classe, soient tenus de signer de nouveau le Consensus, de chargeat lui plus particulièrement, en parlent ici à M. le Thiesmor Steiger, à qui ils doivent présenter leur Memoire. . . . On nous a dit, que Ce Seigneur les avoit assez mal reçus, & depuis ce temps-là nous n'avons entendu parler de rien. Les Auteurs de cette affaire sont quelques-uns des plus ignorans de la Classe.

Barbeyrac to Turretin, 24 November 1715, manuscrits français, vol. 484, fol. 192r.

49. Ibid., fol. 192v.

50. Barbeyrac to Turretin, 9 February 1716, manuscrits français, vol. 484, fol. 196r.

51. Vuilleumier, *Histoire de l'Eglise*, 3:643.

52. Ibid.

53. Sykes, *William Wake*, 2:30.

54. Ibid.

55. Barbeyrac to Turretin, 18 October 1717, manuscrits français, vol. 484, fols. 214r–215v.

56. Geneva MSS, Inv. 1569, fol. 41, in Sykes, *William Wake*, 2:32–33.

57. Ibid., 2:36.

58. Ibid.

59. Ibid.

60. Ibid., 2:41.

61. Ibid.

62. Vuilleumier, *Histoire de l'Eglise*, 3:665–66.

63. Sykes, *William Wake*, 2:45.

64. Turretin, *Nubes testium*. This essay was translated into English and published in 1823 under the title "On Fundamentals in Religion," in *Collection of Essays and Tracts in Theology*, ed. Jared Sparks, vol. 1 (Boston: Oliver Everett, 1823).

65. Budé, *Vie de J. A. Turrettini*, pp. 141–42.

66. Vuilleumier, *Histoire de l'Eglise*, 3:674.

67. Ibid., 3:676–77.

68. Sykes, *William Wake*, 2:54–55.

69. Ibid., p. 49.

70. Ibid., p. 51.

71. Ibid., p. 54.

72. Vuilleumier, *Histoire de l'Eglise,* 3:735.
73. Sykes, *William Wake,* 2:57–58.
74. Beardslee, "Theological Developments," p. 67.

Chapter 6. The Fundamental Articles and Attempts at Protestant Reunification

1. Budé, *Vie de J. A. Turrettini,* pp. 144–46.
2. Ibid., pp. 129ff.
3. Ibid., p. 148.
4. "S'il y a quelque chose, Monsieur, qui nous donne lieu d'en esperer le succès, c'est de voir qu'un Prince aussi puissant et aussi pieux que S. M. s'y applique avec tant de zèle, et qu'il y employe un Ministre aussi habile, et aussi bien intentionné que vous [If there is something, Sir, which can give us hope of success, it is to see a Prince as powerful and as pious as His Majesty, who applies himself with so much zeal, and who employs a minister as able and well meaning as you]." Turretin to Metternich, manuscrits français, vol. 452, 29 April 1707, fol. 222r.
5. The king of Prussia to the Genevan Company of Pastors, manuscrits français, vol. 490, 5 July 1719, fol. 139r.
6. Ostervald to Turretin, manuscrits français, vol. 490, 5 July 1719, fol. 139r.
7. Ibid., 2 March 1718, fol. 125r.
8. Ostervald to Turretin, manuscrits français, vol. 489, 23 October 1706, fol. 153r.
9. Ibid.
10. LeClerc to Turretin, manuscrits français, vol. 487, 15 May 1725, fol. 318r.
11. Leemans to Turretin, manuscrits français, vol. 487, 18 January 1700, fol. 287r.
12. Adams, *Wake's Gallican Correspondence,* 1:8.
13. Ibid., 1:17.
14. Ibid., 1:72.
15. Sykes, *William Wake,* 2:66.
16. Ibid., 2:62–64.
17. Ibid., 2:64.
18. Ibid., 2:65–70; John T. McNeill, "Irenical Treatises by German and Dutch Reformed Writers," in *Ecumenical Testimony,* ed. John T. McNeill and James H. Nichols (Philadelphia: Westminster Press, 1974), pp. 73–74.
19. Sykes, *William Wake,* 2:69.
20. McNeill, "Irenical Treatises," p. 74.
21. Sykes, *William Wake,* 2:84.
22. The term *fundamental article* should not be confused with the fundamentalism of American Protestantism, which was restrictive in scope in response to the development of liberal theology and biblical criticism. Fundamental articles in the Reformation and post-Reformation period, by contrast, were primarily intended to be nonrestrictive and make possible a pan-Protestant union. The term is used in a technical sense by virtually all of the major theologians of the period and Richard Muller defines it as "a doctrinal concept originated among the early Lutheran scholastics and later adopted by the Reformed, according to which the

basic doctrines necessary to the Christian faith are distinguished from secondary or logically derivative doctrines. Thus *articuli fundamentales* are those doctrines without which Christianity cannot exist and the integrity of which is necessary for the preservation of the faith." Richard A. Muller, *Dictionary of Latin and Greek Theological Terms,* p. 45.

23. Preus, *The Theology of Post-Reformation Lutheranism,* 1:151.

24. Otto Ritschl, *Dogmengeschichte des Protestantismus,* vol. 4, *Orthodoxie und Synkretismus in der altprotestantischen Theologie* (Göttingen: Vandenhoeck & Puprecht, 1927), pp. 243ff. See also Timothy Phillips, "Francis Turretin," pp. 434–35. Although it is not fair to lump the Remonstrants and the Socinians into one category as if there were no differences between them, the distinctions between the two groups were often blurred during the period. Furthermore, the Socinians often claimed such great Arminian champions as Simon Episcopius, Etienne de Courcelles, and Hugo Grotius as their own. Pierre Bayle in 1685 labeled the Arminians as "l'égout de tous les Athées, Déistes et Sociniens de l'Europe [the sewer of all the Atheists, Deists and Socinians of Europe]," Guy H. Dodge, *The Political Theory of the Huguenots of the Dispersion with Special Reference to the Thought and Influence of Pierre Jurieu* (New York: Columbia University Press, 1947), p. 168n; *Lettre de M. Bayle à M. Lenfant,* dated 6 July 1685 in *Oeuvres,* 1737, IV, 623.

25. Martin Schmidt, "Ecumenical Activity on the Continent of Europe in the Seventeenth and Eighteenth Centuries," in *A History of the Ecumenical Movement,* ed. Rouse and Neill, pp. 75–78; Phillips, "Francis Turretin," pp. 442–43; Acontius, *Stratagemata Satanae* (Amsterdam: Ionnem Ravestegnium, 1652), pp. 53ff.

26. Schmidt, "Ecumenical Activity," pp. 93–96.

27. Phillips, "Francis Turretin," p. 481.

28. The French national synods of Gap (1603) and La Rochelle (1607) were prime examples of this. Philippe du Plessis Mornay (1549–1623), the advisor to Henry of Navarre, used fundamental articles in his *Traité de l'Eglise* (1578) as a basis for suggesting an accord with the Church of England. James I responded to the French Reformed initiative by sending a letter to the Synod of Toniens (1614) expressing his own desire for union. The Synod went on to adopt a series of procedures designed to set up an international synod that would formulate procedures for establishing a common Reformed-Anglican-Lutheran statement of faith based on the fundamental articles. John T. McNeill, "The Ecumenical Idea and Efforts to Realize It," in *The Ecumenical Movement,* ed. Rouse and Neill, pp. 65–67; LaPlanche, *L'Ecriture,* p. 14. Mornay also used fundamental articles in his description of the true church. Philippe du Plessis Mornay, *Traitté de l'Eglise* 2d edition (La Rochelle: Hierosme Havltin, 1599), pp. 75–77; 172–75.

29. Isaac D'Huisseau, *La Réunion du christianisme; ou La Manière de rejoindre les chrétiens en une seule confession de foi* (Saumur, 1670), pp. 146ff. See also Richard Stauffer, *L'Affaire d'Huisseau: Une controverse protestante au sujet de la réunion des chrétiens (1670–1671)* (Paris: Presses universitaires de France, 1969), p. 14. French theologian Jean Daillé also included his discussion of fundamental articles within the context of defining the true church and even provided a list of fundamental articles that included the mediatorial ministry of Christ and his sacrifice on the cross for sin, the necessity of baptism, and the Lord's Supper, scriptural authority, and the proper worship of God. Daillé even pointed out the errors of the Roman Catholic church on each point. René Voeltzel points out that Daillé did not share the same optimism of D'Huisseau concerning the possibility

of the Roman Catholic church reforming itself on any of these points. René Voeltzel, *Vraie et fausse Eglise selon les théologiens protestants français du XVIIe siècle* (Paris: Presses Universitaires de France, 1956), p. 41. Saumur was by no means the sole center for French Protestant opinions concerning the fundamental articles. Pierre du Moulin, who opposed Saumur on a number of theological topics, emphasized the importance of the fundamental articles on the issue of biblical perspicuity against the Counter-Reformation charge of the obscurity of Scripture. Du Moulin feared that the Salmurian approach compromised too much of orthodoxy by admitting that many distinctive Reformed doctrines were not fundamentals because they are not clearly revealed in the Bible. See Robinson, "The Doctrine of Holy Scripture," p. 140.

30. D'Huisseau rejected those "doctrines qui établissent l'ordre des décrets éternels de Dieu, qui disent précisément quel est l'objet de la prédestination, qui exposent comment les deux natures sont unies en la personne de Jesus Christ, qui approfondissent le mystère de la Trinité, qui prétendent découvrir le moyen par lequel le Saint-Esprit agit [dans l]es coeurs des fidelles [doctrines which establish the order of God's eternal decrees, which state precisely what is the object of predestination, which show how the two natures are united in the person of Jesus Christ, which probe the mystery of the Trinity, which presumes to discover the means by which the Holy Spirit acts in the hearts of the faithful]." D'Huisseau, *Réunion,* p. 55; Richard Stauffer, *L'Affaire D'Huisseau,* p. 14; Stauffer, *The Quest for Church Unity from John Calvin to Isaac D'Huisseau* (Allison Park, Penn.: Pickwick, 1986), pp. 64–66.

31. Alfred Soman, "Arminianism in France: The D'Huisseau Incident," *Journal of the History of Ideas* 31 (1967): 599–600; See also Stauffer's response, "D'Huisseau a-t-il plagié Arminius?" *Bulletin de la Société de l'histoire du protestantisme français* (1972): 335–48. Other treatments of D'Huisseau include Frank Puaux, *Les Précurseurs français de la tolérance au XVIIe siècle* (Paris, 1881), pp. 75–81; Voeltzel, *Vraie et fausse Eglise,* pp. 45–50.

32. The correspondence between Wake and Turretin is housed in the library of Christ Church, Oxford University, and is catalogued under Archbishop Wake Epist. 31.

33. LeClerc pointed out that the English church would need an archbishop of Canterbury who would work tirelessly for such a union in order for the plan to have any success. Even when such a man, Wake, became archbishop in 1716, LeClerc noted that Wake's influence would be limited because of the factions within the English church. LeClerc was also pessimistic about the chances of accord with the Lutherans primarily because they "do not have enough prudence or charity, and because the Princes are not sufficiently enlightened." Barnes, *Jean LeClerc,* p. 199.

34. Beardslee, "Theological Developments," p. 67.

35. Johann Heinrich Heidegger, *Corpus Theologiae Christianae* (Zurich: David Gessneri, 1700), 1.1.53–54; Francis Turretin, *Institutio Theologiae Elenctiae,* 3 vols. (Edinburgh: John D. Lowe, 1847), 1.14.4, 22.

36. Jean-Alphonse Turretin, *Dilucidationes,* 2.3.13. Turretin was an ardent opponent of Enthusiasm primarily on the issue of extra-biblical revelation. In addition, Turretin did not believe in extrabiblical miracles. In his *De Scripturae Sacrae interpretandae methodo tractatus,* Turretin attacked the Quakers for their dependence on internal light. François LaPlanche notes that, on this point, Turretin argued that the Enthusiasts contradicted the clarity and sufficiency of Scripture, thus preventing all rational discussion with unbelievers and subverting both

church and civil order. Turretin, *Opera omnia,* vol. 2, *De Scripturae Sacrae inter-pretandae methodo tractatus,* part 1, ch. 3, p. 17; LaPlanche, *L'Ecriture,* p. 692.

37. Turretin, *Nubes testium,* in *Dilucidationes,* 3.30–31.

38. Ibid., p. 42.

39. Ibid., p. 34.

40. Ibid., p. 44.

41. Ibid.

42. Ibid., p. 42.

43. Jean LeClerc, *Liberii de Sancto Amore Epistolae Theologicae, in quibus varii scholasticorum errores castigantur* (Saumur: Henri Desbordes, 1681). Annie Barnes argues that LeClerc influenced Turretin on a number of topics, an asser-tion that is supported by the correspondence between the two, which lasted from 1705–28. Barnes writes: "One can see how much his [Turretin's] spirit and his ideas came from LeClerc whom he had admired since his youth, when under the direction of his tutor he read the *Bibliothèque universelle* [edited by LeClerc]. The two men were made for a mutual understanding." Barnes, *Jean LeClerc,* p. 199. In addition, an interesting article by J. J. V. M. De Vet shows that LeClerc, in turn, was quite influenced by Grotius. LeClerc edited and republished Grotius's *De Veritate Religionis Christianae* (1629) in several editions starting in 1709. LeClerc included his own marginalia in which he updated Grotius's arguments on a number of points relative to discoveries in science. In addition, according to De Vet's description, LeClerc's position on fundamental articles is almost the mirror image of Turretin's stance. See J. J. V. M. De Vet, "Jean LeClerc, an Enlightened Propagandist of Grotius' *De Veritate Religionis Christianae,*" *Neder-lands Archief voor Kerkgeschiedenis* 64 (1984): 160–195.

44. Turretin, *Nubes testium* in *Dilucidationes,* 3:46.

45. Ibid., p. 50.

46. Ibid., p. 42.

47. Ibid.

48. Ibid.

49. Ibid., p. 48.

50. John Calvin, *Institutes of the Christian Religion,* ed. John T. McNeil, trans. Ford Lewis Battles, 2 vols. (Philadelphia: Westminster Press, 1960), II.ix.1; II.xi.1–5.

51. Dodge, *The Political Theory of the Huguenots,* pp. 165–97.

52. Turretin, *Nubes testium* in *Dilucidationes,* 3:43.

53. Ibid., pp. 50–51.

54. Ibid., pp. 42–43.

55. Ibid., pp. 59–60.

56. Turretin, *Nubes testium,* in *Dilucidationes,* 3:37–38.

57. Ibid., p. 38.

58. Ibid.

59. Ibid., p. 68.

60. See Schmidt, "Ecumenical Activity," pp. 86–87.

61. Ibid.

62. Budé, *Vie de J. A. Turrettini,* p. 88.

63. Turretin, *Nubes testium* in *Dilucidationes,* 3:73.

64. Manuscrits français, vol. 491, fol. 247v.

65. Turretin, *Nubes testium* in *Dilucidationes,* 3:76.

66. Ibid., pp. 78–80.

67. Turretin, *Défense de la Dissertation de Mr. Turretin sur les Articles fonda-*

mentaux; contre une Brochure intitulé, Lettre de M. T. C., c'est-à-dire, de Mr. Théodore Crisnoz, qu'on appelle ordinairement Mr. de Bionens, etc. (Geneva: Fabri et Barillot, 1727).

68. Ibid., p. 1.

69. Ibid., p. 2.

70. Ibid., pp. 4–5.

71. Ibid., p. 5.

72. Ibid., p. 6.

73. Ibid., p. 44.

74. Ibid., p. 45.

75. Ibid., p. 58.

76. Ibid., p. 6.

77. Ibid., pp. 11, 17.

78. Budé, *Vie de J. A. Turrettini,* p. 101; Vuilleumier, *Histoire de l'Eglise,* 4:220–21.

79. Ibid., 4:221; Budé, *Lettres à Turrettini,* 3:302.

80. Budé, *Lettres à Turrettini,* 3:430.

81. Vuilleumier, *Histoire de l'Eglise,* 4:221–24.

Conclusion

1. Kraus, "Calvin's Exegetical Principles," p. 12.

Bibliography

Primary Sources

Manuscript Sources

AMSTERDAM:

Universiteitsbibliothek von Amsterdam:
  Correspondence de Turrettini à LeClerc

GENEVA:

Archives d'Etat de Genève:
  Registres de la Compagnie des Pasteurs. Vol. 19.
Bibliothèque publique et universitaire de Genève:
  Archives Tronchin. Vols. 33, 36, 38, 39, 42, 47, 51–60, 68, 81, 82, 84, 86, 119.
  Collection de manuscrits français. Vols. 452, 481–493.
  Collection de manuscrits latins. Vols. 210, 213.
  Manuscrits de la Compagnie des Pasteurs. Vols. 15–36, 54, 862, 1001, 1072
  Manuscrits Lullin. Vol. 5

CHRIST CHURCH, OXFORD:
  Archbishop Wake Epist. Vol. 31

PARIS:

Bibliothèque Nationale de Paris:
  Fr. 9362 Correspondence de L'Abbé Nicaise

ZURICH:

Zentralbibliothek Zürich:
  F. A. V. Wyss. Vol. 111

Unpublished Treatises by J. A. Turretin

MANUSCRITS DE LA COMPAGNIE DES PASTEURS:

Vols. 15–16 Sermons et paraphrases (1695–1733), 2 vols. in 4o, 314 and 103 pp.
Vols. 17–18 Sermons et sermons de congrégation (1701–20), 2 vols. in 12, 510 and
  411 pp.

Vol. 19 Sermons en italien (1701–09), 1 vol. in pp.

Vol. 20 Dix discours de consécration (1706–26), 1 vol. in 12, 145 pp. Sept discours de censures (1719–25), relié avec les discours précédents, 30 pp.

Vols. 21–22 Praelectiones in concionem Christi, Matth. V, VI, VII (1716–21), 2 vols. in 4o, 523 and 544 pp.

Vols. 23–24 Idem (exemplaire différent du précédent par le texte et par l'écriture), 2 vols. in 4o, 264 and 332 pp.

Vol. 25 Praelectiones Theologicae (1704–13), 1 vol. in 4o, 992 pp.

Vols. 26 and 27 Praelectiones in Epistolas Pauli (1731–34), 2 vols. in 4o

Tome I: Epist. ad Romanos, 644 pp.

Tome II: Epist. ad Thessalonicienses, 536 pp.

Vol. 28 Historiae ecclesiasticae compendium, a Christo nato usque ad annum MDCC, 1 vol. in 4o, 609 pp.

Vol. 29 Praelectiones theologicae, 1 vol. in 4o, 190 pp. De felicitate humana . . . De statu animorum postmortem, chiliasmo, purgatotio, etc . . . De articulis fondamentalibus.

Vol. 30 Tractatus de Dei attributis, 1 vol. in 4o, 327 pp.

Vol. 31 Tractatus: de dei perfectionibus et de Scriptura Sacra, 1 vol. in 4o, 298 and 136 pp.

Vols. 32–33 Theologia naturalis. 2 expl., l'un écrit par G. de l'Escale (1787), 49 pp. l'autre par Gabriel Pasteur, in 12, 264 pp.

Vol. 34 Analyses praelectionum exerptiae a F[rançois] De Roches, 1 vol. in 12, 368 pp.

Vol. 35 Thèses et dissertations théologiques, traduites par P[hilippe] Basset fils, 1 vol. in 4o, 59 pp.

Vol. 36 Manuscrits divers, 416 pp. L'Existence de Dieu demontrée par la structure de l'univers, 64 pp.

Vol. 54 Collection des sermons.

Vol. 862 Dissertatio de studiis recte instuendis, 31 pp.

Vol. 1001 Lettres de J. A. Turrettini.

Vol. 1072 Explications, paraphrases, réflexions sur des textes bibliques.

MANUSCRITS LATINS:

Vol. 210 Tractatus de interpretatione Sacrae Scripturae.

Vol. 213 Praelectionum analyses, 26 pp.

Published Sources

Acontius, Jacob. *Stratagementa Satanae*. Amsterdam: Ionnem Ravestegnium, 1652.

Amyraut, Moïse. *Brief Traité de la prédestination avec L'Eschantillon de la doctrine de Calvin sur les mesme sviet*. Saumur: Isaac Desbordes, 1658.

Bèze, Théodore de. *Traicté des vrayes essencielles et visibles marques de la vraye Église Catholique*. Geneva: Iean LePreux, 1592.

Bionens, Théodore Crisnoz de. *Apologie de Msr. de Bionens contre un Ecrit intitulé Défense de la dissertation de Mr. Turretin sur les articles fondamentaux de la religion.* Yverdon: Jean-Jacques Genath, 1727.

Calvin, John. *Commentary on the Epistles to Timothy, Titus, and Philemon.* Edited by William Pringle. Edinburgh: Calvin Translation Society, 1852.

———. *Commentaries on the First book of Moses called Genesis.* Translated by John King. Grand Rapids, Mich.: Eerdmans Publishing Co., 1948.

———. *Institutes of the Christian Religion.* Edited by John T. McNeill. Translated by Ford L. Battles. Philadelphia: Westminster Press, 1960.

Cappel, Louis. *Critica sacra, sive de variis quae in sacris Veteris Testamenti libris occurrunt lectionibus libri sex . . . cui subiecta est eiusdam criticae adversus iniustum censorem iusta defensi.* Paris: S & G Cramoisy, 1650.

———. *hoc est arcanum punctationis revelatum, sive de punctorum vocalium et accentuum apud Hebraeus vera et germana antiquitate.* Amsterdam: Johan nem Maire, 1624.

Grotius, Hugo. *The Truth of the Christian Religion in Six Books.* Translated by John Claude. London: William Boghes, 1825.

Heidegger, Johann Heinrich. *Corpus Theologiae Christianae.* 3 vols. Zurich: David Gessneri, 1700.

Hobbes, Thomas. *De cive; or the Citizen.* Edited by Sterling P. Lamprecht. New York: Appleton-Century-Crofts, 1949.

———. *Leviathan; or the Matter, Form and Power of a Commonwealth, Ecclesiastical and Civil.* Edited by Michael Oakshott. New York: Collier Books, 1962.

Huisseau, Isaac D'. *La Réunion du christianisme: où, la Manière de rejoindre les chrétiens en une seule confession de foi.* Saumur, 1670.

Jurieu, Pierre. *Traité de l'unité de l'église et des points fondamentaux.* Rotterdam: Abraham Archer, 1688.

———. *Examen du livre de la Réunion du Christianisme.* Orleans, 1671.

LeClerc, Jean. *Défense des Sentimens de quelques théologiens de Holland sur l'Histoire critique du Vieux Testament.* Amsterdam: Henri Desbordes, 1686.

———. *De l'incredulité ou l'on éxamine les motifs et les raisons générales qui portent les incrédules à rejetter la religion chrétienne.* Amsterdam: Henri Desbordes, 1696.

———. *Five Letters Concerning the Inspiration of the Holy Scriptures.* Translated by [John Locke] London, n.p., 1690.

———. *Parrhasiana ou pensées divers sur des matiers de critique, d'histoire, de morale et de politique avec la défense de divers ouvrages de M. LeClerc.* Amsterdam: Henri Schulte, 1701.

———. *Sentimens de quelques théologiens de Hollande sur l'Histoire critique du Vieux Testament.* Amsterdam: Henri Desbordes, 1685.

———. *Vita et opera.* Amsterdam: Johannus Luduricum, 1711.

Limborch, Philippe van. *The Remarkable Life of Uriel Acosta, an Eminent Freethinker; With his Reason for Rejecting all Revealed religion. To which is Added Mr. Limborch's Defense of Christianity in Answer to Acosta's Objections.* London: John Wheston, 1740.

———. *Theologia Christiana ad praxin pietatis ac promotionem pacis Christianae unice directa.* Amsterdam: George Arnold, 1735.

Locke, John. *Familiar Letters Between Mr. John Locke and Several of his Friends. In which are Explained, his Notions in his Essay Concerning Human Understanding.* London: F. Noble, 1742.

Moray, Philippe du Plessis, *Traitté de l'Eglise.* 2d ed. La Rochelle: Hierosme Havltin, 1599.

Musculus, Wolfgang. *Loci Communes Sacrae Theologiae.* Basel: Ex officina Heruagiana, 1567.

Pictet, Benedict. *Lettre sur ceux qui se croyent inspirez.* Geneva: Fabri & Barrilot, 1721.

————. *La Morale chrétienne ou l'art de bien vivre.* 2 vols. Geneva: La Compagnie des Libraires, 1710.

————. *La Théologie chrétienne.* 3 vols. Geneva: De Tournes, 1721.

————. *Traité contre l'indifférence des religions.* Geneva: Cramer et Perrachon, 1716.

Simon, Richard. *Histoire critique du Vieux Testament.* Rotterdam: Renier Leers, 1678.

————. *De l'inspiration des livres sacrés avec une réponse au livre intitulé Défense des Sentimens de quelques théologiens de Hollande sur l'Histoire critique du Vieux Testament.* Rotterdam: Renier Leers, 1686.

————. *Réponse au livre intitulé Sentimens de quelques théologiens de Hollande sur l'Histoire critique du Vieux Testament.* Rotterdam: Renier Leers, 1686.

————. *Lettres choisies de M. Simon.* 2 vols. Amsterdam: n.p., 1730.

Socinus, Faustus. *An Argument for the Authority of Holy Scripture; from the Latin of Socinus, after the Steinfurt Copy. To which is fixed a Short Account of his Life.* Translated by Edward Combe. London: W. Meadows, 1731.

Spanheim, Friedrich. *Controversiarum de Religione cum Dissidentibus Hodie Prolixe & cum Judaeis Elenchus Historico-Theologicus.* Amsterdam: Joannem Wolters, 1694.

Spinoza, Benedict de. *The Chief Works of Benedict de Spinoza.* Edited by R. J. M. Elwes. 2 vols. London: George Bell and Sons, 1883.

Suarez, Francis. *On the Various Kinds of Distinctions.* Translated by Cyril Vollert. Milwaukee, Wis.: Marquette University, 1947.

Turretin, Francis. *Institutio theologiae elencticae in qua status controversiae perspicue exponuntur, praecipua orthodoxorum argumenta proponuntur, et vindicantur, et fontes solutionum aperiuntur.* 4 vols. Geneva: Jacobum a Puolsum, 1734.

————. *Institutes of Elenctic Theology. Volume 1: First Through Tenth Topics.* Translated by George M. Giger. Edited by James T. Dennison, Jr. (Phillipsburg, N.J.: P & R Publishing, 1992).

Turretin, Jean-Alphonse. *Abrégé de l'histoire écclesiastique depuis la naissance de Jesus-Christ jusqu'à l'an MDCC.* Neuchâtel: S. Fauche, 1765.

————. *Cogitationes et dissertationes theologicae. Quibus principia religionis, cum naturalis, tum revelatae, adstruuntur & defenduntur; animique ad veritatis, pietatis, & pacis studium excitantur.* Geneva: Typis Barrillot & filii, 1711–37.

————. *Commentarius theoretico-practicus in epistolas Sancti Pauli ad Thessalonicos.* Basel: J. Brandmullerum, 1739.

———. *Défense de la Dissertation de Mr. Turretin sur les Articles fondamentaux; contre une Brochure intitulé, Lettre de M. T. C., c'est-à-dire, de Mr. Théodore Crisnoz, qu'on appelle ordinairement Mr. de Bionens, etc.* Geneva: Fabri et Barillot, 1727.

———. *Dilucidationes philosophico-theologico-dogmatico-morales, quibus praecipua capita tam theologiae naturalis, quam revelate demonstrantur et ad praxin christianam commendantur accedunt, I. Orationes panegyricae et varii argumenti item henoticae de pace ecclesiae II. Commercium epistolicum inter regem borussiae Frider I. et Pastores Genèvenses de syncretismo protestantium.* 3 vols. Basel: J. R. ImHoff, 1748.

———. *Dissertation on Revealed Religion.* Translated by William Crawford. Belfast: James Magee, 1778.

———. *Dissertations on Natural Theology.* Translated by William Crawford. Belfast: James Magee, 1778.

———. *Nubes testium pro moderato et pacifico de rebus theologicis judicio, et instituenda inter protestantes concordia. Praemissa est brevis & pacfica de articulis fundamentalibus disquisitio.* Geneva: Fabri & Burrillo, 1719.

———. "On Fundamentals in Religion." In *Collection of Essays and Tracts in Theology,* edited by Jared Sparks, vol. 1. Boston: Oliver Everett, 1823.

———. *Opera omnia theologica, philosophica et philologica.* 3 vols. Franeker, the Netherlands: H. A. de Chalmot et D. Romar, 1774–76.

———. *Orationes academicae. Quibus multa ad scientiarum incrementum. Christianae veritatis illustrationem pietatis commendationem, pacemque Christianorum, pertinentia continentur.* Geneva: Typis Barrilot & filii, 1737.

———. *Pyrrhonismus pontificus sive theses theologico-historicae de variationibus pontificorum circa ecclesiae infallibatem.* Leiden, 1692.

———. *Sermon sur ces paroles de l'Evangile de notre Seigneur Jesus-Christ selon Saint Jean Chap. XII. v. 35–36.* Geneva, 1719.

Ursinus, Zacharius. *The Sume of the Christian Religion.* Translated by Henrie Parrie. Oxford: Joseph Barnes, 1587.

Werenfels, Samuel. *Opuscula Theologica, Philosophica et Philologica* Lausanne: Michaelis Bousquet, 1739.

Secondary Sources

Adams, Leonard, ed. *William Wake's Gallican Correspondence and Related Documents, 1716–1731* 2 vols. New York: Peter Lang, 1988.

Allen, Don C. *Doubt's Boundless Sea: Scepticism and Faith in the Renaissance.* Baltimore: The Johns Hopkins University Press, 1964.

Allison, Leon M. "The Doctrine of Scripture in the Theology of John Calvin and Francis Turretin." Th.M. thesis, Princeton Theological Seminary, 1958.

Archinaud, A. "Les Théologiens du nom de Tronchin." *Bulletin de la Société de l'histoire du protestantisme français.* 13 (1864): 175–83.

Armstrong, Brian. *Calvinism and the Amyraut Heresy: Protestant Scholasticism and Humanism in Seventeenth Century France.* Madison: University of Wisconsin Press, 1969.

———. "The Changing Face of French Protestantism: The Influence of Pierre

Du Moulin." In *Calviniana: The Ideas and Influence of John Calvin,* edited by Robert V. Schnucker. Kirksville, Mo.: Sixteenth Century Journal Publishers, 1988.

Auvray, Paul. "Richard Simon et Spinoza." In *Religion, Erudition et critique à la fin du XVIIe siècle et au début du XVIIIe,* edited by René Voeltzel, pp. 201–14. Strasbourg: Presses Universitaires de France, 1968.

———. *Richard Simon (1638–1712): étude bio-bibliographique avec des textes inédits.* Paris: Presses Universitaires de France, 1974.

Bangs, Carl. *Arminius: A Study in the Dutch Reformation.* Grand Rapids, Mich.: Francis Asbury Press, 1985.

Barnes, Annie. *Jean LeClerc et la République des Lettres.* Geneva: Droz, 1938.

Battles, Ford L. "God was Accommodating Himself to Human Capacity." *Interpretation* 31 (January 1977): 19–38.

Beardslee, John W., ed. *Reformed Dogmatics.* New York: Oxford University Press, 1965.

Beardslee, John W. "Theological Developments at Geneva under Francis and Jean-Alphonse Turretin (1648–1737)." Ph.D. diss., Yale University, 1956.

Biographie universelle, ancienne et moderne. Edited by M. Michaud. 2d ed. 45 vols. Paris, 1843–65.

Bizer, Ernst. *Früorthodoxie und Rationalismus.* Zurich: EVZ Verlag, 1963.

Bohatec, Josef. *Die Cartesianische scholastik in der philosophie und reformierten dogmatik des 17. jahrhunderts.* Hildesheim, Germany: Georg Olms Verlagsbuchhandlung, 1966.

Bonno, Gabriel, ed. "Lettres inédites de LeClerc à Locke." *University of California Publications in Modern Philology* 52 (1959).

Borgeaud, Charles. *Histoire de l'université de Genève: L'Académie de Calvin, 1559–1798.* Geneva: George & Co., 1900.

Bourchenin, P. Daniel. *Etude sur les académies protestantes en France aux XVIe et XVIIe siècles.* Paris: Grassart, 1882.

Bouwsma, William J. *John Calvin: A Sixteenth Century Portrait.* New York: Oxford University Press, 1988.

Bray, John S. *Theodore Beza's Doctrine of Predestination.* Nieuwkoop, the Netherlands: B. de Graaf, 1975.

Bredvold, Louis A. *The Intellectual Milieu of John Dryden: Studies in Some Aspects of Seventeenth-Century Intellectual Thought.* Ann Arbor: University of Michigan Press, 1934.

Breen, Quirinius. *John Calvin: A Study in French Humanism.* 2d ed. New York: Archon Books, 1968.

Brooks, Richard S. *The Interplay Between Science and Religion in England, 1640–1720: A Bibliographical and Historical Guide.* Evanston, Ill.: Garrett Theological Seminary, 1975.

Budé, Eugene de. *Lettres inédités adressées de 1686 à 1737 à J.A. Turrettini, théologien genevois* 3 vols. Geneva: Jules Carey, 1887.

———. *Vie de Bénédict Pictet, théologien genevois (1655–1724).* Lausanne: Bridel, 1874.

———. *Vie de François Turrettini, théologien genevois (1623–1687).* Lausanne: Bridel, 1871.

———. *Vie de Jacob Vernet, théologien genevois (1698–1789)*. Lausanne: Bridel, 1893.

———. *Vie de J. A. Turrettini, théologien genevois (1671–1737)*. Lausanne: Bridel, 1880.

———. *Vie de Jean-Robert Chouet, professeur et magistrat genevois (1647–1731)*. Geneva: Reymond et Cie, 1899.

Burnett, Stephen G. "The Christian Hebraism of Johann Buxtorf (1564–1629)." Ph.D. diss., University of Wisconsin, Madison, 1990.

Butler, R. J. *Cartesian Studies*. Oxford: Basil Blackwell, 1972.

Cellérier, J. E. *L'Académie de Genève: Esquisse d'une histoire abregée de l'Académie fondée par Calvin en 1559*. Geneva: A. Cherbuliez, 1872.

Chadwick, Owen. *From Bossuet to Newman: The Idea of Doctrinal Development*. Cambridge: Cambridge University Press, 1957.

Colie, Rosalie L. *Light and Enlightenment: A Study of the Cambridge Platonists and the Dutch Arminians*. Cambridge: University Press, 1957.

Collin, Jacques. *Etude biographique sur Jean LeClerc (1657–1736)*. Geneva: Rivern & Dubois, 1884.

Copleston, Frederick A. *A History of Philosophy*. Vol. 4, *Descartes to Leibniz*. Garden City, N.Y.: Image Books, 1963.

Cragg, Gerald R. *Puritanism in the Period of the Great Persecution, 1680–1688*. New York: Russell & Russell, 1957.

Cramer, Marguerite. *Genève et les Suisses: Histoire des négociations préliminaires à l'entrée de Genève dans le corps helvétique, 1691–1792*. Geneva: Librairie A. Eggimann, 1914.

Cronin, Timothy J. *Objective Being in Descartes and Suarez*. Rome: Gregorian University Press, 1966.

DeKoster, Lester. "Calvin's Use of Scripture." *Reformed Journal* 9 (1959): 3–6.

Dillenberger, John. *Protestant Thought and Natural Science: A Historical Interpretation*. London: Collins, 1961.

Dodge, Guy. *The Political Theory of the Huguenots of the Dispersion with Special Reference to the Thought and Influence of Pierre Jurieu*. New York: Columbia University Press, 1947.

Donnelly, John P. *Calvinism and Scholasticism in Vermigli's Doctrine of Man and Grace*. Leiden: E. J. Brill, 1976.

———. "Calvinist Thomism." *Viator* 7 (1976): 441–45.

———. "Italian Influences on the Development of Calvinist Scholasticism." *Sixteenth Century Journal* (1976): 81–101.

Dorner, J. A. *History of Protestant Theology Particularly in Germany*. Translated by George Robson and Sophia Taylor, 2 vols. Edinburgh: n.p., 1871. Reprint. New York: A. M. S. Press, 1970.

Dowey, Edward A. *The Knowledge of God in Calvin's Theology*. New York: Columbia University Press, 1952.

Dufour, Alain. *Histoire politique et psychologie historique suivi de deux essais sur humanisme et réformation et le mythe de Genève aux temps de Calvin*. Geneva: Droz, 1966.

Fatio, Olivier. *Méthode et théologie: Lambert Daneau et les débuts de la scholastique réformée*. Geneva: Droz, 1976.

————. *Nihil pulchrius ordine: Contribution à l'étude de l'établissement de la discipline écclesiastique aux Pays Bas (1581–1583).* Leiden: E. J. Brill, 1971.

Faulenbach, Heiner, *Weg und Ziel der Christi: Eine Untersuchung zur Theologie des Johannes Coccejus.* Neukirchen: Neukirchner Verlag, 1973.

Fazy, Henri. *Procès et condemnation d'un déiste genevois en 1707,* Geneva: L'institut national genevois, 1877.

Forstmann, H. Jackson. *Word and Spirit: Calvin's Doctrine of Biblical Authority.* Stanford, Calif.: Stanford University Press, 1962.

Frei, Hans W. *The Eclipse of the Biblical Narrative: A Study of Eighteenth and Nineteenth Century Hermeneutics.* New Haven: Yale University Press, 1974.

Gaberel, Jean Pierre. *Histoire de l'Église de Genève depuis le commencement de la réformation jusqu'à nos jours.* 3 vols. Geneva: J. Cherbuliez, 1855–62.

Ganoczy, Alexandre. *La Bibliothèque de l'Académie de Calvin.* Geneva: Droz, 1969.

————. *La jeune Calvin: Genèse et évolution de sa vocation réformatrice.* Weisbaden: Franz Steiner Verlag, 1966.

————. *La Bibliothèque de l'académie de Calvin.* Geneva: Droz, 1969.

Gautier, Jean-Antoine. *Histoire de Genève, des origines à l'année 1690.* 8 vols. Geneva: Rey et Malvallon, 1896–1919.

Geiger, Max. *Die Basler Kirche und Théologie im Zeitalter der Hochorthodoxie.* Zurich: Evanglischer Verlag, 1952.

Geisendorf, Paul F. *Théodore de Bèze.* Geneva: Alexandre Jullien, 1967.

————. *L'Université de Genève (1559–1959).* Geneva: Alexandre Jullien, 1959.

Geisler, Norman L., ed. *Inerrancy.* Grand Rapids, Mich.: Zondervan Publishing House, 1980.

George, Timothy. *Theology of the Reformers.* Nashville, Tenn.: Broadman Press, 1988.

Gerrish, Brian A. "Biblical Authority and the Continental Reformation." *Scottish Journal of Theology* 10 (1957): 337–60.

————. *Grace and Reason: A Study in the Theology of Luther.* New York: Oxford University Press, 1962.

————. *Tradition and the Modern World: Reformed Theology in the Nineteenth Century.* Chicago: University of Chicago Press, 1977.

Gibson, A. Boyce. *The Philosophy of Descartes.* London: Methuen & Co., 1932.

Godfrey, W. Robert. "Biblical Authority in the Sixteenth and Seventeenth Centuries: A Question of Transition." In *Scripture and Truth,* edited by Donald A. Carson and John D. Woodbridge, pp. 225–43. Grand Rapids, Mich.: Zondervan Publishing House, 1983.

————. "Tensions Within International Calvinism: The Debate over the Atonement at the Synod of Dort, 1618–1619." Ph.D. diss., Stanford University, 1974.

Gohier, Henri. *La Pensée religieuse de Descartes.* 2d ed. Paris: Vrin, 1972.

Golden, Samuel A. *Jean LeClerc.* New York: Twayne Publishers 1972.

Gonin, Louis. *Les Catéchismes de Calvin et d'Ostervald: Etude Historique et Comparative.* Montauban, France: J. Granie, 1893.

Good, James I. *History of the Swiss Reformed Church Since the Reformation.* Philadelphia: Publication and Sunday School Board, 1913.

Grabmann, Martin. *Die Geschichte der scholasticichen Methode.* Friburg im Breisgau, Germany: Herdersche Verlagshandlung, 1909.

Gretillat, Robert. *Jean-Frédéric Osterwald: 1663–1747.* Neuchâtel: Paul Attinger, 1904.

Grohman, Donald D. "The Genevan Reaction to the Saumur Doctrine of Hypothetical Universalism: 1635–1685." Ph.D. diss., Knox College, Toronto, 1971.

Gründler, Otto. *Die Gotteslehre Girolamo Zanchis und ihre Bedeuting fur seine Lehre von der Pradestination.* Neukirchen: Neukirchner, 1965.

Haag, Emile and Eugène, eds. *La France Protestante.* 1st ed. 9 vols. Paris, 1847–59. 2d ed., revised and compiled under the direction of Henri Bordier. 6 vols. (to the letter G). Paris: Sandoz et Fischbacher, 1877–88.

Hagglund, Bengt. *History of Theology.* Translated by Gene J. Lund St. Louis, Mo.: Concordia Publishing House, 1968.

Hall, Basil. "Calvin Against the Calvinists." In Courtenay Studies in Reformation Theology, vol. 1, *John Calvin,* pp. 19–37. Berkshire, England: Sutton Courtenay Press, 1966.

Harrison, Archibald W. *The Beginnings of Arminianism to the Synod of Dort.* London: University of London Press, 1926.

Hazard, Paul. *The European Mind: 1680–1715.* Translated by J. Lewis May. London: Halles and Carter, 1953.

Heppe, Heinrich. *Reformed Dogmatics: Set Out and Illustrated from the Sources.* Translated by G. T. Thompson. Grand Rapids, Mich.: Baker Book House, 1950.

Heyd, Michael. *Between Orthodoxy and the Enlightenment: Jean-Robert Chouet and the Introduction of Cartesian Science in the Academy of Geneva.* The Hague: Martinus Nijhoff, 1982.

———. "Cartesianism, Secularization and Academic Reform: Jean Robert Chouet and the Academy of Geneva, 1669–1704." Ph.D. diss., Princeton University, 1974.

———. "Jean-Robert Chouet et l'introduction du cartésianisme à l'Académie de Genève." *Société d'Histoire et d'Archéologie de Genève* 15 (1972–73): 125–53.

———. "Orthodoxy, Non-Conformity and Modern Science: The Case of Geneva." In *Modernité et non-conformisme en France à travers les ages,* edited by Myriam Yardeni, pp. 100–119. Leiden: E. J. Brill, 1983.

———. "Un Role nouveau pour la science: Jean-Alphonse Turrettini et les débuts de la théologie naturelle a Genève. *Revue de théologie et philosophie* 112 (1982): 25–42.

Heyer, Henri. *L'Église de Genève (1535–1909).* Geneva: Librairie A. Jullien, 1909.

Hodge, Archibald A. *Outlines of Theology* New York: Robert Carter, 1860.

Hooykaas, Reijer. *Religion and the Rise of Modern Science.* Edinburgh: Scottish Academic Press, 1972.

Jellema, Dirk W. "God's 'Baby-Talk': Calvin and the 'Errors' of the Bible." *Reformed Journal* 30 (1980): 25–27.

Jensen, Paul T. "Calvin and Turretin: A Comparison of their Soteriologies." Ph.D. diss., University of Virginia, 1988.

Keizer, Gerrit. *François Turrettini: sa vie et ses oeuvres et le consensus.* Kampen, the Netherlands: J. A. Bus, 1900.

Kennedy, Earl W. "An Historical Analysis of Charles Hodge's Doctrines of Sin and Particular Grace." Ph.D. diss., Princeton Theological Seminary, 1969.

Kent, John H. S. "Socinian Tradition." *Theology* 78 (March 1975): 131–40.

Kickel, Walter. *Vernuft und Offenbarung bei Theodor Beza. Zum Problem des Verhaltnisses von Theologie, Philosophie und Staat.* Neukirchen-Vluyn: Neukirchener Verlag, 1967.

Klauber, Martin I. "The Context and Development of the Views of Jean-Alphonse Turrettini (1671–1737) on Religious Authority." Ph.D. diss., University of Wisconsin, Madison, 1987.

———. "Continuity and Discontinuity in Post-Reformation Reformed Theology: An Evaluation of the Muller Thesis." *Journal of the Evangelical Theological Society* 33–34 (December 1990): 467–75.

———. "The Helvetic Formula Consensus: An Introduction and Translation." *Trinity Journal* (Spring 1990): 103–23.

———. "Jean-Alphonse Turrettini and the Abrogation of the Formula Consensus in Geneva." *Westminster Theological Journal* 53 (Fall 1991): 325–38.

———. "Reason, Revelation and Cartesianism: Louis Tronchin and Enlightened Orthodoxy in Late Seventeenth-Century Geneva." *Church History* 59 (September 1990): 326–39.

Klauber, Martin I., and Glenn Sunshine. "Jean-Alphonse Turrettini on Biblical Accommodation: Calvinist or Socinian?" *Calvin Theological Journal* (April 1990): 7–27.

Kot, Stanislaus. *Socinianism in Poland: The Social and Political Ideas of the Polish Antitrinitarians in the Sixteenth and Seventeenth Centuries.* Translated by Earl M. Wilbur. Boston: Starr King Press, 1957.

Kraus, Hans-Joachim. "Calvin's Exegetical Principles." *Interpretation* 31 (January 1977): 8–18.

Kreter, Harmut. *Calvinismus und franzosische Monarchie in 17. Jahrhundert: die politische besonderer Berucksichtigung von Pierre Du Moulin, Moyse Amyraut und Pierre Jurieu.* Berlin: Drunker & Humblot, 1975.

Kümmel, Werner G. *The New Testament: The History of the Investigation of its Problems.* Translated by S. McClean Gilmour and Howard Kee. Nashville, Tenn.: Abingdon Press, 1972.

Labrousse, Elizabeth. *Pierre Bayle.* Vol. 1, *Du Pays de Foix à la Cité d'Erasme.* The Hague: Martinus Nijhoff, 1963. Vol. 2, *Hétérodoxie et rigorisme.* The Hague: Martinus Nijhoff, 1964.

LaPlanche, François. *Orthodoxie et prédication: l'oeuvre d'Amyraut et la querelle de la grâce universelle.* Paris: Presses Universitaires de France, 1965.

———. *L'Ecriture, le sacré et l'histoire: érudits et politiques protestants devant la Bible en France au XVIIe siècle.* Amsterdam: Holland University Press, 1986.

———. *L'Evidence du Dieu Chrétien: Religion, culture et société dans l'apologétique protestante de la France classique (1576–1670).* Strasbourg: Association des Publications de la Faculté de Théologie Protestante de Strasbourg, 1983.

LeBrun, Jacques. "Meaning and Scope of the Return to Origins in Richard Simon's Work." Translated by T. D. M. Carson. *Trinity Journal* 3 (1982): 57–70.

Lee, R. W. *Hugo Grotius.* London: Humphrey Milford Amen House, 1930.

Léonard, Emile, G. *Histoire générale du Protestantisme.* 3 vols. Paris: Presses universitaires de France, 1964.

Mailhet, E. André. *Jacques Basnage: théologien, controversiste, diplomate et historien.* Geneva: Charles Schuchardt, 1880.

————. *La Théologie protestante au XVIIe siècle: Claude Pajon, sa vie, son système religieux, ses controverses.* Paris: Fishbacher, 1883.

Manschreck, Clyde L. *Melanchthon: The Quiet Reformer.* New York: Abingdon Press, 1958.

Margival, Henri. *Essai sur Richard Simon et la critique biblique au XVII siècle.* Paris: n.p., 1900. Reprint. Geneva: Slatkine Reprints, 1970.

Maurer, Armand. *Medieval Philosophy.* New York: Random House, 1962.

McAdoo, Henry R. *The Spirit of Anglicanism: A Survey of Anglican Theological Method in the Seventeenth Century.* London: Adam & Charles Block, 1965.

McCoy, Charles S. "Johannes Cocceius: Federal Theologian." *Scottish Journal of Theology* 16 (December 1963): 252–70.

McLachlan, H. John. *Socinianism in Seventeenth-Century England.* Oxford: Oxford University Press, 1951.

McLelland, ed. *Peter Martyr Vermigli and Italian Reform.* Waterloo, Ontario: Wilfred Laurier Press, 1980.

McNair, Philip. *Peter Martyr in Italy: An Anatomy of Apostasy.* Oxford: Clarendon Press, 1967.

McNeill, John T. *The History and Character of Calvinism.* New York: Oxford University Press, 1957.

Merzeau, E. *L'Académie protestante de Saumur (1606–11685).* Alençon: Guy, 1908.

Metayer, L. J. *L'Académie protestante de Saumur.* Paris: "La Cause," 1933.

Miegge, Giovanni. "Il Problema degli articoli fondamentali nel Nubes Testium di Giovanni Alfonso Turrettini." *Genevra e l'Italie* (1959): 505–38.

Montandon, Albert. *L'Evolution théologique à Genève au XVIIe siècle.* Le Cateau: J. Roland, 1894.

Monter, E. William. *Studies in Genevan Government: 1536–1605.* Geneva: Droz, 1964.

Muller, Richard A. "Arminius and the Scholastic Tradition." *Calvin Theological Journal* 24 (1989): 263–77.

————. *Christ and the Decree: Christology and Predestination in Reformed Theology from Calvin to Perkins.* Grand Rapids, Mich.: Baker Book House, 1988.

————. "The Debate over the Vowel Points and the Crisis in Orthodox Hermeneutics." *The Journal of Medieval and Renaissance Studies* 10 (1980): 53–72.

————. *Dictionary of Latin and Greek Theological Terms.* Grand Rapids, Mich.: Baker Book House, 1985.

————. *God, Creation and Providence in the Thought of Jacob Arminius: Sources and Directions of Scholastic Protestantism in the Era of Early Orthodoxy.* Grand Rapids, Mich.: Baker Book House, 1991.

————. *Post-Reformation Reformed Dogmatics. Volume 1: Prolegomena to Theology.* Grand Rapids, Mich.: Baker Book House, 1987.

————. "Scholasticism Protestant and Catholic: Francis Turretin and the Object and Principles of Theology." *Church History* 55 (June 1986): 193–205.

Nicole, Roger. "John Calvin and Inerrancy." *Journal of the Evangelical Theological Society* 25 (December 1982): 425–42.

————. "Moyse Amyraut (1596–1664) and the Controversy on Universal Grace: First Phase (1634–1637)." Ph.D. diss., Harvard University, 1966.

Niesel, Wilhelm. *The Theology of Calvin*. Translated by Harold Knight. London: Lutterworth Press, 1956.

Noll, Mark A., ed. *The Princeton Theology, 1812–1921: Scripture, Science, and Theological Method from Archibald Alexander to Benjamin Breckinridge Warfield*. Grand Rapids, Mich.: Baker Book House, 1983.

Parker, T. H. L. *Calvin's Doctrine of the Knowledge of God*. Grand Rapids, Mich.: Eerdmans Publishing Company, 1959.

Pelikan, Jaroslav. *From Luther to Kierkegaard: A Study in the History of Theology*. St. Louis, Mo.: Concordia Publishing House, 1950.

————. *Reformation of Church and Dogma (1300–1700)*. Chicago: University of Chicago Press, 1984.

Petersen, Peter. *Geschichte der aristotelischer Philosophie im Protestantischen Deutschland*. Leipzig: Meiner, 1921.

Phillips, Timothy R. "Francis Turretin's Idea of Theology and its Bearing upon his Doctrine of Scripture." Ph.D. diss., Vanderbilt University, 1986.

Pitassi, Maria. C. "L'Apologétique Raisonnable de Jean-Alphonse Turrettini." In *Apologétique 1680–1740: Sauvetage ou naufrage de la théologie*, edited by Olivier Fatio and Maria C. Pitassi. Geneva: Publications de la Faculté de Théologie de l'Université de Genève, 1990.

————. "De la censure à la réfutation: L'Académie de Genève." *Révue de Metaphysique et de Morale* 93 (1988): 147–64.

————. "L'echo des discussions metaphysiques dans la correspondence entre Isaac Papin et Jean LeClerc." *Revue de théologie et de philosophie* (1982): 259–75.

————. *Entre Croire et Savoir: Le problème de la méthode critique chez Jean LeClerc*. Leiden: E. J. Brill, 1987.

————. "Jean LeClerc bon tacheron de la philosophie: l'enseignement philosophique à la fin du XVIIe siècle." *Lias* 10 (1983): 105–22.

————. "Un Manuscrit Genevois du XVIIe Siècle: La Réfutation du Système de Spinosa par Mr. Turrettini." *Nederlands Archief voor Kerkgeschiedenis* 68 (1988): 180–212.

Platt, John. *Reformed Thought and Scholasticism: The Arguments for the Existence of God in Dutch Theology, 1575–1650*. Leiden: E. J. Brill, 1982.

Popkin, Richard. "The Development of Religious Scepticism and the Influence of Isaac La Peyrère's Pre-Adamism and Bible Criticism." In *Classical Influences on European Culture A. D. 1500–1700*, edited by R. R. Bolgar, pp. 271–80. Cambridge: Cambridge University Press, 1976.

————. *The History of Scepticism from Erasmus to Descartes*. New York: Harper and Row, 1964.

————. *The History of Scepticism from Erasmus to Spinoza*. Berkeley: University of California Press, 1979.

Preclin, E. *L'Union des Eglises Gallicane et Anglicane: une tentative au temps de Louis XIV*. Paris: Librairie Universitaire J. Gamber, 1928.

Preus, Robert. *The Inspiration of Scripture: A Study of the Theology of the Seventeenth Century Lutheran Dogmaticians* London: Oliver and Boyd, 1957.

————. *The Theology of Post-Reformation Lutheranism: A Study of Theological Prolegomena*. St. Louis, Mo.: Concordia Publishing House, 1970.

Prost, Joseph. *La philosophie à l'Académie protestante de Saumur (1606–1685)*. Paris: H. Paulin, 1907.

Raitt, Jill. *The Eucharistic Theology of Theodore Beza: The Development of Reformed Doctrine*. Chambersburg, Penn.: American Academy of Religion, 1972.

———, ed. *Shapers of Religious Traditions in Germany, Switzerland and Poland, 1560–1600*. New Haven: Yale University Press, 1981.

Reventlow, Henning G. *The Authority of the Bible and the Rise of the Modern World*. Translated by John Bowden. Philadelphia: Fortress Press, 1985.

Reverdin, Olivier et al. *Genève au temps de la révocation de l'édit de Nantes 1680–1795*. Vol. 50 in *Mémoires et documents publiés par la Société d'histoire et d'archéologie de Genève*. Geneva: Droz; Paris: Champion, 1985.

Rex, Walter. *Essays on Pierre Bayle and Religious Controversy*. The Hague: Martinus Nijhoff, 1965.

———. "Pierre Bayle, Louis Tronchin et la querelle des Donatistes." *Bulletin de la Société de l'histoire du protestantisme français* 105 (1959): 97–121.

Ritschl, Otto. *Dogmengeschichte des Protestantismus: Grundlagen und Grundzüge der theologischen Gedanken und Lehrbildung in den protestantischen Kirchen*. 4 vols. Leipzig: J. C. Hinrichs, 1908–12; Göttingen: Vandenhoeck & Rucht, 1926–27.

Robinson, John R. "The Doctrine of Holy Scripture in Seventeenth Century Reformed Theology." Ph.D. diss., Université de Strasbourg, 1971.

Rogers, Jack and Donald K. McKim. *The Authority and Interpretation of the Bible: An Historical Approach*. New York: Harper and Row, 1979.

Rosen, Edward. "Calvin's Attitude Toward Copernicus." *Journal of the History of Ideas* 21 (1960): 418–39.

Roth, Jean. "Le 'Traité de l'inspiration' de Jean LeClerc." *Revue d'histoire et de philosophie religieuse* 36 (1956): 50–60.

Rouse, Ruth and Neill, Stephen C., eds. *A History of the Ecumenical Movement: 1517–1948*. Philadelphia: Westminster Press, 1967.

Sabean, David. "The Theological Rationalism of Moïse Amyraut." *Archiv für Reformationsgeschichte* 55 (1964): 204–16.

Schaff, Philip, ed., *The Creeds of Christendom*. Grand Rapids, Mich.: Baker Book House, 1959.

Schweizer, Alexander. *Die Protestantischen Centralgogmen in ihrer Entwicklung innerhalb der reformierten Kirche*. Zurich: Orell, Fuessli, 1856.

Scholder, Klaus. *Ursprung und Probleme der Bibelkritik im 17. Jahrhundert: Ein Beitrag zur Entstehung der historisch-kritischen Theologie*. Munich: Chr. Kaiser Verlag, 1966.

Scharlemann, Robert P. *Thomas Aquinas and John Gerhard*. New Haven: Yale University Press, 1964.

Senebier, Jean. *Histoire littéraire de Genève*. 3 vols. Geneva: Barde, Manget et Co., 1786.

Shapiro, Barbara J. *John Wilkins 1614–1672: An Intellectual Biography*. Berkeley: University of California Press, 1969.

Sinnema, Donald. "The Issue of Reprobation at the Synod of Dort (1618–1619) in Light of the History of this Doctrine." Ph.D. diss., University of St. Michael's College, 1985.

Snoeks, Remi. *L'Argument de tradition dans la controverse eucharistique entre catholiques et réformés français au XVIIe siècle.* Louvain: Publications Universitaires de Louvain, 1951.

Solé, Jacques, "Rationalisme chrétien et foi réformée à Genève autour de 1700: les derniers sermons de Louis Tronchin." *Bulletin de la Société de l'histoire du protestantisme français* 128 (1982): 29–43.

Stauffenegger, Roger. *Eglise et société: Genève au XVIIe siècle.* Geneva: Droz, 1983.

Stauffer, Richard. *L'Affaire d'Huisseau, une controverse au sujet de la Réunion des Chrétiens (1670–1671).* Paris: Presses Universitaires de France, 1969.

———. "Un Précurseur français de l'oecumenisme: Moyse Amyraut." *Eglise et théologie* 24 (December 1961): 13–49.

———. *The Quest for Church Unity from Calvin to D'Huisseau.* Allison Park, Penn.: Pickwick, 1986.

Steinmann, Jean. *Richard Simon et les origines de l'exégèse biblique.* Paris: Desclée de Brouvier, 1960.

Steinmetz, David. *Luther and Staupitz.* Durham, N.C.: Duke University Press, 1980.

Strehle, Stephen A. "The Extent of the Atonement Within the Theological Systems of the Sixteenth and Seventeenth Centuries" Th.D. diss., Dallas Theological Seminary, 1980.

Stromberg, Roland N. *Religious Liberalism in Eighteenth-Century England.* Oxford: Oxford University Press, 1954.

Sunshine, Glenn. "Accommodation in Calvin and Socinus: A Study in Contrasts." M.A. thesis, Trinity Evangelical Divinity School, 1985.

Sykes, Norman. *Church and State in England in the XVIIth Century.* Cambridge: Cambridge University Press, 1934.

———. *William Wake: Archbishop of Canterbury, 1657–1737.* 2 vols. Cambridge: Cambridge University Press, 1957.

Tavard, George H. *Holy Writ or Holy Church: The Crisis of the Protestant Reformation.* London: Burns & Oates, 1959.

———. *La tradition au XVIIe siècle en France et en Angleterre.* Paris: Les Editions du Cerf, 1969.

Van Stam, Franz Pieter. *The Controversy Over the Theology of Saumur, 1635–1650. Disrupting Debates Among the Huguenots in Complicated Circumstances.* Amsterdam: Holland University Press, 1988.

Vernière, Paul. *Spinoza et la pensée française avant la révolution.* 2 vols. Paris: Presses Universitaires de France, 1974.

Voeltzel, René. "Jean LeClerc (1657–1736) et la critique biblique." In *Religion, érudition et critique à la fin du XVIIe siècle et au début du XVIIIe,* edited by René Voeltzel, pp. 33–52. Strasbourg: Presses Universitaires de France, 1968.

———. *Vraie et fausse église selon les théologiens protestants français du XVIIe siècle.* Paris: Presses Universitaires de France, 1956.

Von Allmen, Jean-Jacques *L'Eglise et ses fonctions d'après Jean-Frédéric Ostervald: Le Problème de la théologie pratique au début du XVIIIe siècle.* Neuchâtel: Delachaux & Niestle, 1947.

Von Leyden, W. *Seventeenth-Century Metaphysics: An Examination of Some Main Concepts and Theories.* London: Gerald Duckworth, 1968.

Vreeland, Williamson Up Dike. *Etude sur les rapports littéraires entre Genève et L'Angleterre jusqu'à la publication de la "Nouvelle Heloise."* Geneva: Librairie Henry Kundig, 1901.

Vuilleumier, Henri. *Histoire de l'église réformée du Pays de Vaud.* 4 vols. Lausanne: Editions la Concorde, 1930.

Watson, Richard A. *The Downfall of Cartesianism 1673–1712: A Study of the Epistemological Issues in Late 17th Century Cartesianism.* The Hague: Martinus Nijhoff, 1966.

Weber, Hans Emil. *Reformation, Orthodoxie, und Rationalismus.* Beitrage zur Forderung Christlicher Theologie, vols. 37 and 51. Gütersloh: Bertelsmann, 1937, 1951.

Weir, David A. *The Origins of the Federal Theology in Sixteenth-Century Reformation Thought.* Oxford: Clarendon Press, 1990.

Wendel, François. *Calvin, sources et évolution de sa doctrine.* Paris: Presses Universitaires de France, 1950. Translated by Philip Mairet. *Calvin: The Origins and Development of His Religious Thought.* New York: Harper and Row, 1963.

White, Andrew D. *A History of Warfare of Science with Theology.* 2 vols. New York: D. Appleton, 1898.

————. *Seven Great Statesmen in the Warfare of Humanity with Unreason.* Garden City, N.J.: Garden City Publishing Company, 1976.

Wilbur, Earl M. "Faustus Socinus, Pioneer." *Hibbert Journal* 33 (1935): 536–48.

————. *A History of Unitarianism: Socinianism and its Antecedents.* 2 vols. Boston: Beacon Press, 1945.

Willey, Basil. *The Eighteenth Century Background: Studies on the Idea of Nature in the Thought of the Period.* New York: Columbia University Press, 1950.

————. *The Seventeenth Century Background: Studies in the Thought of the Age in Relation to Poetry and Religion.* Garden City, N.Y.: Doubleday, 1953.

Williams, George H. *The Radical Reformation.* Philadelphia: Westminster Press, 1962.

Woodbridge, John D. *Biblical Authority: A Critique of the Rogers/McKim Proposal.* Grand Rapids, Mich.: Zondervan Publishing House, 1982.

————. "Biblical Authority: Towards an Evaluation of the Rogers and McKim Proposal." *Trinity Journal* 2 (Fall 1980): 165–236.

————. "History's Lessons and Biblical Inerrancy." *Trinity Journal* 6 (1977): 73–93.

————. "Some Misconceptions of the Impact of the 'Enlightenment' on the Doctrine of Scripture." In *Hermeneutics, Authority and Canon,* edited by Donald A. Carson and John D. Woodbridge, pp. 241–70. Grand Rapids, Mich.: Zondervan Publishing House, 1986.

Index